SUNDAY'S CHILD

Second edition

A Memoir
By Anne Lyken-Garner

Contact: http://www.getconfidence.net

Authors Note

To give Sunday's Child the gift of dialogue, I condensed the things the people around me said over the years. I then used their personalities, the way they spoke, and the tones they used to give them words to 'speak' in my story. This is very much like the way you relate the things your mother used to say to other people. You can remember the manner in which she used her hands to speak, the phrases she revisited, and even her tone of voice.

I tried to recreate, to the best of my human ability, the speech patterns and the words for the people included in Sunday's Child.

You will also notice that this book is written in my childhood voice. This perspective changes and progresses as time passes in the book. I wanted to give you my thoughts and feelings – free from adult analyses.

CHAPTER 1

JONESTOWN, GUYANA, AND THE CHASE

My usual shortcut through the building site for the new school seemed like a good idea, on account of it being so late and all. The evening sunlight glowed orange, signalling that dusk was crouching round the corner.

Piles of rubbish and concrete were scattered everywhere, but the men weren't working anymore – something about shortage of materials or other. Even the grass had packed up and left the parched ground, leaving the entire site something of a mountain of brown and grey mess.

I mustn't get home late, but with after-school lessons every day, I don't know how I could help that. At least I only have one more year at primary school, after which . . .

A noise behind me snapped me out of my thoughts. It was coupled with panting – loud panting – and heavy, running footsteps on the hot, hard concrete.

The familiar, large hands of fear grabbed hold of my insides and squeezed them like play dough. It took me just one tiny instant to look behind me, but before I did I knew – I just knew I was in trouble.

When my head finally creaked around, the man's eyes were dead set only on me.

That dreaded, unforgettable, dirty red cap!

Those blood shot eyes.

The mad stare.

I and all the other girls my age had seen him a hundred times before, slinking around the village.

Looking at us.

Looking for us.

Oh no!

My heart spilled over itself for one breathless moment. I took a hesitant intake of hot air before my whole body bulleted forward.

'Please God, don't let him catch me. Please don't let him catch me.'

The pounding footsteps grew louder. I didn't want to, but I had to take another glance – just a little one – over my shoulder. He was not alone! There was now a second man.

I sprawled on the ground when my knees buckled under me, and as I clawed the crisp grass to try to scramble up, I took another look back but I still couldn't get up for crippling fear. I started to crawl away. Getting up was no good. I couldn't use my dead legs anymore.

Dirty Red Cap, who was closer to me, turned, looking back when the second man yanked his belt off with a mighty swish. The bald man behind him raised his hand above his head and swung his belt as Dirty Red Cap straightened his body and picked up his speed.

Swoosh!

Dirty Red Cap stopped and grasped his whipped arm. His eyebrows shot up, as his mouth began to form an 'o.' Snarling, he barely ducked the second blow then darted back and ran away in the direction he came from.

He would live to fight another day,
And wait to catch me another way.

The other man looked in my direction then walked towards me, but the only message showing up in bright letters behind my eyes was, I should really go back to get my school bag.

"Child!" he shouted. "Yuh alright?"

"Yeah, Mister," I whispered.

"Do you know who that is," he asked, while picking up my old, green hand-bag-turned school sac.

"Yes, Mister."

"He's always hanging round here," he said as he handed me my bag. "They can't lock him up because he's proved insane. Doan walk through here anymore. It not safe at all. I doan want to think what couldda happened to yuh if I wasn't 'round here. Brush yuhself off and tell your parents what happened when you get home. What's yuh name, eh?"

"Ann."

"You shaking real bad, Ann. Look, I'll hold your bag and walk you out of the site, right?"

"Thanks, Mister."

"Make sure you tell your parents when you get home," he said again.

I had a feeling that if he had been looking at me when he said this instead of buckling his belt around the tyre in his belly, he would've seen through the emptiness in my words when I said, "Yes, Mister, I will."

A minute later I was boring through the hole in the fence and walking away in the dry dust, legs still porridge-like. I was already making notes in my head of the details I would leave out when I did my nightly letters entitled, 'Dear Aunty or Mister,' to no one and everyone.

In the two minutes it took me to walk to the house I wished I didn't live in, I tried to work out where the bald man had come from and why he was there. He had to have been an angel. Maybe even children who get themselves attacked have angels to save them.

I was really sure of this, just like I was sure that I had to stand under the house until I stopped shaking. Today, Red Cap was not the only bolt that penetrated through to the insides of my senses. At least it was lighter on my chest than the message I was carrying which hung like a sandbag from my stomach. This bag had started to fill up at lunchtime over at Aunty Meena's house with something I heard on the radio.

***

"Breaking news of what appears to be a mass suicide in Jonestown. Reports that over 900 members of a sect known as 'The People's Temple' are said to have lined up to be served what they knew to be a deadly mix of poisonous Kool-aid. Early reports suggest that this sect was led by the American, Jim Jones, who may or may not be dead along with his followers.

"The aftermath of this totally horrific incident was witnessed by one of our reporters who said that groups of people, who appeared to be members of families were found dead, still huddled together with their babies and children in little bundles. This is the most shocking…"

"Did you hear that, Ann?" Aunty Meena asked, turning up the radio. "Can yuh believe that? How on earth can yuh get people to line up to take poison? That can't be right." Aunty Meena's small, youthful face creased in thought, her eyes stared, but not at anything in particular.

"Is Jonestown in Guyana, Aunty?" I asked.

"Seems so, child," she whispered, putting her finger to her lips as if she was about to kiss it. "Never heard of it before."

I waited in silence, and eventually when the man on the radio said, "More coming up in our next news bulletin," I asked, "Who's Jim Jones, Aunty?"

"Some American, it seems," Aunty Meena said, swiping her sentence away with a flick of her wrist. "The Comrade Leader invited all these people here and we only know about it when there's trouble." She had that look on her face and that shrug in her shoulder which said there was yet another thing she couldn't do anything about.

"Anyway," she continued, calling out to her daughters, "if you children finish yuh lunch, clean up and get back to school. Rafza and Tasleema, make sure you go to the toilet before you go."

The even breathing I was allowed in Aunty Meena's house was always squeezed out of my chest when it was time to leave. One nod – even half a nod – was all it would take from her, and I would stay. There would be no broken skin, no swollen face and no aching joints anymore. I could help her look after baby Nafeeza and do the washing.

But I knew that *'She'* would never allow that.

"Bye, Mammy," Tasleema and Rafza said five minutes later. "See you after school."

"Bye kids," Aunty Meena answered, then turned to me. "Ann, see that they cross the road properly."

"I am seven," Rafza exclaimed, pulling out stray hairs from the end of her long pony tail. "I know how to . . ."

"I know, I know, Rafza," Aunty replied, as she stood in the doorway. "But Ann is the oldest, right?" A light wind touched her forehead and she shook her head and lifted her chin as if she was looking up to heaven and asking it to do it again.

"Last one downstairs is a big fat rat," shouted Tas, as we all raced down the stairs.

"Oh, Ann," Aunty Meena shouted after us. "When you get home this afternoon, tell yuh grandmother that I got to talk to her about something."

I stopped in mid-step. My foot suddenly froze, not quite remembering what to do next. Heaven did it again for Aunty and breathed another burst of the November wind – strong and steady, but hot as usual.

I haven't done anything! I checked, I checked all my movements, every minute of my movements. Why does she want to see Mammy? I know I didn't do nothing.

Oh God, no, not . . .

"Oh, nothing 'bout you, child. My fault, I shoudda said that first. You gone really pale. It's . . . It's about me and Uncle Nizam and the girls. You all right?"

"Yes, Aunty Meena," I answered, breathing a big sigh of relief as my heart briskly made up for the beats it had missed.

"I'll tell her," I said, showing her all of my teeth, hoping the flash of whites made a good enough smile. "Bye."

I followed the girls down the stairs.

We skipped to school hand in hand, the three of us – best friends – and decided that tomorrow at lunch time we would eat quickly so that we could go under the house to play hopscotch on the hot concrete.

Rafza said that we could all take three posts each, of the nine that held up their house, to use as scoreboards. Then we could count them up at the end of the year.

We walked out of Stanleytown where Raf and Tas lived, past the tiny houses perched on four posts, which were scattered across grass on either side of the thin, tarred road. Five minutes later we had entered Islington, where the tar suddenly ran out. The road was hurriedly dressed with Bauxite waste from the nearby plant where many of my classmates' parents worked. The fly-away red dust caked on the bottom of our shoes when it rained. A few children from our school came drizzling out from Singh's corner shop at the top of the village. Their freshly bought ice lollies were already dribbling wet exclamation points onto their green school uniforms.

"Run up, y'all," I said, hitching my school bag onto my shoulder. "I hear the bell." It took us a minute to get through the village and into Overwinning, to the wide, sandy, flat stretch of land on which our wooden school was built.

"I won't see y'all this afternoon," I said breathlessly as we stomped across the wooden bridge at the school gates. "I got Common Entrance lessons, awright?"

The two girls skipped away together, and in the bright midday sunlight reflected off the peeling white paint on the front of the school building, they looked paler than usual.

As I turned away from them and walked up the long, creaking stairs into my classroom, Mr. Williams was getting the class ready for the afternoon by making us stretch before saying the Lord's Prayer.

"Hands up, down, in, out, clasp your hands and close your…" I quickly scuffled into my space next to Jan, his daughter, closed my eyes and chorused with the others:

"…Who art in heaven,
Hallowed be Thy name,
Thy Kingdom come,
Thy will be done on earth as it is in Heaven.
Give us this day our daily bread
And forgive us our trespasses
As we forgive those who trespass against us.
And lead us not into temptation.
But deliver us from evil,
For Thine is the kingdom, the power and the glory
Forever and forever Amen."

"Hands up, down, in, out, sit down," Mr. Williams said again.

"Yes, Sir," we all sang after we had followed his directions.

"Now, I want to talk to you all today about your upcoming Common Entrance Exams, especially to those of you who are in this class for the first time . . ."

Mr. Williams had a dense black beard, which itched with excitement whenever he was breaking into one of his 'very important' speeches.

". . . As Liddle, my own son, Geff, and others will tell you, this will be your hardest class in primary school. I know most of you are only eleven but unfortunately, what you do in these exams and the grade of high school you attend will follow you throughout your lives. This is why some of us teachers have come together to give you free extra lessons after school."

Scratch, scratch went his long, dark fingers. He had placed the other hand in his trouser pocket, and as he spoke he not only managed to look at all of us at the *same* time, but at the light blue, galvanised zinc ceiling which covered the high roof of our little school and every other building I'd ever been into.

"I will speak to you in groups so when I call your names come up to my desk. The rest of you do your revisions quietly. The first group is: Lyken, Ricardo Singh, Sanjay Singh, Geff and Jan and McAlman . . ."

***

Hiding under the house to calm the thoughts of why Red Cap wanted to catch me didn't work as planned. *I'll have lots to write in my letters to no one and everyone, but scary things are mostly kept in my heart. 'Dear Aunty or Mister' it would say . . .'*

"What you doin' down there?"

At the sound of her voice, the breath I was about to take shot up through my shoulders and into the air.

"Bring yuhself upstairs," my grandmother shouted in my direction from the front bedroom window. "You know how long ah been looking out for yuh?"

The tight crease in her forehead pointed accusingly at me as always. "Guilty! Guilty! Guilty!" it cried, still pointing.

"Yes, Mammy," I answered, running up the stairs. The thoughts of Red Cap were already held captive somewhere else in my mind, a trailer saved for later re-plays.

"Ah run outta cigarettes. Go next door to Grimmond Bar and buy two Bristols for me."

"Yes, Mammy," I said again, swallowing dry air and getting ready to deliver the sandbag message. "Aunty Meena said she got to see you, she . . ."

"What you gone and do now, Eh?" My grandmother put her hands on her hips. That crease was never going to let me go. "You lucky I get Meena, a stranger, to cook yuh lunch every day, and this is how you repay me?"

"No, she said it's about her and Uncle Nizam," I answered quickly, but quietly under my breath, like, just in case . . . .

"Don't you answer me back, just go and get me cigarettes. Ah can't see Meena this week, ah got to go to court again. The landlady want us out!"

I hoped the side stable door was open so I wouldn't have to go inside the bar today. I closed my eyes and wished hard: *Please be open, please be open. Please be open.*

But as I already knew, I'd used up my portion of good luck for today. I kept my eyes focused on the concrete floor as I walked inside. I didn't want to step into one of the beer-ish, pee-ish looking puddles *again* in my bare feet. Hardworking flies and their children zipped from table to table. They reminded me of the cockroaches that came out in our kitchen at nights. The smell of rum hit my nostrils, but the piles of cigarette butts on the floor and in the ashtrays on the sticky counter proved that my sniffer had gone a bit wonky. Stale cigarette smoke couldn't smell of rum. But in a bar which transformed into a loud disco three nights a week, maybe anything is possible.

I hoped none of the drunkies were in as I made my way around to the main entrance at the front of the bar.

"What you want, girlie?" the day barman wanted to know.

"Two Bristols please, Mister," I answered, trying to hold in my breath to block out the stench of last night's activities.

"Two packs, or two singles as usual?"

"Two singles, thanks."

With that ritual done, it was time to go back home to face my fate. The beating stick that Mammy kept behind the front door had found me only yesterday, so maybe I was safe for now. But the landlady's news and Aunty Meena's message were enough to put Mammy in a spitting bad mood.

CHAPTER 2

THE DEAD BODY

"Ann, you hungry," my aunt Theresa asked after I got home for the second time that afternoon and walked into the kitchen. "You must be. What you have fuh lunch today?"

"Eggplant and chicken with rice," I answered.

"Sounds nice. You had lessons again, ah see." She blew her nose on the little rag cloth she kept in the band of her skirt, her smooth, black, marble-like skin almost mirroring the light from the open back door. A whisper of air sailed into the tiny kitchen and I could almost hear the leaves on the guava tree in the back yard wriggle in delight.

"Hmm," was all I managed to say.

"They should really excuse you sometimes. You wouldn't even be going to that school if we were living here when yuh started Prep A. None of the other children live all the way out here."

"I feel very tired walking all that way," I said, hoping for some of her sympathy – my dose of love for the day.

"I would too. Is nearly two miles."

"I miss picking you up from sewing class and walking home together. When yuh going back?"

"I can't really go back now I got Franc to look after," Theresa answered. She sniffled and wiped her nose with the back of her hand, then on the side of her faded skirt. "Maybe when she goes to nursery school I can, but even then I'd have to go to a different class because the teacher's going to live overseas soon."

"You used to have fun laughing and talking with the other girls at the class."

"Yes," she said, smiling a sad kind of smile. "I cooked bora and rice today. Do you…?"

"Theresa!" Mammy's voice shot from the bedroom, almost shooting – I imagined – a straight line of cigarette smoke through the thin kitchen wall. "Franc woke up! Mek a bottle!"

"What she say?" Theresa asked me.

"You got to make a bottle for Franc."

"Awright!" Theresa shouted back. The sad look hadn't left her eyes, and as I stood and watched the back of my mother's young sister's head, I could see emeralds of perspiration running down her neck. Mammy's always said that Theresa had good skin. Good skin and a sweaty head, but what else could you expect from someone who was always working, scrubbing, and cooking?

***

"The reason I called you today," began Aunty Meena, "Is because I…um, we got something important to say to you."

Aunty Meena has always been a quiet speaker. Even when she was telling her children off, I had to listen hard to hear what she was saying. I didn't know if it was because she was a Muslim. Her family was the only Muslim people I knew, so I couldn't really know for sure if I had no one else to measure her with.

"Umm…we moving back to Georgetown for a while, then moving out of the country for good. This country's getting from bad to worse with all them murders and robberies and stuff, and we getting out now, um…we really sad, and the children, too."

I didn't want to hear this, so I stared at her face instead, at her dark eyes (though not as dark as Rafza's) and tiny nose. I studied the way she played with the hair on her arms while she talked with Mammy. I wished I had that much hair on *my* arms.

"They really like playing with Ann," Aunty Meena said running her fingers through her short, dark hair. "They been friends ever since we moved in here when you guys were living in the mechanic's house opposite. They'll miss her – and all of you – we all will."

I could almost see Mammy's brain wheels going round and round, with bitter brain juice dripping from every side. Her head was turned towards Aunty Meena, but her eyes were staring inwards. I'd seen that look before. It was the same look she'd have when she'd tell Theresa, through her bubbles of smoke, about how God's punishing her by "dropping *that one* on me hands."

"By the way, we going to Georgetown on business next week and the kids are staying with our relatives in Overwinning."

Turning to me, Aunty Meena said, “Ann, you know where that is, don’t you? It’s the house right opposite the school with the combine harvester parked in the yard.”

I nodded. She nodded. I looked at my lap and decided that I didn’t hear any of it. I searched around inside my head for a conversation. Any conversation, even one I could join which was already half way through.

Nothing.

“Don’t worry,” Aunty Meena continued, turning back to Mammy. “I arranged for them to do lunch for Ann as well.”

No one said nothing – or is that ‘anything?’ No one said anything or nothing for a long time. Then we walked home.

In silence, with Mammy’s eye-look intact.

Dear Aunty or Mister,

Yes, you. You, right there, reading my story. I hope you don’t mind me calling you this. In my village, children have to respect grown-ups at all times and this also means calling men ‘Uncle’ or ‘Mister’ and women ‘Aunty.’ I haven’t got many big words, coz I’m only ten years old, but I will try to describe this the best I can.

Three straight roads run through the village of Stanleytown and the town of New Amsterdam. They are the Back Dam Road, where the scheme was cut out of the woods; the Main Road, where you find most of the shops; and Water Street which runs alongside the Berbice River.

These three streets all meet up like two knots, one at Berbice High School (or B.H.S.) which is at the end of the town called New Amsterdam. The other knot is at the end of the village of Stanleytown. The Main Road, however, goes on past the knots through several villages. Now, lots of little streets run crossway through these three roads like plaids on a skirt.

These streets in Stanleytown are numbered from thirty-nine, where the burial ground is, to sixty where the village ends and Islington begins with Mr. Singh's corner shop. Beyond Islington is Overwinning. This is where our Primary school is. Beyond the burial ground on the opposite side of Stanleytown is a little town called New Amsterdam.

I live on the very edge of this town with my grandmother Martha (who calls herself Elizabeth, because when you say Martha in a Guyanese accent, it sounds like 'Mahta,' which is too common) my nineteen-year-old Aunt Theresa, whose real name is Mayleen (she is the one who saves me), and my baby sister Francoise. Well, she has a French name coz she was born in French Guyane, you see, but her name's too hard to say, so we call her Franc.

My mother . . . (I'll have to tell you later. I gotta hide this book because Mammy's coming this way. Oh, and I'll tell you about Dirty Red Cap and Jonestown as well).

Best wishes xxx

* * *

"We late now girls," I said, breathing heavily. "We gotta run."

We were panting as we left Stanleytown, the village in which Raf and Tas lived. We were on our way to school on the day after we got the bad news about them leaving.

"Ann, look," Rafza shouted. "Look at all them people. What they looking at?"

"Let's go see," said Tasleema. "Quick!"

So we went over to the river wall, a concrete structure that runs alongside the muddy Berbice River.

"It's a dead body," someone at the edge of the crowd whispered to someone else.

"The police coming," another voice said. "But it's just after lunch time so they sure to be a while yet."

"Probably takin' an after-lunch smoke and a nap," said the first person, and the crowd burst out laughing.

"Or arrestin' someone for smuggling in wheat flour," another voice shouted.

"Hey, that ain't so funny," came the answer.

Rafza, Tasleema and I managed to get through the legs of the adults still making various jokes about the police. Peeping over the wall, we saw what looked like a massive, stuffed, scarecrow-like dummy, face down in the river. Someone said that it was a woman "coz only drowned women floated face down."

Somebody else said it was surely the other way round, that it was "actually and positively women who floated face up."

We didn't know, but we understood that whatever that floating thing was, if we had seen it without the crowd, we would've surely thought it was a bag of laundry.

"The body had to be in there for at least three days."

"Why yuh say that, mon?"

"Well, can't you see how swollen it is?"

"It stink bad, no."

"It can't come up to float unless it's been there for three days."

"Ah see."

A very loud woman said, "De woman must have killed sheself."

"Yuh can't know that."

"Well, she is Indian, ain't she? Look at the long, black hair."

"Yes, them Indian women kill themselves a lot 'round here."

We couldn't drag ourselves away even though we knew we were late for school. My eyes stapled themselves on the little four-eyed fish which were busy feasting on the dead person's already smelly flesh. Nibbling, picking, napping like thieves, back and forth, twice again.

A nip there, swim away, swallow, another nip, same place. My stomach turned over as I watched their little eyes, the top two on the crowd, the bottom two on their lunch.

"Wot you doing here, girlies?" a woman suddenly said behind us, and shooed us away.

"Off you go, or yu'all will get nightmares."

When I got into class Mr. Williams was lecturing about the exams again.

"Our school really has to increase its number of good grades. We haven't had many passes for Berbice High School in recent years and we must change that. I don't have to tell you that it's the best secondary school in the whole county of Berbice. Some people who live far away have their kids stay with relatives here just so they can go to that school. I know it's not easy to obtain the marks for B.H.S., kids, but I have faith in you."

Mr. Williams used his eyes like the four-eyed fish I had just seen, looking at everyone, everywhere, while he scratched his beard – something I had grown to find very comforting and safe, maybe because that was the one thing I was always sure of happening, or maybe, just because it was.

"I know that some of you have the potential to do it," he continued. "Remember those of you who are not twelve yet, that you may have two chances to do it. My own son Geff had two chances last year. He didn't do it the first time and now he is trying again. Same for Liddle and the Mercy twins, so do not let nervousness get to any of you…"

What's going to happen when we have to move again? If the landlady wants us out, where will we go? Mammy said that her son and son-in-law are convicts and that they go in and out of jail. What if they come back and shout at us again? I could probably sneak out and go to the police station in town, only it's so far away, the bad men could do something terrible to Franc and Theresa before I get back with the police.

"Time for your break, kids," said Mr. Williams later on, drawing me back into the real world.

Everyone rushed outside to play in the sand and heat. As usual, I went over to where the girls were playing Chinese Skipping to watch. Of course, I wasn't allowed to play. Why would they want me to? I wasn't that good at it really, so it shocked me when I heard a voice asking, "You want a game?"

"Me?" I asked in surprise.

"Yes, you," she asked again, pointing at me. "Want a game or not?"

I recognised her as one of the twin sisters in my year. So far, I'd only spent two months in my present class so I didn't know her first name, but her last name was certainly Mercy.

"Come," she ordered.

I was already wobbling as I made the first jump, and it didn't surprise anyone, including myself, when I toppled and sprawled in my second.

"You see!" Sandra Europe shouted in her fourth gear voice. "She got two left feet. Stupid! Doan let her play again!"

"Stop it, Sandra," the Mercy girl said with a knit in her brow. "She's never played before."

"Yeah. And you see why we don't let her play in our games," she continued.

The group laughed. I knew she was right. Even Mammy knew I was awkward and stupid. Even *I* wouldn't have let me play, if I were them.

I turned away while the group laughed.

"Come back, fire ant. Come back and sting me, nuh. Sting me nuh, fire ant. Come back and sting me!" Sandra screamed with laughter, wriggling her hips in time to the 'beat' of her stupid little song.

I hurried away towards the classrooms wishing I could poke a finger into all the staring eyes plastered onto my back. Shaking my shoulders made it feel a little better, as I imagined I was able to shrug some of the eyeballs off.

I wished I *could* go back and sting her. What's the point of looking like a giant red ant, from the tip of my toes to the end of my frizzy, springy hair, if I wasn't given any sting? My hair was red-ish, orange-ish, and boinged out from the plaits. My body stood long, straight and thin with skinny, red-honey coloured arms and legs sticking out from either end. And I walked funny, sort of like an ant who was scared that its next step would be under some giant, grindy boots.

I heard running footsteps behind me and whirled around. That Red Cap thing happened weeks ago but running footsteps behind me were now equally as frightening as seeing a ghost. Well, I supposed that it was. I'd never seen a ghost. Didn't think so, anyway.

That sound made my heart swell up like a water balloon, getting ready to pop, pop, whoosh!

"Hi, my name is Marleen…"

"Mercy," we said together.

"Never mind those girls, 'specially Sandra. She is mean to everybody. She teases me and my sister because we talk funny." She stopped and looked at me intently, probably looking to see if I was crying again like I did the other day when I tripped over and tore my uniform as I fell. Only, I didn't cry because of the fall, you see. When you get used to pain, you don't cry every time you get hurt. Besides, I wasn't supposed to shed tears because I'd get more licks if I did.

I cried about the uniform thing coz I was meant to keep it clean so I could wear it all week. I was crying the tears I wasn't allowed to cry later on, when I *did* get home that afternoon.

"I see you went up with the bright group the other day," Marleen said in her sing-song voice. "What did Sir say to you?"

"Just stuff about high school, you know," I said, wiping my eyes quickly, now I had the chance. "Which high school did you put on your 'First Choice' list?"

"Marla, that's my sister, and I are down for B.E.I. or B.H.S. Last year we passed for Tutorial, but our aunt said we should try again. What about you?"

"Same one . . . I mean B.H.S., but I'm only ten so I got two chances to do it," I told her, looking across to her train lines of corn rows and wishing I could get my crazy, fire-ant-coloured curls into such artistic patterns.

"So how come you only ten and writing Common Entrance," Marla asked frowning. "You supposed to be eleven."

She said 'En-rance' and 'wri-ing' almost as if she was jumping across a bridge right in the middle of her words.

"They let me skip one of the infant classes," I answered.

"Really?" Marlene said in her hiccupping, musical way again. "Your mam must be proud."

"Um, ah doan know. Maybe."

That afternoon, after lessons Marla, Marleen and I walked home. We planned that we would all try our very best to go to B.H.S. because we would be too embarrassed – just like the rest of our class – to wear the green uniform of the Community High or the khaki of the Tutorial Academy. Blue, we said. Blue was definitely the colour for us.

"You live at Fifty-four Stanleytown, right?" Marla asked.

"No, but I used to," I answered.

"One day we missed school coz we went out with our aunt, and we saw you at lunch time, coming out of Fifty-four with two Indian girls."

"I have lunch at their house."

"How come?" asked Marleen.

"Yeah," Marla said, "How come?"

I looked from one to the other and started to see little differences in their twin faces. Marla's little nose flared when she asked a question, and while she waited for the answer, it was almost as if she bored inside your soul with her large dark-copper eyes.

"We used to live in a house opposite theirs and we became friends. We moved about a couple a years ago to the scheme."

"You mean you have to pass the burial ground every day to go home?" Marleen asked excitedly. "You not 'ared?" She missed out 'sc' in scared.

"Yeah," I said smiling. "I try to run pass real quick."

"Ever see funerals going in?" Marla asked even more loudly, her little nose twitching. "You know if you cut through a funeral and not wait until they all pass by, you'll die," she said, whispering the 'die' bit.

"No you don't, silly," her sister told her. "It's just bad luck."

"Bet you never walk through the burial ground, eh?" Marleen asked again.

"You mad? Never!"

We came to Forty-eight Stanleytown and they showed me their house, which you could see from the Main Road, hiding behind a huge tamarind tree. It was a large, unpainted, wooden house built on posts. I'd never even been inside a house that grand before. Even with the paint all washed away from years of rain and baking humid heat, it was the handsomest house any friend of mine had ever lived in.

They told me that they had a Chinese Skipping rope, which I could borrow some time to learn to skip at home. I lied and said yes, but couldn't really. I wasn't allowed to take home anything that belongs to anyone else. Besides, I wasn't allowed to go outside to play. I would get too dirty, and get up to all sorts of nonsense if I wasn't watched with a close eye.

When I got home, Mammy said that she had to go to 'Shop Lady' to get some goods on credit.

"Shop Lady, she knows the whole village on account that she's at her shop in the market every day, six days a week. Maybe, she'd know someone who got an empty house to rent. Ah can't understand," Mammy fretted, "how it's getting so hard to find a vacant house when so many people escaping the country every day."

I ran quickly to get her Bristols from the bar, and to fetch her slippers from the kitchen. I didn't even care that Grimmond's side stable-door was shut. Mammy was going out and I didn't have to go with her. That was enough for me to be brave about going inside the bar and walking past the men drinking at the tables, who always tried to talk to me.

"Reds," they would say, and then smile as if I had a big, fat, terrible secret written across my forehead.

CHAPTER 3

THE PRISONERS' BREAK-IN

"Theresa, why does Mammy call 'Shop Lady' by that name?" I asked after dinner. Outside the crickets were singing their usual evening worship-song to the approaching sunset.

"Well, ah think Mammy believes that she'll make people less important if she don't call them by they given name," Theresa answered, her dark eyes deep in concentration. "She only uses the names of people she likes, that's why she refers to most people by some made up name or the other."

"But Shop Lady gives us food from her shop that we don't pay for right away," I said. "Aren't we meant to like her?"

"I suppose. But when Esther comes back she always pays her off, and then buys loads of food stuff only from her shop."

"Is Shop Lady rich?" I asked.

"Wot you say?"

"Is Shop Lady rich?" I repeated, making sure that Theresa could see my lips move.

"Ah doan know, but maybe…ah think so. She owns the house Meena and Nizam and the girls live in, the shop, and a larger house in Canjie where she lives now."

"I remember her old husband before he died," I said. "I used to watch him through our window from across the street when they lived in Aunty Meena's house – well – his house. Rafza told me that they saw him once."

"But they don't know him," Theresa answered. She tried to crease up her forehead like Mammy does – although Mammy didn't have to try – but her forehead remained tight, except for one thick eyebrow which went up into a sort of 'comma' shape. "He died before they moved in."

"Yeah, but she said that the house is haunted, and that's why Shop Lady moved out and went to live in her other house."

"That's the story, but no one knows for sure," Theresa answered, but she was clearly not thinking about old-men ghosts anymore. "Look, Ann, ah really got to clean up this kitchen before Mammy come back. Go watch yuh sister 'til I ready to give her a bath, no."

Theresa played 'pat-a-cake' on the back of my neck and steered me out of the kitchen. Her palms rested on the flesh of my neck for a tick. The insides of her hands were Velcro-like. I'd heard the grown-ups say 'cool hands, warm heart' or something like that, but they should have made up one for Theresa that said 'rough hands, smooth girl.' Or maybe something like, 'strong arms, tender girl.' Yeah, Theresa should have had something made up for her.

"All right," I said, looking over my shoulder, straining my neck to look up into those deep, dark eyes. "When…um…you have your own house like Shop Lady, can um…can…I live with you?"

Theresa looked me in the eyes and said, "When I dream of me own house, I always dream of you there."

She saves me.

* * *

Dear Aunty or Mister,

I promised to come back and talk to you, and here I am. You see, we live in a house – like all the other houses – that had been built on posts (some people call them stilts), so to come into our front door, you have to first walk up the long stairs, go past our veranda (where Mammy keeps her rocking chair), then open the door on your left. We have back steps as well, with another little veranda sticking out at the top like an odd plunging board.

Having a 'bottom house' means that if you are allowed to play outside, you could play under the house where it's cool without having to run around in the blazing heat all the time. My friends play hopscotch, cricket, football and even dollies at their bottom house. I don't though. You see, my father left me with my mother, who's called Esther, when I was a baby, and then my mother left me with her mother when I was three, and since then they've both left me.

I only see my mum once in a while, and haven't been visited by my father for years. The last time I saw him I was seven years old. He gave me twenty dollars then, but I had to give it to Mammy to help buy food. The last time I saw my mother I was nine, when she brought my sister, who was two weeks' old, from French Guyane.

My aunt Theresa, my mother's sister, who was then eighteen, became my sister's carer.

My mum works in a bar in this French principality, and she brings some of her money for us when she comes back to Guyana. I remember well the morning she last came. It was the day I woke up from a very strange dream. In this dream, my mum was outside the house and I was looking out the window when she arrived.

She smiled up at me and the morning sunlight flicked off her teeth. Then she beckoned me downstairs to help her bring in the carload of baggage she had saved up to bring over for us.

I had just finished telling Mammy about this dream when we heard a car horn outside our house. When I found myself looking out the window – and this is real life now – my mother was standing in exactly the same place with the sun in her face (but not bouncing off her teeth, because that would've been way too freaky).

Mammy and I and Theresa rushed downstairs to meet her. Of course, by this time we had been surviving on very little food for weeks, so we were really excited. That's when I saw that my mother was holding this soft, peachy, tiny baby in her arms. She introduced my sister and said that her name was Francoise.

Later she told us that a French nurse at the hospital where she had given birth had given her that name. When they came upstairs, I was able to inspect the new baby. She was very pink and soft and had no hair. Mind you, I'd never seen a baby with no hair before, but my mother said that a lot of white and mixed race babies were born without hair. Francoise was so cute and smooth, and best of all, she was my very own little baby sister. It was nice to have her.

My mother had also brought a record player. She said it was so small because it was portable. She said this meant that you could carry it around with you. You had to put six big batteries into it to make it play. But that's not all.

She also brought some records to play on it. There was one with a very handsome man on the cover. He had piercing eyes and black hair that was high in the front, but sort of tapered off at the back, he also had these long, amazing sideburns.

My mother said he was a king. I think she said that his country was called Rockandroll. I don't quite know how to spell that (even though I'm a very good speller and all that), but then again, I'd never heard of that place before.

When I heard the king's record, his voice sounded like it was coming from another person, in a kind of 'ver-trillion quest' (I think that's what you call them) act. His voice was mighty, wide and deep, but the picture of him looked so smooth and soft. Mammy said she liked Jim Reeves and Tom Jones best, but Theresa said that the handsome king one sounded better to her because she could hear some of his 'grrrs.' There was one called 'Heartbreak Hotel' that Theresa said she could actually hear.

Best wishes xxx

* * *

After Mammy came back from Shop Lady, we went to bed that hot night as usual, Theresa and Franc in the back bedroom so Franc doesn't disturb Mammy when she wakes up for her porridge in the night, and me and Mammy in her bed in the front room.

Mammy would say that she couldn't open the windows to let air in because they opened out onto the veranda. She'd say all a thief would have to do to rob or kill her was to step inside from the veranda, onto the window sill, and then into the front bedroom.

Maybe she was right about this, because she was right about everything. Maybe this was how she knew that I looked out the windows when I couldn't remember doing it myself. Theresa would say I should refuse to put my hands on the beating chair when Mammy found the curtains weren't the way she'd left them, but I was too scared to do that. Maybe tomorrow when I wake up, Esther would arrive and I could have a break until left again. I was glad that even though Mammy slept right beside me, and I could feel her breath, she couldn't hear me when I talked in my mind to myself.

I was safe there.

Sleep,

Silent sleep . . . .

* * *

Loud, crashing, splintering sound, then broken glass on my face!

Oh Gawd! What's happening to us?

Franc was crying. Mammy was screaming, "Get up! Get up!"

I was still half asleep. Theresa was shaking my kite-like, little frame. "Ann! Ann! They breakin' in! Run!"

Franc started to scream. She was in spasms. I knew her mouth was open, but I couldn't hear anything but a hissing "whoop." I waited for the next burst of scream. It came, and with it I was lifted out of my bed and rushed out of the room. The last thing I saw in the shadow of the street lamp as I was dragged from the bedroom was a dark boot stepping through the now-broken window pane, into the bedroom, and onto the bed. The owner of the boot was holding a cutlass in his hand. *Mammy won't like that. No shoes allowed in the house!*

* * *

"Ah think he went back out," Theresa whispered, grasping the baby as we all stood trembling together in the safety of living room. "He only want to scare us," she said, pulling the bedroom door shut.

"It's the two of them," Mammy shouted-whispered. "Derek wid him!"

I knew who Derek was straight off. He was our landlady's crazy-hair son who'd run away from the prison. I supposed that the other one was his sister's mad, criminal husband. Mammy always said, "Them's dangerous people to get mixed-up with."

One time Theresa had asked her, "Why you say that?"

Mammy had a very long answer to that. I can't remember all that she said, but one thing that stood out in my mind was when she explained that the landlady was a dark spirits' worker, and that people went to her when they wanted to put bad, Obeah spells on someone.

"Ann, you go out the back door and call fuh help," Mammy instructed me, jerking me back into the terror before us.

"No, doan send her out," Theresa pleaded. "They still in front there shouting. One of them can easily run under the house and find her on the back steps."

"No," Mammy said. "They won't hurt a child. Go, shout for help. Mr. Barry will come."

"But yuh said that Derek is a murderer. She can't…I'll…I'll go," Theresa told her.

"You make the baby keep quiet," Mammy shouted, and this was no whisper-shout either. "Go," she said, and she and I crept through the dark kitchen to the back door.

She shoved me out.

Then I heard the bolt click.

* * *

I was screaming before I could hear my own voice. I was wailing and crying, spewing like a volcano – a lava of tears running down my face.

"Help! Help! Somebody please help us!" The louder I screamed the harder I wept. My body wanted to do this so much. My voice was breaking, but it was not because of the shouting. I was crying so hard I could barely say *'Elp.'* I was exposed and only had moments before the two men walked under the house and came to deal with me.

I almost imagined footsteps getting nearer and nearer, closing in on me. I thought of all the things they could do to me, and I saw my half-grown body chopped up into tiny pieces with the cutlass the person who stepped into the bedroom was holding. A bizarre voice in my head shouted louder than I ever could, *'But would that be so bad?'*

I was shivering in the hot night air, feeling the not so foreign hand of fear take hold of my heart and squeeze and squeeze. I knew my heart was going to spurge its contents all over the hand in seconds. *That'll teach it.*

I looked for the men through my tears, while I reasoned with that voice, *'But see, I am only little.'*

'Is that why I catch yuh thinking of dying?'

'I don't want to die, please, I don't want to die. I'm really only little.'

Heavy tears were streaming down my face when I heard him. He was blowing his whistle through the curtain of the night. *It had to be Mr. Barry!* By the time he reached our house still dressed in his pyjamas, he had most of the street behind him.

* * *

The two men had run away, leaving us with a bedroom full of glass and a lifetime's worth of fear.

We survived the night of terror with the mad men from the prison. We each packed a little plastic bag. Theresa packed two, one for herself and another bigger one for the baby. We slept the rest of the night in Mr. Barry and his wife Shirley's living room. I couldn't go to school the next day because the police wanted to question everyone who lived in the house, bright and early in the morning.

"So we start from the top and tell me what happened," said the big puffy policeman. I thought of him chasing after criminals and wondered how hard he would wheeze after five minutes of hard running.

Mammy began, and told them how the landlady's son and son-in-law smashed our window with their cutlasses, but the police wanted to know how we were so sure it was them. Of course Mammy saw them clearly and they didn't hide who they were either.

"So what did they say to you?" the big one asked again.

"They shouted down the house and cursed us about our so and sos, and then said we'd better move soon or else."

"Or else?" he asked again.

"Or else they will do worse than break a window," Mammy answered.

"Did they enter the house at any time?" the smaller policeman asked. His voice was a lot bigger than I thought it would be. Even Theresa heard him.

"One of them stepped into the bedroom window from the veranda," Theresa answered, "but ah think he must 'av stepped right back out because he never come through the bedroom door, and into the living room where we were. Ah think their voices were coming from outside most of the time they were here, even when Ann was outside."

"Who's Ann?" Big Puffy said, and my heart leaped into the wall of my bony chest which barely held it inside my body.

"Me niece here," she said, pointing at me.

'Please don't ask me, please don't ask me, I not allowed to talk when grown-ups speaking. Besides I don't know nothing.' I screamed in my stupid head like I always did, too afraid to say anything out loud.

"What were you doing outside, child? You obviously saw their cutlasses, you . . ."

"Well," Mammy cut in. "She rushed out shouting for help, and then Mr. Barry come 'round and they run away."

"Mr. Barry? Oh, the P.N.C. Neighbourhood Watch chap from up the street," he answered his own question.

"So," the little, loud-voice policeman said, turning to Mammy, "At which point did you call the police?"

"We doan have a phone, you see," Mammy answered. "Mr. Barry went back home when he was sure they were gone and called you."

"I think we have enough to charge these men with aggravated assault with a dangerous weapon, breaking and entering, and disturbing the peace," the bigger policeman said. "Maybe more. Just one more thing. Do you know why they want you to move?"

"They doing it for their mother," Mammy said. "They just come out of jail and she send them." A tiny ball of spit appeared on her bottom lip, and when she said 'them,' it transferred onto the upper lip.

"She got someone else she want to rent the house to, and she want me out. I pay her rent, and when she tek me to court, the magistrate said she got no grounds for throwing me out, that she got to wait until I find somewhere else to live. She threatened to get me out in the court yard." Her ball of spit – which I named 'blit' – rested finally on her top lip.

"As the magistrate said, she can't throw you out."

"But ah can't stay here now, can I? And she know that, she show me what they can do. I got a young lady daughter, and if anything happen, you know how fast gossip will travel 'round this place about what shame happen to me."

"We are very sorry," said the bigger policeman. "We will do what we can. Do you have anywhere to stay?"

"No, but Mr. Barry say that we can sleep in his living room until the end o' the week."

"Then what?" he continued.

She shrugged, dejected like. Even I could see that she knew this was far from the end. I found I wasn't scared. I had buried worse than this inside the soft bits of my own body. After all, I didn't even get beaten today.

"Strange," said the smaller policeman, "How people will destroy their own property."

Was I Mammy's property?

CHAPTER 4

MOVING HOUSE

"Ann, I wrote a note to yuh grandmother to ask if you could spend a day with the girls next week during the Easter holidays," Aunty Meena said, handing me a folded piece of paper. "You know that we leaving in a few weeks." I was on my way back to school after another of her tasty lunches.

Ever since that day we got kicked out from the house opposite the one she now lived in, she decided that because I was going to be so far away from school, she would make me lunch, and in exchange, I could help bring her little girls home.

Rafza was two years younger than me, and her sister, three. Their house was about ten to fifteen minutes' walk from our school, which made it perfect to get there and back in the hour's break we had at lunch time.

Our old house opposite theirs was the nicest house we'd ever lived in. Built on stilts, it had two bedrooms and a big enough sitting room for Mammy to run a little nursery school out of. She only had seven children, but Theresa, the only person who did any teaching, managed to keep them all under control. The landlord had sold the house with us still in it. It was as if he had sold us, the house and the things inside. The new owners, a mechanic and his new wife, were going to run a car repair and re-spray service out of the yard.

"Thanks, Aunty Meena," I answered. The word 'holiday' has always grated on the edge of my teeth. I wished I had to go to school every day, always.

It was the rainy season again which meant that my thin cotton shirt became my second skin almost every day going to, or coming from school. It didn't matter though, because the sun came out so hot after the rain that, before I knew it, I was well and truly parched again. Besides, a shower from heaven was a lot better than the little bucket of water I carried upstairs to wash with every afternoon after school.

Marla, Marleen and I had found a spot behind the school where no one else played, so every break time we would hurry down the long slats which made up the stairs to our classroom to go outside to draw our own hopscotch.

You had to be very careful coming down the stairs for two reasons. One, your foot could end up between the slats, and someone like me could easily slip through – head and all, onto the dust, ten or twelve feet below. Two, you had to hold your skirt tightly around your knees so that no-one standing under the stairs could see your underwear.

The twins had taught me how to play hopscotch, and I was becoming quite good. Well, obviously not as good as they were.

Today when Mrs. MacAlman, our little, circular deputy head rang the bell, we raced out. There was still a chance to play a game or two before the rain came.

As I was rushing down the stairs, I happened to run past Sandra Europe, the worst person to overtake because she owned the playground and hated me, I might add. She insisted that either me or my 'wind,' had brushed past her skirt and that I had no right to do so.

"Look where yuh going, stupid!" she shouted.

"You look where *you* going, picky head!" Marla shouted back from behind me.

"Yuh have yuh bodyguards today," Sandra hissed poisonously, pointing a very angry finger at me. "But I know you walk on the Back Dam road to go home, I'll catch you alone and beat you up, you scrawny fire-ant."

"If you stop fighting so much your hair might grow," Marla shouted back at her. Go flush your head down the toilet. That might help!"

Even under the circumstances, laughter came bounding out of me. I found that it felt good. Sandra Europe has always had very, very short, matted, knotty hair, too short to even plait in cornrows, so it was left to porcupine in every direction on her head.

"You black so and sos hanging round with her." Sandra had one hand on her hip and the other pointed at Marla's head. "What she gat? The biggest thing on her red, fire-ant face is she two bony cheeks. What she gon do with them? Sting me?"

Sandra turned to me.

"Come sting me, na!" she said, thrusting her hips out and making tiny hops in my direction. Then she faced Marla and said, all quiet-like, "When I finished with her, I gon beat you and yuh tie-tongued sister up!"

The warrior finger had finally left me and was switching from side to side like a steel cobra, to where the twins stood.

"What? Both of us? Together?" Marleen asked. We laughed. We knew they went nowhere without each other.

The three of us walked away together in the rain. So much for our game.

"Let's go buy some tamarind sour from the stall ladies," said Marleen. "I got five cents."

"I got ten," said Marla.

"Where'd you get the extra five?" demanded Marleen.

"Remember? I didn't spend mine yesterday, silly."

"Oh yeah," giggled Marleen.

"How come you never get any spendin' money, Ann?"

"My grandmother never give me any."

"Race you to the stalls," my friends shouted together. They'd talk at the same time sometimes, you know. They say twins do that.

My friends. That sounded cool.

* * *

"I in a good mood – I got paid today," my grandmother declared when I walked into the house this afternoon, late again no doubt, from Common Entrance Exams lessons. As I was beginning to change out of my worn green skirt, she said to me, "Go and buy a shot of rum for me at the bar."

I was glad that the money had put her in a good mood. It meant that she had bought batteries for the radio, which would be playing constantly. Pleasant music, coming from a world which existed outside of my experience and imagination, gave me a bridge of hope that one day I would be allowed to explore. It gave me a different background music to the one I'd gotten used to which played night and day inside my head, the kind of music you'd hear in horror films that'd set your toes tingling as you waited for something scary to jump out of the dark and do something bad to you.

Music on the radio dulled the nasty tunes playing in my head, which meant I didn't have to listen to them all the time. It also gave Mammy a distraction to take her attention off me a bit.

Money also meant that I could have some milk in my green tea tomorrow.

"Milk so expensive these days," Mammy always said.

This is why only Franc could be allowed any, and sometimes even she had to drink her porridge without.

"Count this money and make sure there's two hundred and seventy-five dollars," Mammy told me. She'd say she gets mixed up counting her salary, so it was better that I do it to make sure it was all there. It was, and as I was leaving to go to the bar with an empty rum bottle in my hand, I heard Ray Peterson singing his heart out on the radio:

". . . Tell Laura I love her . . ."

"Grimmond's bar don't do 'loose' rum anymore, Mammy," I said from a safe distance when I arrived back home. "You got to buy the whole bottle now if you taking it away."

"What yuh say?"

"The bar man said you had to buy the whole bottle if you taking it away."

"Ah hear what you said, stupid. Ah not deaf. How come they doing that now? They didn't do that the last time."

"Ah doan know."

"You never know anything. Ah want me rum, and I can't afford a whole bottle." Mammy's forehead-crease was pointing at me again. I shifted from foot to foot, then remembered that there was something I could do to redeem myself out of this one.

"Um . . . I could go to Vrymon's if you want."

I'd suggested another disgusting bar which was more than a mile away, with every intention of walking there with an empty rum bottle in my hand, so that Mammy could have a drink with her curry. If I made her happy, she would be pleased with me, you see.

"Awright, but hurry, Ah doan want to eat too late," Mammy replied.

As she walked away from me, I stared at her back. Her narrow shoulders seem to reach all the way to the ceiling, as they carried her very stiff, proud head out to the veranda. Her short, feathery, jet black hair seemed very odd on a body that smelled a lot older than it looked.

It was getting dark by the time I got back home, so Mammy said I should have my dinner before I did my homework. With a watering mouth, I galloped down even the sweet aroma of the most beautiful curry ever made, a dish that no one could ever make as well as Theresa. The only thing I savoured was the one piece of meat I had on my plate. After months without meat, I couldn't let my serving go without chewing into the bone. I then took the fragments of bones apart and licked all the brown stuff off from the inside. Marrow, Theresa said it was called. Marrow, the sweetest bit, the bit you savour and keep for last.

After dinner, Mammy went to have her cigarette in her rocking chair on the veranda. Theresa had to give Franc her bath, and I cleared the table. This was turning out to be a nice day after all. Tiring, but nice. Maybe if we're lucky Mammy would even tell us a long-time story.

As I was taking the last few dishes into the kitchen, I caught my foot in the mat, slipped, and let go of the glass I was holding.

Tick, tock, tick, tock

Rewind!

Now slow it down.

As the glass fell, my eyes saw it tumble a few times before it finally hammered the floor.

Splinters! Don't walk! Don't walk!

So many things went through my mind, it was as if my brain had kept a film of the last time this had happened and was playing it back -- frame by clicking frame in front of my eyes -- in very small black and white pictures *tinged with spots of red.* The glass crashed on the wooden floor, and I felt my heart dive there with it.

Tick, tock, tick, tock.

Now speed up.

Within a fraction of a second, Mammy was standing there with that familiar look on her face, wide nose flaring. She glanced at the broken glass with a look of satisfaction. This look would've puzzled me, except that there was too much terror racing through my blood to be anything but terrified.

Before she looked behind the front door where she kept the two-by-four, I knew what was coming.

Mammy picked up the wood and walked towards me. I didn't actually see her move, one second she was at the door; the next, right in front of me. There was nowhere for me to run. What was I talking about? I'd never run – too scared. Besides, she'd always said if I make her have to run after me, I'd get a lot more licks.

CHAPTER 5

BREAKING GLASS

She twists my arm behind my back and my knees hit the floor. The blows come straight after in a downpour of, *Thud! Thud!*

My arms, they're way too small, way too thin, but the *thud, thud,* they keep coming.

The pain – electricity through my bones – rockets me to my feet and I jump around on one foot. The more I jump around, the more the hits rain on, and the more she chews her lips.

Thud! Thud!

I cry in pain but not loudly. I always keep it in. She grabs my wrist as she starts to beat my legs all over, again and again, speeding up. I try to turn again, but this time she's holding me so tightly that my whole arm is twisted over and above my head.

I can't move, I can't get away from the fire on my skin, charring me all over. I can't get loose.

Pain. Too much pain!

It's in this position that she hits me again, again, again. Every time the licks land on my skin, I feel – rip.

The lashes come harder and harder. I hear them in my head and I cry out inside, *please stop, please stop. Oh my God please make it stop, please, please.*

My knees are now giving away I can't stand. But, yank! She yanks my little body up by the arm and keeps beating.

"You want to break her?" Theresa demands. I think she has Franc in her arms because she very carefully puts down something which is wrapped up in a bath towel and comes over. At this point I'm half sitting on the floor, tears streaming down my face, body fire-working into flames of red, sizzling pain.

Theresa pulls the piece of wood from Mammy's hand. Mammy drops me and goes for her, punching her several times in the face and chest.

"Don't you take me on!" Mammy shouts, spit flying from her mouth. "She know that she get licks when she break me things."

“People don’t beat children for accidentally breaking things, and they not your things, they Esther’s things!” Theresa shouts, leaning in dangerously close to Mammy. “I hate this wood. Ah getting rid of it!” She storms out of the house.

“Clean up that glass!” Mammy shouts at me. “And you, sit down!”

It’s only at this point I notice naked Franc, with a green towel draped round her shoulders, standing in the biggest of our three chairs – the ones with steel legs – staring at us.

Taking it all in and swallowing it down.

* * *

Later:

I cleaned up the glass with limbs that felt like they had hot, wriggly porridge in them. Five minutes later, as I was sitting at the table, trying to do my homework, my legs were shaking so badly because of all the pain, I couldn’t keep them on the floor.

My dear God

I do try to be good but she always gets me. I really do try. You know I try to exist only in my mind, because I know she doesn’t want me to be, and sometimes I not even sure if I am *real. I don’t want to be a bad person and I don’t want to get licks, please let it stop.*

Amen.

“You got any splinters?” Theresa asked me.

“I took them out already,” I said. “I had some in me hands, coz I held on to the wood, and some in me knees.” I still found it hard to breathe and took in four little breaths instead of one, the way you’d do if you’d been crying too much for too long.

“Can’t you put your feet flat on the floor?” asked Theresa, looking under the table to where my violently shaking legs were resting on my toes.

“No,” I replied. “They making a rapping sound on the floor and she won’t like it.”

“I threw the wood away,” Theresa whispered and patted me gently on the back.

"I hope she doan hit you for that," I whispered, fresh tears pouring down my cheeks.

"Doan you worry about that," she said. "At least she only hits me now and again these days. With you, it's almost every other day."

I'm sorry, but I have to escape now.

* * *

I've now gone back to the day I spent with Aunty Meena and the girls because it was the best day of my life, ever. Luckily, Mammy was busy at the court with the landlady and her fugitive, window-smashing son and son-in-law, and surprised me by saying yes to the note Aunty Meena had written to her.

"Doan you go and shame me. And mek sure you ask if she can leave me something when she go," was her warning to me when I stepped out to leave.

Outside in the warm air the neighbours' children were testing out their kites for Easter Sunday. Almost everyone made a kite during the Easter holiday.

A long time ago when my uncle Christopher lived with us, he made several, and even managed to sell some of them.

"Is really easy, mon," he told me once. "All you need is some light wood, a bit of kite paper, some thread, a long piece of twine and some scrap cloth for the tail. The hardest part is picking the glue off the glue tree."

"There's a glue tree up by my school," I'd told him.

"Really? I gat to go up there later to get some, then."

That afternoon he'd come in with a bunch of tiny green fruit, the size of goat's dung. He'd let me peel them with my finger nails and hand them to him, after which he squeezed the water-coloured paste from the fruit onto his multi-coloured kite paper. It stuck fast instantly. Afterwards, it took me days to finally get all the glue off my fingers.

"That's why ah let *you* peel them," he laughed a few days later. What I didn't tell him was that I'd eaten some of the sweet flesh of the glue fruit. Me and my friends had learned about the taste of the fruit last year at Easter (this is when the glue tree is in fruiting season). I wondered about how it was gluing my insides together, but didn't dare ask anyone what would happen to me. This was a long time ago, though. My uncle doesn't live with us anymore.

Rafza, Taz and I, on the day we spent together, had helped bathe baby Nafeeza, then we went downstairs to play. We didn't go into the little store room under the house, though. Raf said it was haunted. It did give you a strange feeling when you looked in through the window, like someone was watching you, but you couldn't see them. I can't explain this properly, but it was almost like the window was simply a pair of big eyes, and when you looked through it, you were meant to gaze into something secret – but not a good kind of secret.

After we had lunch, the girls taught me the Arabic alphabet. It started like this: Alef, Ba, Ta, Tha, Jeem. We climbed up the mango tree and picked several of the ripe, juicy fruits. 'Little Spice,' they're called. Soft, cinnamon-like, sweetish and very delicious.

They were not like the large ones which are sometimes sour. These are always sweet, even when they're green. We had to be careful on the tree because there was a large bees' nest high up in the very top. After our pickings, we took the mangos upstairs, cleaned them, then cut them into tiny pieces. We mixed some red chilli sauce with a sprinkle of salt, and oohed and aahhed our way through the tongue-throbbing snack, but it was good.

Aunty Meena said we could help pick up the washing off the line before our dinner of curried chicken – my most favourite in the whole wide world. There was only happiness, and no one was afraid. It made me wish I was going with them.

When I was very little, I used to think that our house was normal, but I was beginning to learn that maybe it just wasn't. If happiness was available to Aunty Meena and her family, then it must also be available to me. If it was, I was going to find it.

Days after the breaking glass, I returned to what was real to me. I walked up my own stairs, pulling my legs behind me. I've never been back to the shortcut I'd used when I was nearly attacked. Fifteen minutes less walking wasn't enough to make me less scared of what could've happened to me.

There was a strange pair of slippers on the veranda. Good, somebody was here. I walked into the house and there, sitting on the big blue chair with Mammy, was someone that looked like Shop Lady, but I wasn't sure.

"Good afternoon, Aunty," I said, then walked into the kitchen to put away my school bag.

Franc was sitting on Theresa's hip as she tried to cook dinner with one hand. Theresa silently handed her to me. Her wet cotton nappy made a dark patch on my thin shirt as I took her and sat her on the scrubbed, wooden floor.

"Ah washed all the nappies and hang them out, but the rain wet them again," Theresa said breathlessly. "I got to find something to put on her. Play with her for me until ah finished here." She placed the palm of her hand on her forehead and took a deep breath.

I turned to Franc.

"Wanna sing?" She now had little wisps of light brown hair sticking out from the top of her milky head.

"Dak, dak," she answered. So I sang:

"Jack and Jill went up the hill
To fetch a pail of water,
Jack fell down and broke his crown
And Jill came tumbling after."

"Atta," Franc shouted, and we did it again.

Theresa said that dinner was almost ready and we were going to eat as soon as Shop Lady was gone. So it *was* her.

After what seemed like one hundred 'Dak and Dills,' Theresa left to go and find a suitable piece of old bedding to use as a nappy for Franc. On her way out, Mammy was saying goodbye to Shop Lady in a rather loud and excited voice. Before the tip of her skirt had hit the back of the door, Mammy said that we were moving.

"Shop Lady come to say that she heard in the village about what happened with the break-in and stuff," Mammy told us.

"She too hear that?" Theresa asked, stopping with Franc for a minute.

"Yeah," Mammy answered, nodding heavily. "And she say she wanted me to move into her house now that Meena and Nizam and the girls gone and it's empty. She said that she always admired how clean and tidy I kept the house we lived in when we lived opposite her in Fifty-four."

I looked at Theresa, and I knew that if she had a crease on her forehead, it would've been pointing at Mammy now, and not in a nice way either. After all, it was me and Theresa, mainly Theresa, who did all the house work.

"What you tell her?" Theresa asked.

"What you think ah tell she? She so happy that ah say yes."

The next day I couldn't wait to tell Marla and Marleen about our good news.

"I'm going to be closer to school than you," I sang excitedly.

"So you moving back to the same street you lived in before," Marla said. "Cool!"

"Wait," said Marleen, "If you pass for B.H.S, that is at the other end of New Amsterdam. Where you live now would be far away, let alone if you move back."

However, I couldn't allow myself to worry about that. I'd have to do that later. I was happy that we were going to live in Aunty Meena's old house. That way I could be close to her and her happiness.

* * *

Marla and Marleen and I had another 'un-popular' playing with us now. Marla said that we might as well get together with her since we're all in the same boat. Dianne lived in the next street up from Marla and Marleen, and had five younger brothers and sisters. A lot of the children in my class wouldn't play with her because they said she was a dunce. I thought the only reason she couldn't do better in school was because she sometimes had to miss classes to take care of her younger brothers and sisters, like my mother used to do when Mammy had to go to parties. It wasn't really Dianne's fault. She told us so, and she said that her mother was pregnant, and because she was the oldest, she'd have to help take care of the baby when it came.

Dianne had a younger sister in third year in our school and sometimes when she wasn't playing with her own friends, she'd play with us. These days we had to wait a long time for our turn to come around in hopscotch because there were more of us. Instead of three walking home after lessons, we sometimes had four. It was nice before, but it was so much better now. I was glad I had my friends. School wasn't as lonely as it used to be.

CHAPTER 6

MAMMY'S GOT A NEEDLE GOING TO HER HEART

Dear Aunty or Mister,

It's time I came back and have a little chat with you, to pick up from where I left off.

My mother's name is Esther and my father is called Steve. My grandmother, whom I have to call Mammy, is a nursery school teacher but this is a mistake, you see. After we moved here from the country, Mammy opened a little nursery school.

If you know Mammy, you'll be aware that she's well-schooled in stiff-necking about and taking praise from parents, but not in teaching. None of the parents knew this because when they dropped off their kids, Mammy would be all peacocking about in the lessons' area.

However when they left, my aunt Theresa was the one doing all the teaching and other things teachers do. She was only about twelve and didn't know what exactly to teach, so she taught the kids - me included - everything she knew, like counting, writing, spelling and stuff (this is why I knew how to count and write my name and had to skip an infants' class at primary school, because the teachers said I was too bright for it).

Even though Mammy's had no teaching certificate or training, her school became very popular and had a good name around the village, because we (the students) knew lots and lots of stuff other children our age didn't. Years later when the government took over all the private schools (right about when people started calling each other Comrade this and Comrade the other), one teacher from each of the best private nursery schools in the same area had to come together to make up one big Government school. My grandmother chose to jump into this big curry pot of schools, instead of sending Theresa.

Poor Theresa.

I'm trying really hard to go to B.H.S. because this is a really good school. Well, me and everyone else, that is. Sadly, only people with enough points on their Common Entrance Exams are allowed in. The Canadians set up this school when they were here, and the harder it became for the locals to get in, the more people wanted their kids to go there, especially when they started working towards doing the Cambridge Junior and Senior Certificate Exams. Everything was different and special. You even had to wear a posh tie despite the blistering heat.

Before the Government and the ruling PNC party took over all the schools, you had to pay to go to this one, but fees have all been scrapped, so that means I am allowed in – as long as I get the marks, that is. The only thing is that B.H.S. is so far away. It is on the edge of this very long road I told you about, on the very end of New Amsterdam. This means that it is about two miles from where I live now. When we move back to Fifty-four, I'll be about four miles away from the school. We can't afford transportation so I'll have to walk, but it's major worth it.

Best wishes xxx

* * *

A week before we moved from the scheme, we had to go to the people in our street to say goodbye, but not everyone, because not all of them were good enough for Mammy to speak to.

We went to see Mr. Barry and Shirley and the Persauds – they had a big house, and talked to you from behind a mighty iron fence guarded by four giant, evil dogs. I'd buy ice from them every day because we didn't have a fridge, you see. However, I stayed as far away from the fence as possible and called "Upstairs!" at the top of my voice.

As soon as the dogs heard this, of course they'd come a'runnin', barking and gnashing, with spit flying from their opened teeth-filled mouths. Mammy always said that if she didn't know me, she'd always be able to tell when I was standing at the Persauds' gate.

"Gruff! Gruff!" the four of them would shout at me.

"Gruff! Grrruff! We will kill to rip you up!" No really, they would. Their teeth always glittered as if they had just cleaned them to impress me, terrify me. It worked.

When someone came down to bring me the ice, I would hand over the money as quickly as I could, and pull my hand away real fast, because the dogs were so determined to get me that they jumped all the way to the top of the gate.

I would still be shaking by the time I walked up our back stairs. Of course I wasn't allowed on the front steps with the ice dripping through the little, old plastic bag, but this did give me extra time to cool down my racing heart.

We also went next door to see Mrs. Dhanpaul who had her bottom house converted and enclosed to make a nursery school. This was where Mammy now worked. Mrs. Dhanpaul had lodgers, a man and his two teenage sons who both went to B.H.S. and studied all the time. Mammy said this man married a white woman, a German, but something happened and they broke up. His sons were 'red' like me.

I really don't understand why we're 'red,' I don't *look* red. Okay, I agree that I have red hair, so I can't argue with that part of it, but if I were to pick a colour for my skin, I'd say it was honey. Well, perhaps 'honey' ain't a colour, but neither is 'red' if you're referring to skin colour. Come to think of it, neither is 'white,' but people still call themselves 'white,' don't they? Ah well, I suppose I'll have to stick with 'red.'

Mrs. Dhanpaul looked sad all the time. I always tried not to look at her because I'd become soaked with guilt. Firstly, because I thought she'd heard when I got licks and must think I was a very bad girl, and secondly, because Mammy always said such bad things about her, silly things, like she does Obeah on account of her constant use of Red Lavender. Mammy said that White Lavender was good, but that the Red one was bad – like Black and White magic or something. Maybe Mammy didn't like her because she was the headmistress.

"That big foot that she gat," Mammy said, turning down the sides of her mouth, "Is what they call elephantiasis." Then she turned to me and said, "Is a Portuguese curse, coz your other grandmother, got one as well."

I don't know about this though, because she lives in Canada and I've never seen her. I was told that my dad has lots more children. Mammy said that he left Esther for an Indian woman who was already pregnant, and then went on to have loads more children, some with his new wife's sister, but I have no idea.

I felt like I should go to Grimmond's bar to say goodbye to the drunkies and the barman. Maybe when I was sent for cigarettes, I could.

When we got home from the visits, Mammy got a needle out of the sewing box and asked me to thread it so that Theresa could mend her work trousers for tomorrow, but first I had to go get the Bristols. When I came back into the bedroom, with the front window boarded over making it slightly dark in the upcoming twilight, Mammy was standing there in a panic.

"The needle went up me foot," she kept on saying.

I went down on my hands and knees and tried to look for it.

"It went up me foot, stupid. You not gon find it there!"

"I . . . um . . ." I too was panicking.

"You could've threaded it for me *before* you run over to Grimmond. Now look what happen. It fall down, and when I went to look for it, I stepped on it by mistake, and it got sucked up into me foot."

Mammy had always told me to be careful with needles. She said that if an unthreaded needle went into your skin, your blood took it straight to your heart and it killed you.

"You got to run to the hospital," she screamed. "Run and bring back a doctor!"

I scooted off in a panic straight away, without even telling Theresa where I was going. I ran as fast as I could, which probably wasn't very fast on account that I'm very awkward at doing physical things. That's why I always get picked last for P.E. stuff unless Marla or Marleen was picking. I ran out of the scheme, and cut through the burial ground because it would be quicker. I had to be extra fast before the needle found its way to Mammy's heart. I didn't want her to die, especially not because of me.

When I got to the hospital, puffing like a fireworks factory aflame, no one seemed to be in a hurry. Injured people were sitting around in a waiting room that smelled of seeping sores. There were white people with black sores and black folk with white ones.

There were hundreds of flies caught on the old fly trap which hung from the middle of the white, wooden ceiling. The first nurse I saw – a woman wearing a badge which said 'Geeta' – told me, "You got to take a ticket. These people been waiting for hours. You just can't barge in and demand attention."

"But my grandmother's got a needle going to her heart."

"What?"

"She got stuck with a needle. You got to help her."

The nurse straightened her blue belt which lay on her bleached white uniform and said, "What?"

"She wants to see a doctor," I went on.

The nurse looked at me, then glanced around her as if to make sure that she wasn't the only one hearing all this. Then she stuck a thumb inside the 'V' on the neck of her uniform, blew down it, and started to fan herself with some important-like looking papers.

"Wait here," she warned, with a short, fat finger. "And doan go nowhere, mind."

I wiped the sweat off my forehead and waited, rooted on the same spot. The nurse with the 'Geeta' name tag came back a few minutes later and told me that there was only one doctor working tonight (must be one of the Cuban doctors the grown-ups said The Comrade Leader was bringing in, because of his connections with Cuba's President, Feedel, or someone like that). He wasn't due until nine p.m., in about two hours, and was only called in for emergencies.

I thought I *had* an emergency.

I left the hot, fly-buzzing hospital to Geeta, and ran all the way back home, back through the burial ground again. When I got back to the house it was dark. Theresa was sitting in one of the small blue chairs on the veranda mending Mammy's trousers under the naked, moth-covered bulb. She jumped up when she saw me coming. I was never out this late, you see. Mammy was sitting in her rocking chair smoking her cigarette.

"Theresa find the needle on the floor," she said, through a grey cloud of rising smoke.

When I told Theresa later about my trip to and from the hospital and got to the part about the burial ground, I started to shake. Did I really do that? I was so, so stupid. Mammy did say I was very stupid. Maybe she was right.

* * *

The rainy season was still batting in its innings. This season offered the perfect opportunity for the truanting boys from our school to get away and go swimming in the overflowing trenches on the Back Dam Road. This morning Terrance and Charlie got caned on their bottoms in front of the whole class. Mr. Williams is not like the other teachers, he said that his "policy was to beat it out only if he can't speak it out."

"Let this be a lesson to everyone in this class," he said after the caning, wiping the sweat from his top lip with the back of his hand.

"If you take part in dangerous sports like swimming in the Back Dam trenches, that…," and here he pointed at the two boys who were still making hissing sounds with their teeth and rubbing their bottoms with the palms of their hands, "…is what you're asking for."

The boys had a very organised way of getting out of school to go swimming. They planned it all the day before, when one of the gang was told to bring a blob of Vaseline, wrapped up in a bit of old newspaper.

Sometimes in the midst of classes, Mr. Williams would say, "Alright! Everyone down tools. Time for spot-checking and convicts-caking."

I knew that the last two words meant he was going to seize their stuff and bin them, but I didn't know why he called it 'convicts-caking.' It made me think of our landlady and her convict son.

When Mr. Williams found bits of stowed-away Vaseline in the boys' bags, he made a big deal out of holding them as high above the bin as he could, then dropping them with a dull 'thud' into the black, galvanised rubbish bucket.

The trenches were totally muddy, you see, and going for a swim in them meant that when you finally surfaced, you'd be as grey as…as a…what was the greyest thing? Well, as grey as that thing. As you dried off in the heat, you'd become greyer and greyer and soon everyone and their neighbour knew you'd gone swimming, including your parents when you get home in the afternoon.

To find a way 'round this grey, dead giveaway, the boys took off all their clothes for the trench-bath. Once the swim was over, they got dressed again and rubbed the Vaseline on the bits of exposed skin like their legs under their shorts, arms, faces, and so on.

After Mr. Williams began to convicts-cake their Vaseline, they had to change tactics, and found that spit worked just as well as, if not better than, the Vaseline.

After that magical discovery, they spat on their skin, in nice little splotches then rubbed it all in. Pah, rub in, pah, rub in.

A grey spot there, not to worry. Pah, rub in, pah, rub in.

Now you could hardly see the grey at all.

* * *

". . . For the power and the glory,

Forever and ever. Amen," we all said for the second time.

"Hands up, in, out, down, sit down," Mr. Williams said as we went through the motions.

"Yes, Sir," we all replied as we sat down. The girls, as always, neatly tucked our skirts under our bottoms and over our knees – just like we were taught.

There was a sort of rumble in the classroom as we took our seats on the scrubbed wooden benches. The kiss-ka-dees were singing outside in the hot, damp air. "Kiss, kiss, kiss-ka-dee," went their song. One of them landed on the windowless window sill for a moment, saw forty eyes staring at its wet, brown and yellow feathers and quickly flew away.

"Them kiss-ka-dees is good bird meat," my uncle Christopher had said to me once when I was very little.

"But they so small," I'd said. "How d'you get any meat under them feathers?"

"Ahh," he had said, but never answered my question until some time later when he had managed to catch a blue-sakie (another tiny bird) and roasted it on a spit. He didn't have to use his sling-shot that time. All he did was put some old chewing gum out in the sun on the fence with a bit of bird seed next to it. Soon enough, the bird came by to eat the seeds, and bingo!

"See?" he asked when he'd given me a taste of the tiny, charred leg. "They got meat, mon. Ah tell you they got meat."

Usually, Mr. Williams would take the afternoon register straight away, but he didn't today. He told us that Errol, who was absent from school yesterday, didn't get home at all last night. Mr. Williams said that he was going to call each of us, one by one, and that we should not be afraid to tell him if we knew anything about Errol and why he disappeared.

Mr. Williams was the only grown up I wasn't afraid of.

He was really nice, and a photographer as well. He was the person who took my photograph for the Common Entrance Exam form we all had to fill in. I had to go to his house after school one day. He made Jan bring me to their front room, she helped set up the stuff, and then he took my picture, just like that.

He lived in Stanleytown as well, and had a powerful motorbike. He'd bring Jan and Geff to school on it every day. Jan sat in the middle and Geff on the end, so they both had to hold on for dear life.

The only thing I knew about Errol was that he lived in Stanleytown and liked to run away from school to swim. I really couldn't help at all.

CHAPTER 7

MOVING HOUSE

"That's the way . . ."

KC and the Sunshine Band were rocking away on the radio when I walked in today.

"*. . . Uh huh, uh huh."*

Mammy was whistling as she was packing to move. She was the best whistler and singer I have ever heard – not that I'd heard many, mind. I had to go and get some Bristols from Grimmond's bar, then some ice from the Persauds from down the street. Gruff! Grrruff!

Theresa was cooking Mammy's vegetables.

"They not really vegetables," Theresa had said to me some time back.

"Is things like bora, ochra, and pumpkin that are vegetables. Cassavas, eddoes, sweet potatoes and plantains are actually called ground provisions."

Whatever they were, they gave Mammy a lot of satisfaction because she ate them all the time. Theresa had to boil them in a large pot every two days. Mammy would then dip into this store all week long. As long as she had money, she had her store of 'vegetables.'

I was really curious to find out what pleasure Mammy obviously got from these provisions, so one day I slurped up a large serving spoon of the water they were boiled in, when she was out of the kitchen. I was surprised to find – and this was only when it was half way down – that all it tasted of was salt. I gulped and retched a bit, but by then it was too late to bring anything up.

Mammy always said that she wished Shop Lady would sell 'vegetables' and not just groceries so she could get them on credit when we ran out of money.

"Ah bought a cane today!" Mammy announced to the room while we were having dinner.

"Why?" Theresa asked, but I guessed that she already knew why.

Mammy put another spoonful of the boulanger and eddoes into her mouth, the tip of her nose pointed downwards into the spoon as if it was set to sniff the world around her with a permanent dislike. The wide sides flared out dangerously, and I wondered for a moment if she'd ever inhaled food instead of swallowing it.

"For that one, na," Mammy answered. "From now on, when she tempt me, she gon be in for a good caning."

Theresa did one of her sighs, and I felt my stomach turn over, then knot. That was the end of my dinner. My stomach had made up its mind that it was going to take no more food.

"The cane better for beating she than the wood anyway, because it stings for a long time. Woods only hurt, and then they cool off. Not canes," Mammy shook her head, smiled and wagged her forefinger.

"Ah been watching them at the market for a long time, and hoping for enough money to afford one for ages. They say that if you know how to hit with it, it can really make a person dance."

Mammy got up, took the cane out from behind the front door, and proudly showed it to us. She whacked the air with it and it made a horrible swishing sound. This was the same type of thing they use in school. The boys get whacked two lashes on their bottoms and the girls, one in each hand. I didn't know what it felt like, but I knew that it hurt like hell. That was why Mr. Williams hardly ever gave more than two licks.

Inside my belly, I knew that Mammy was going to give me more than two licks. For the first time since I was about seven, my stomach felt just like it did when I used to vomit every day after breakfast. Whenever I brought up any food, more was brought out and put on my plate. The more I tried to keep down the vomit, the more the nervousment overtook me.

My chest drummed, my throat locked and my stomach used to turn itself upside down. Nothing I did would allow any more of the food inside my mouth to go pass my neck.

Mammy used to take up her place standing behind my chair at breakfast time. Wood in hand.

"Chew faster. I got things to do."

I used to try passing the heavy, flowery bakes from one side of my mouth to the other, but this only made it worse because it got all splattery and yucky.

My throat made this sound, then the food splashed out of me and onto the floor.

Then we started all over again.

Sometimes I ate and vomited twice before I went to school.

Every morning of every day, yes, every morning of every day.

Mammy said that I was stubborn, but that was one thing I knew she wasn't right about. What was strange was that as I got bigger, I found more and more things she wasn't right about. She thought I was really ugly, but my friends thought I was nice. They thought my long neck and stupid cheeks weren't so bad. Could it be that I wasn't stupid either?

Please God, please make it so that I'm not stupid.

* * *

Three days later, Errol was found. Not good news though, he was found floating in the Back Dam trench, naked, with lots of his soft bits like his ears and stuff, eaten off by crabs. What was worse was that two boys from the other fourth year went swimming with him.

The three of them were trying to see who could make the biggest splash. When it was Errol's turn to plunge in, he made a giant splash, only he didn't come up again. When the two other boys realised that he wasn't going to, they jumped out of the water, got dressed and went back to school. They kept quiet when their teacher asked if anyone knew anything because they were scared.

We were told that Errol dived in right on top of a big boulder, hidden by the muddy water in the trench. They told us that he was knocked unconscious when his head hit the boulder, which is why he couldn't swim back up. At his funeral, held at his parents' bottom house, his Mummy passed his baby sister over his coffin. Marla said this was so his spirit could always take care of her.

Errol's two friends, the boys who went swimming with him, held on to each other and wept loudly. There were other friends from his class, looking on and wiping their eyes. Old people with black head-ties wailed, hanging on to the side of the dark brown, wooden coffin. People were stamping loudly upstairs in the house. Dust fell on us downstairs and onto the lapel of Errol's brand new suit.

His face looked like old concrete – grey, dead and crumpling. His nose and ears and parts of his cheeks looked almost plastic. I wondered for a moment if they *were* plastic. Did they fix them to cover up where the crabs had eaten him?

Marla and Marleen said that their aunt told them that his friends will suffer more than he did. I didn't understand how. But Marleen's aunt Mayleen said you remember the things which hurt you for longer than you remember the good stuff that happened to you. She said this is why even very old people can remember how they got even the littlest scar, and not many of us can remember what we got for birthday presents each year. I didn't know about this. Not all grown-ups knew everything, I didn't think. Well, I should say, *I hoped.*

* * *

"So how come you live with your aunt?" I asked Marleen and Marla on our way home one afternoon.

"Our Mum couldn't look after us when we were born," Marla said. "We were very small coz we were born premature and very ill. We couldn't speak until we were five years old. That is why we talk like this." Marla used her forefinger to scrape sweat off her forehead, then off her sister's, and flicked it on the asphalt. It dried up immediately in the afternoon heat. "I was second, that's why Marleen's bigger and taller than me now."

"Aunt Mayleen was so good, she said she was going to take us and raise us as her own, even though she was already looking after Granny and Aunty Elsie who are both ill," Marleen continued where her sister had left off.

"She is a good Aunty, and even though she never had any children or married, she just takes care of everyone and the family properties and everything. She is real good."

"My aunty is good too, and you know what?" I asked. "Her real name is Mayleen, too."

"So what you call her?" Marla asked.

"Theresa," I replied, kicking yet again the little pebble I had brought all the way from school. Pit, pit, pit, it said, as it stopped a few paces away, waiting for me, daring me to do it again.

"How come you call yuh aunt by her name?" Marla asked loudly. "That's rude."

"She doan want me to call her Aunty. She is only nine years older than me."

"Isn't it way cool that our aunts have the same name?" Marla asked.

"Yeah," I agreed. "And we're all the same size, too."

"Well, not really," Marleen answered, with a serious look on her face. "I'm taller than you two."

"Spoil sport!" Marla shouted.

"What's 'spoil sport'?" I asked.

"Is when someone takes away all the fun," Marleen answered, all grown-up like, in a posh accent. "I'm not a spoil sport. I'm just the sensible one."

"She not asking you," Marla told her. Then she turned to me and said, "Is when someone takes all the fun away from everything."

"But that's what *I* said, silly!"

I looked at both girls and couldn't help smiling.

I knew that the three of us were going to be friends forever, even if we didn't get passes for the same high school.

"Oh gosh, we got to run!" Marleen gasped, suddenly glancing nervously behind us.

"Why?" we asked.

"Doan look back now, but Weird Harold's behind us."

"What?" I said in panic, as Marla and I immediately looked back.

And yes, he was. He was wearing the same dirty red cap. I don't think he ever took it off. He walked all over the villages close by, looking for trouble, poking through the neighbourhoods for lone little girls. He wasn't looking at us yet, or perhaps he had already seen us.

We held onto our bags and ran, the warm wind brushing our faces, until he was a good distance behind us. I couldn't breathe properly but tried to calm myself. I couldn't tell them. I hadn't told anyone. I didn't know why, but I couldn't. I felt guilty, but again, I didn't know why.

The reason weird Harold brought so much fear in the neighbourhood was because a long time ago he was sent to prison for rape and assault on his mother. She now lived in the scheme and people said she never left her house because she was so embarrassed. Her son did all the shopping and stuff.

A while after he'd left prison, the grown-ups said he was charged with assaulting a little girl. He didn't go to prison again because he was 'disturbed' and didn't really know what he was doing.

Marleen and Marla got to their street, and from there on I took another route home, making sure I looked behind me as I went. I even walked some of the way backwards – just to make sure. But he had disappeared again.

My feet ached when I got home. We were still packing to move, and I was studying for my upcoming Primary school-leaving exams.

Mammy said she had already hired the donkey cart and that it should come later when it got dark, because that's when everyone moves. Theresa was busy packing, so I had to sing to Franc to keep her occupied. I never had any toys except for one big doll, but Mammy thought that I would break it, so she never allowed me to touch it.

It spent its years standing against the wall in the living room. Two feet high she stood, white skin - covered in grey dust - and blue eyes. Her hair was short and uneven in bits where her previous two owners had first cut, then tried to repair the damage.

So it was nice to play with Franc because she was like my own big doll, the one I did get to touch and help change. Like Cliff Richard said, I had a living doll.

Recently though, I hadn't been able to play with her much because when I was home, I spent most of my time standing in a corner waiting for instructions, getting licks, running to the shops, going to buy ice or cigarettes, or studying a little.

Franc's hobby was to fight sleep for as long as she could. Whenever it was time for her nap, her habit was to scream the street down in a piercing, shrill bird-cry. Then she would rub and claw her face until her little eyes were red and her face, bright pink.

"Stop trying to fight it," Theresa would say.

"I'm half deaf and I can still hear yuh inside me head. You must be the loudest baby around. Why don't you like sleep?"

Franc also never went to anyone but Theresa. If anyone outside the family tried to hold her, she'd scream until she left herself breathless, then she'd scream some more just to make sure they understood they shouldn't try to do it again. Theresa worried Franc wouldn't even go to Esther when she saw her again.

Franc was beginning to cry, so I thought it was a good idea, since Theresa was busy, to take her out to the veranda before the screams came. She was way heavy. She ate a lot, you see, and drank lots of porridge. Not like me. I was skinny, jumpy and weak.

"Look at yuh," Mammy said sometimes when I passed by her. "A strong wind will blow yuh away. Ah won't put it past you to starve yuhself so that people would say ah not taking care of you properly."

Then sometimes she would lash out at me with whatever she had in her hand because I annoyed her with the way I walked about the house. Years ago, I learned to walk past her only when she had her back turned.

It wasn't easy trying to hide from someone who lived in the same house, so I had to time it right. I thought maybe she couldn't beat me if she couldn't see me.

I had just managed to get Franc into my arms after picking her up from the floor when she let fly a sudden kick into my tummy and propelled herself out and away from me. I thought she was playing, but this made her fly out of my hands and drop back to the floor. My stupid skinny arms couldn't hold onto her. She started to scream and scream her painful scream. I dropped to the floor and tried to gather her up.

Had I broken her?

I quickly looked at her arms and legs for red marks to see if she had hurt herself, and breathed a sigh of relief when she stopped crying. It sounded like a sudden cut off. She still had little pearls hanging from the bottom of both eyes, and she was staring at something behind me.

I didn't have to look back to see what was behind me. I could feel it even with my back turned – the cold presence of hate standing as a shadow of the person behind me.

Mammy sailed towards me with the new cane. She yanked me into the house and away from Franc, who had started screaming again, just as suddenly as she had stopped.

"Ah gon teach yuh a lesson!" she shouted. "Yuh measuring yuh skin colour with Franc. Yuh see she whiter than you, so you push her down!"

I could hear the very loud swishing of the cane as it hit me. The sting surprised me so much that it stopped my breath inside my throat. As if out of my body, I could see Mammy raising her arm way high, over, and behind her shoulders. As she bent over me, she was chewing on her lip when she landed every hit with that awful bee-like, swishing sound. The cane, working like a whip, cracked my skin in many places.

I didn't know that such a narrow thing could hurt so much. I could feel moisture on it as it hit my skin, but I didn't know how it could get wet. She beat me so much that the cane broke. It was so frayed at the end that she said, "Ah can't use this anymore. Yuh skin like rubber, you nah feel a thing."

Then she dropped it, but she was breathing hard and fast.

"Yuh know what I find her doing?" Mammy told Theresa, who had probably just heard Franc's screams and came to see what was happening. She kicked the cane to one side. "She measuring skin colours with Franc now."

"She not doing that!" Theresa dared to say the words I was crying out inside me.

"What *you* know?" Mammy answered, pulling apart the curtain and spitting through the open window. I noticed she didn't close them again.

"Ah know that you been itching to use that cane since the day yuh brought it home!" Theresa shouted, and turned her back to go get the screaming baby.

I looked at the cane later on as it lay like road-kill in the corner of the kitchen floor. There was some brownish, pinkish stuff on the frayed ends of it. Theresa said she had never seen a cane take off skin before. I hadn't either, but apart from the insides of hands, I had never seen a cane used on bare skin before. Some of the little broken pieces from the cane were even stuck inside the skin of my thigh.

"Ah worried about these two cuts," Theresa said. "I had one that looked like that when I was little, and the mark never ever went away."

"I wasn't looking at colours, I . . ." I finally managed to get out, but she wouldn't let me finish.

"Don't say such a stupid thing," Theresa sshhed me. "Of course yuh weren't."

At dinner in our new house in Fifty-four Stanleytown, Mammy said, "Yuh nothing like yuh mother."

She said I was scrawny and feeble and told us a story of when Esther was little and she had just beaten her.

"Ah had just beat Esther and Daniel with a burning piece of wood ah tek out of the fireside where ah cooked. Man, it was a nice, fat piece and it was still red in bits, and smoking."

I swallowed hard and thought that maybe it felt like the sting of the cane. Theresa turned her head away. Only Franc could manage to say anything. She went, "Ba."

Theresa would've normally smiled, but she didn't this time.

"When ah finished, ah put Daniel to kneel down on two graters and mek him hold two irons, one in each hand. Then ah send Esther to wash the dishes straight away with she sore hands."

No one wanted to listen to this story, but we all sat still waiting for the rest of it, even though we knew it as well as Mammy did. I thought of the heavy irons Theresa sometimes used to press the clothes, the ones Mammy was talking about. They were two pressing irons, made of real iron, which you had to heat up on the stove. When they got hot, you cleaned the soot off the bottom then pressed the clothes until they got cold. You always had to have two irons so you could leave one heating on the fire while you used the second.

"Esther, she's always the hero, and love she brother coz they only one year apart, yuh know."

We knew.

"Esther went back and forth to do the dishes and then came back to help she brother with his heavy irons. When she think ah not looking – but nothing gets past me – she came back and mek him put the irons on the floor. When she think ah coming back, she mek him tek them irons back up, to pretend he was holding them all the time.

Esther always did this when ah put Daniel to kneel on those graters. He never learned.

One time after ah beat them, ah went out and left Esther to look after the other children - and Daniel on the grater. Ah warned him not to get off, right, but ah know that as soon as I left the house that he put down them irons.

While ah was out, me brother, Emmanuel – you never met him – came to visit. When he saw them children like that, he break down and cried. What an idiot! He say to me…," and here Mammy put on a whiny sort of voice, "'*Ah not coming back here. Ah can't bear to see me nephew and niece in such pain.*' Then he helped pull the splinters out of Esther's hand. Is her fault really, for holding on the wood ah beat her with. She know it had splinters on it, mon."

Franc was nodding. It wasn't a story she could understand.

Yet.

Mammy continued her story, and told us that her brother never visited again, even when he was leaving the country to go to England to become an architect. She didn't even know if he was alive because he never contacted her again. This was a very sad story - one Mammy had told before. She said that Esther was tough like that. *I wasn't.*

CHAPTER 8

CHRISTOPHER!

My Dear God,

I know I always come to you when I'm confused. This is why I'm here now. I hear grown- ups saying that the older you get the more confused you become. Well I'm not that old, but I'm growing up and becoming more sensibler, and I think that if my mother knows how cruel her mother was, she should not have left me with her. I know you listen to me because Theresa saves me, so please, please don't let her crush us, and please don't let her start beating on Franc.

Amen.

* * *

Our new house was a little bigger than the one we'd lived in before. It had the same two bedrooms, but there was an extra corridor space that we used as a dining room. Also, the shower was not in the kitchen, but slightly away from it, so Mammy couldn't listen to us when we peed, like she did before.

Aunty Meena had left me a desk to do my homework on, which they had taken apart and dropped off at our old house.

She'd said at the time, "Now you have somewhere to put all your papers and homework books. I also left the big mirror for your grandmother, so now you can look at yuh cute face."

It was the first time I'd looked at myself in a mirror, I think. I'd searched in that mirror one day when Mammy was out. I'd searched for the cute girl Aunty Meena had told me was about, somewhere. All I saw staring back at me was a girl with a pair of nearly-copper eyes set in a heart-shaped face. The neck supporting the face was as long as Mammy had described. A gaulin's neck she had called it. Not a stork's, and certainly not a swan's. It was the neck of a despised bird who lived to eat the bugs off dirty cattle's backs and bottoms.

This girl stared with her red face and gaulin's neck, and I stared back. I asked her silent questions, hoping that she'd be able to give me some answers, or that she'd know about how I hoped my life would be, but she didn't have any ideas.

She turned away from me and I saw tears in her shiny, nearly-copper eyes, tears that were about to fall on her little, scarred nose. I didn't let her know that I noticed it. She'd be embarrassed, I thought. She didn't like to talk about the day she got that scar, the day she nearly bled to death.

It was nice having a desk. Mammy said that I could use the bottom drawer coz she had some stuff she wanted to put in the others. Our old house opposite was a lot bigger now. The mechanic and his once-new wife, who'd bought it from our old landlord, had it extended. They ran a car-shop in the bottom house. Several cars were parked under his house and on his side of the street. If I stood at our front window, I could see inside their living room. Mammy said no one was to ever part the curtains or look outside coz she didn't want the people opposite seeing into *our* house. I was never allowed to look out anyway, so this didn't really bother me.

Hire car drivers from all over the village and the town brought their tired, banged-up, rusty Morris Oxfords (at least this is what my uncle Christopher used to call them) and left them with the mechanic, expecting miracles when they returned. He'd sand and weld and solder and stuff, until everything was just right.

He'd sweat on them for days, labouring on his knees on the side of the tiny, dusty street. It was okay to stand in the street since cars never really drove down it. The children in the neighbourhood played all-day, weekend cricket matches with their little rubber balls and pieces of sticks for bats, sometimes even with the wide end of a coconut branch (this made a solid bat, you know) and hardly ever got interrupted by traffic.

The mechanic, when he was done and content that the old patchy surface was perfectly smooth, all hammered in and hammered out, he'd put newspaper on the windows, then spray the whole car in a brand new colour. You couldn't tell that the cars were ever used when he was finished with them. A miracle was just what the owners got when they came back; a solid, sparkling, brand new, four-wheel miracle.

* * *

At school today, Marleen, Marla and I decided to stay in to do some revision. They were sick yesterday so I described to them our lesson about how the Amerindians made Pepper Pot.

We learned that the Amerindians, the original people of Guyana, are relatives of the Incas and Aztecs in the rest of South America. They were here even before the White people arrived. Mr. Williams told us that the White Guyanese first came to Guyana as colonial land owners.

I didn't understand how they owned the land if they had never even seen it before, or knew it existed, but it must have been nice to go to a new place and own something. Or maybe the Amerindians didn't really know how to take care of their land properly.

After the Amerindians, scared of being killed, ran away into the jungle, there was really no one left to work the land for the new owners, so they had to buy some Black people all the way from Africa.

Some time later, the Black people said, "Uh, uh, we ain't working for free, no more."

So then the land owners decided that they would invite some Indians and Chinese to work as labourers. This was all a long time ago.

The Whites stayed on, and so did the Blacks. Most of the labourers did, too. So that was why Guyana was a country of many races. My dad's mother came when the Portuguese all arrived, and her family got a good bit of land. However, no one knew any background for my mother's family.

Mr. Williams said our country was the most special in this part of the world because we had all the races as one, equal Guyanese people.

"It's really weird," I told Marleen and Marla, before our revision.

"In some of the Amerindian tribes the men go out to hunt, right, and when they catch something, they bring it home for the women to cook."

"Catch something like what?" Marla asked.

"Oh, labba, or wild hog, or rabbit and stuff like that," I answered. "The women make the cassareep – which is the sauce for the pepper pot – with cassava."

"I like cassareep. One time, right, Aunty Mayleen put molasses in the pepper pot coz she thought it was cassareep." Marleen laughed.

"Stop interr-optin, Marleen," her sister said.

"It's *inter-ruptin'*, silly," Marleen corrected. "Ain't it, Ann? Tell her."

"It's none of them. It's in-ter-rup-ting," I answered. "I know, coz I read it in a dictionary."

"Yes, Miss Big Words," Marleen sang.

"Marleen!" her sister cried again.

"Anyway," I continued. "Well, the Amerindians all have to stamp on the cassava with their bare feet, for hours, to make it into the cassareep."

"Yuk," Marla said.

"Yes, and when it's all ready, right, they put the fresh meat into the pepper-pot sauce," I continued. "They keep putting meat into the same sauce over and over again, for months and months."

"Yuk," Marla said again.

"We always have pepper pot at Christmas time, but I never realised that we got it from the Amerindians," I told the girls.

"Me neither," said the twins, and we all agreed that their way was a very yuk way to cook food.

Our exams start next week, so we decided to start our revisions with Social Studies. We sat in the hot classroom on our own and took turns in asking ten questions each. Marleen went first because she was the oldest ("but only by a few minutes," as Marla would say). She opened her book and began.

"Question one," she said, in her best serious voice. "And pay attention, numb skulls. What is the position of Guyana on the map?"

"In the Northeast of South America, and is the only English speaking country in the continent," Marla said.

"Right, silly, but you don't have to know the bit about the English speaking," Marleen answered, turning the page of her exercise book. She held it up close to herself, and I could see the face and blue shirt of our Comrade Leader on the front cover. That picture of him, which was also on the wall of our classroom, was one I naturally expected to see everywhere.

"When in doubt, learn everything," Marla giggled, in her best Mr. Williams' voice.

“Question two,” Marleen said, turning the pages of her book while making a kissing sound with her teeth. Marleen and I looked at each other and rolled our eyes.

“What are the two main products that Guyana exports?”

“Bauxite and sugar,” I said. “And, and, we’re the only English speaking country in South America.”

We all screamed in laughter until Marleen said between giggles, “Okay, quiet now and be serious.” She cleared her throat. “Question three. Who is the leader: the President or the Prime Minister?”

“Both,” Marla answered.

“The President,” Marleen said. “That’s why he is called Comrade *Leader*.”

“Wot we got them both for?” I asked, but no one knew.

“Question four: what is the capital?”

I knew this one right away, “Georgetown.”

“Question five . . .”

“But you not telling us when we’re right, Marleen,” I said.

“When you wrong, I’ll tell you.”

“Alright,” we said but we weren’t so sure about this. After all, we did want to be told if we got stuff right so we could count them all up. Marleen said the revision was not a test, just a revision.

“Question six: when did we gain independence from the British?”

“May, twenty-sixth, 1966,” we answered together.

“Question seven, but ah not sure of this one,” Marleen began.

“Well doan ask it then, Mar-le-en,” her sister sang, leaning her head from side to side, her fresh corn rows hung on like little black ropes glued onto her scalp.

“What type of government do we have?” Marleen said, showing us the tip of her tongue.

I wasn’t sure I remembered this one from class revision, but there was a programme on the radio while I was doing my homework. Mammy usually didn’t like the talking bits on the radio (she’d say that they were just wasting her batteries), but she was on the veranda in her rocking chair smoking and didn’t realise the music had stopped.

“Socialist Demo-pratic Republic?” Marla asked.

“What does that mean?” Marleen asked, puzzled.

"I heard these people on the radio, right," I said. "They said that The Comrade Leader was a dictator because, well, remember when all these people who went on strike lost their jobs and they were told, 'Go back to work or you won't have work to go back to' or something like that?"

"Where'd you hear all that?" Marla asked.

"Oh, on the radio," I said. "Anyway, I not sure what a dictator is, but the man made it sound like somebody bad. And when the radio guy said he had to play some music, the man said that he was taking him off the air because The Comrade Leader and the PNC owned all the radio stations as well. It was all grown-up politicking stuff and I didn't understand most of it."

"And this ain't one of your made-up words, Ann," Marleen asked.

"Yeah, you like making up words," Marla joined in before I could answer. "You must be putting dicta-something with gator-something else, and making up that word."

"Nah, I'm not," I pleaded. "Honest, I ain't making up this word, promise. Besides, 'dicta' and 'gator' will go together to make up, 'dicta . . . actually, it *can* make up 'dictator.' Hmmm."

"Well, I'm confused," Marla said. "So is it a Socialist Demo-pratic Republic, or what you said?"

"Dunno," I shrugged. "Or maybe it's both. Oh, oh, and they also talked about when The Comrade Leader banned apples and things."

"Aunty Mayleen told us that before The Mr. Leader . . ."

"*Comrade* Leader," I corrected Marla.

"Before the *Comrade* Leader, they used to get apples from overseas, and grapes and all kinds of nice tinned things like corned beef," Marla said.

"Yes," Marla agreed. "And split peas too."

"I would really like to know what apples and grapes taste like," I continued.

"Dianne said that at Christmas time last year, her Daddy's brother from America sent some apples in the post, just for them to taste, right, and he packed some split peas and other banned stuff in the box too. She said that they were opened at the post office and taken away, but that they were lucky that her Daddy knew one of the men at the post office and gave him a bribe, or else they would've been in big trouble."

"Or be shot," Marleen said.

"You doan get shot for smuggling, silly," I said.

"Don't you?" Marla asked.

"Ah was only jokin'," Marleen said, flipping her book towards our heads. "Anyway, my Aunty Mayleen said that she won't bribe anyone, coz everyone wants a bribe, and you would have to bribe *everyone* to get anything done."

"One time my mother smuggled in walnuts between her dirty clothes in her luggage when she came in at the stelling," I said.

"Which stelling?" Marla asked. "I thought yuh mother lived in French Guyane?"

"Yes, she does," I answered. "But she travels from there to Suriname by boat, then from Suriname to Guyana by another boat."

"Oh!"

"What it taste like?" Marleen asked. "Them walnuts."

"They were hard," I said. "We had to hit them with a hammer and then take out the nuts inside. They taste like peanuts. But we only had four, so I not sure."

"Don't she smuggle wheat flour as well?" Marla asked me.

The bell rang and there ended our revision. We promised to do it on the way home but were so busy talking about my new house, we didn't.

Today I was first to get home.

* * *

My Dear God,

Today is my first exam and it is my weak subject. Please help me to do well and go to B.H.S. I am really nervous, please help me. In Jesus' name.

Amen.

* * *

"So how did you do?" Christopher asked. "I hear yuh had English and Maths exams today."

"Good," I answered.

I liked it when he came to visit. He was my uncle and only about eight years older than me. He was sent to the Guyana Defence Force to become a soldier because Mammy said he was a 'bad seed'. He was finally on leave from the army, and told me that he was a *'Private'*. I didn't know what this meant. Maybe he had to work by himself all the time.

"Ah glad I didn't do that nonsense exams. Study is not my thing at all," Christopher chuckled. "So which is yuh best subject?"

"English, but Maths is m' worst and I had them both today."

"Well that's good," Christopher said, patting me playfully on my shoulder. "So now you only have the ones you not nervous about."

"Yes," I said, looking around to see where Mammy was.

"Relax," he said, laughing his big booming laugh with the clicking sound. "Mammy gone out. Ah gave her some money to do extra shopping coz she wasn't expecting me. Ah gave her 'nuff money, she gon be in a good mood."

I moved away from him so he wouldn't touch me again. He had to have read my mind when he touched my shoulder to know that I was looking for her. Or maybe he knew.

"You look so tall," I said.

"Yeah, I grew taller. I now more than six foot tall and still growing. Don't worry, you only small now, but you will get tall, ah sure. Esther is the shortest in the family and she is five foot seven, and yuh father's very tall."

"Yeah," I agreed, and to tell the truth, that was all I could remember about my father. He was tall.

"Come," he said. "Let meh look at yuh face."

* * *

Dear Aunty or Mister,

I have to tell you about my uncle, Christopher. He used to live with us when we lived at the house opposite this one. That's when Mammy still had her school. I remember that he and Mammy were always arguing and shouting at each other. He didn't pay me any attention at all then, but now he's changed coz he talked to me so much today.

I remember him saying that they didn't get along because they were too much alike.

One time, he went off to Woodwork class and didn't come home till late. To punish him, Mammy locked him out, but when she got up the next morning he was sleeping in his bed. She shook him awake and asked him what on earth was going on. He said that he went to the neighbour's and told them that he had to borrow their ladder (we didn't have one) to fix our window early in the morning before school, coz he didn't want to disturb them then. He climbed up the ladder, removed a pane off the window, and climbed in. Nobody heard anything.

Next day when he took the ladder back, the neighbour said what a good boy he was, that she couldn't get her grown up son to do anything for her.

Another time, he had a big row with Mammy and she complained to Esther about how much trouble he was (she was back from Suriname that time – this was before she started going to French Guyane). Esther and him had a big fight, and Christopher ended up with his leg in a cast.

I was in the kitchen with them when it happened and it wasn't nice. I wish I didn't see it. A few weeks later, I woke up to a scrubbing sound in the bathroom. When I went to see what was going on, Theresa told me that Christopher was in the shower and wouldn't come out. About half an hour later he did, but he wasn't wearing his leg cast any more. Theresa said, "You stupid boy! What you gone and done?"

"Me leg was too itchy, mon. Is better like this."

"It better like that? Is that why you leaning on yuh crutch like that? You almost fifteen, you should know better than that."

"And what? You know better than me because yuh all of. . . sixteen?" he'd replied.

Then he had made that kissing sound with his teeth and hopped away. I could see the sweat trickling down his big, black-as-molasses back as he limped off.

Mammy had once asked him, "How come you so black? Look at me. Ah got good hair and light brown skin. How come you so tar-black eh?"

"I black on the outside, like you black on the inside," he had laughed, and then licked his thick lips as was his habit.

Christopher only really liked two things, his Woodwork and his chickens, but I will have to tell you about them later. Now, I want to tell you why he wanted to look at my face. Excuse me for beating around the bush all this time.

When I was seven, Christopher was sleeping in his bed one morning while Mammy was doing what she calls a general cleaning. This is a really, really bad time – as you too will soon find out. Anyway, when she's into this cleaning thing, I have to stand by to run for stuff, and hand her things. Everything has to be done straight away, or else. The moment Mammy puts out her hand for something, she expects that thing inside her hand. Right then. No waiting, no hanging around.

Mammy don't wait for things.

So, I was standing there being scared, waiting for the next punch, when she sent me to Christopher's room to tell him to get up. I did so. I always do what she tells me, and straight away. The thing was though, he didn't get up. I only found out later that Mammy thought I didn't tell him. This is the reason I ended up with the hole in my face.

CHAPTER 9

THE DAY I GOT A HOLE IN MY FACE

"Go downstairs and bring that wood!" Mammy shouts, while pointing at an old abandoned wood at the bottom of the stairs.

I take the steps one by one, and walk into the dry dirt at the bottom of the stairs. My bare leg brushes against the lemon grass bush whose leaves we use to make tea. I feel the stinging cut from its sharp leaves, but don't react.

Instead, I glance at the wood. It had been used to patch up the chicken coop a long time back, so it has nails sticking out from various parts of its used body. I walk past it to look for another, a smaller one maybe.

"Ah say bring *that* one! Look! Doan try me faith here today!"

"But . . ." I can't follow that with anything else, I don't think. My mind is a muddy trench with hidden boulders. I'm drowning in the confusion. Why? Why? Why?

I see my fingers pick up the wood, the one with the nails sticking out from it in all those different directions.

Maybe she only wants the wood, maybe it's not to beat me with at all. She won't beat me with a wood with nails in.

Yeah, she just wants the wood for something else.

* * *

She is beating me everywhere as she chews on her bottom lip. The top of the stable door is open, letting some warm air into the room, which is packed with the furniture from the rest of the house – 'general cleaning' stuff. She's holding in her hands, both hands, a piece of wood which is fatter than my arm. I can hear 'conk', 'conk,' as the wood hits my bony parts and it makes a kind of 'ta' sound when it contacts with flesh. I reel over with pain and the pressure of the heavy wood on my body. It pounds on my fingers as I move my skinny arm up to my face.

I'm sure that one or all of them are broken. The sound's so loud inside my head. I stumble backwards into the wall from the sheer force of the hit and the pain. Ta! Ta! Conk!

But I don't scream out.

"Stretch out yuh hand!"

I try, but when the wood's about to connect, it yanks itself back.

"Stretch out yuh hand!"

I try – the other hand this time – the wood connects.

Too late.

"Stretch out yuh hand, I tell yuh!"

By now the smell of hate is so frothed in the woman's nose – the tall woman standing by the stable door whom the child is looking up to – that she grabs the tiny arm and makes the hand stay put.

I weep like a baby, but not loudly, my dry mouth hardly open.

I cry my soul free, but more on the inside than out.

I hold my hurting hand with the other as I look up again, this time to see if there is a chance of forgiveness. Then one of the nails connects with my face.

It sticks into flesh.

That was then.

* * *

Back to now:

You know, when Christopher came to visit, he brought some big records to play on the little portable record player which my mother had brought to Guyana about a year ago. She'd only brought one needle with it, so it didn't work very well now. It stuck into the records just like the nail stuck into my flesh.

"Jailhouse, Jailhouse, Jailhouse, Jailhouse, Jailhouse, Jailhouse," it would go. Then Mammy would send me to lift the little thingy up so that the record could move from the stuck position and keep on playing. If I didn't move it far enough, it would stick again, "Rock, Rock, Rock, Rock, Rock, ock, ock, ock, ock," so I would have to lift the thingy again.

Christopher had also brought a small record, he said it was called a 45. It was a song about the Jonestown Kool-aid stuff, but the one he liked best was the big yellow, double one by Bob Marley. He said that the record only looked yellow, but it was really gold because Bob Marley sold so many of them.

All the words of the songs were written out on the jacket. Mr. Bob Marley seemed to be very, very clever. His words are so sweet. I'd never heard anyone talk about such great things before.

"Schism," he said on his record. I asked what it meant, but Christopher didn't know.

"Schism, schism, schism, schism, schism," Mr. Marley went for a long time before Christopher sent me to lift that thingy.

* * *

Back to then again:

Mammy pulls the wood, then bright red blood starts to spurt out of my face. Theresa drops the bowl of rice she's cleaning, screams, runs me to the shower at the back of the kitchen and begins to wash the blood away. But it keeps coming and coming and coming.

Why won't it stop?

Theresa is only a young teenager so she doesn't know what to do. I am crying and she is running the water, but the red water keeps on escaping.

My eyes watch me bleed down the drain hole.

"Ah can't get the blood to stop, Mammy!" Theresa shouts. "Ah can't get it to stop!"

I'm shivering, but not from cold. I'm sure that this is where I die. After hungrily clawing onto this lifeless life for so long, I still die.

I still die?

I still die?

I feel a faint coming on, as the red water runs down into wherever drain water goes.

Christopher is awake again, this time by all the noise, and gets up to see what all the commotion is about. He sees us in the shower and tiptoes on the wet, wooden floor outside the little enclosure. He looks at me for a while, then steps in on the wet, red concrete and says, worried like, "Ah didn't know yuh had so much blood in yuh, mon." He tiptoes out again, but we – Theresa and I – still cry.

Mammy comes to the shower door and says to Theresa, "Stop running the water now. Yuh want she to bleed to death on me hands?"

Theresa takes me out and gives me a towel to put on my face. She uses the edge of it to dry her eyes.

* * *

Back to now:

I didn't know which part of my face was cut. I thought it was my eye at first but I could still see, so it had to be my nose. I couldn't feel any pain on my face. How was that possible? I knew there was pain in my back where I got some of the beating, but none on my face.

"We gat to finish this cleaning," Mammy said. "Ah warn you, to stretch out yuh hand, but you too stubborn to listen to me. Let that be a lesson to yuh, that next time I give yuh a message, mek sure yuh deliver it."

"Wot message?" Christopher asked. He was well into his morning body-scratching ritual, while looking for something to have for breakfast.

"Ah send she to go and wake you. If she wasn't so stubborn, she wouldn't be standing there like an idiot with a towel on she face."

Christopher turned to me, "Is that when you come in and shake me out me sleep?"

I nodded my head.

"Ah tired mon," he said. Then he turned away to put the tea pot on the stove.

Mammy said nothing.

Later that day Mammy realised that my face wasn't getting any better. The skin on the side of my nose, just under my right eye, was wide open. She said that we would go to the hospital that night when it got dark. I think we had to wait till it was dark because Mammy said she didn't much like that whitish stuff she could see when she looked inside the tear.

She said the nail that ripped me was a rusty one and the next thing I would do was to get tetanus on her hands. This made me wonder if I would've had to go to hospital if the nail was brand new.

"We got to walk up to the hospital when it get dark," she said. Her forehead-crease was pointing at me, so I couldn't tell if we were friends now or not.

"You should go sooner or that thing gon bleed she out." Christopher was the only one not shocked enough into complete silence.

Theresa said later that it looked like I had a new mouth under my eye, but I wasn't allowed to look at it in the small, hand-mirror we had on the kitchen shelf.

"We not going now," Mammy said sternly. "People will talk. Look at she, she look like she lost an eye. It all puffy and hhhggg . . . ." She made this sound with her throat, then she turned her eyes away from me.

After twilight, the four of us set out for the hospital. It was the first time I'd gone out at night and it was exciting. Diamonds winked at me from the black sky. I just knew that somewhere out there was another world, another place where I belonged.

Not here.

No, not here at all, not with my second evil-clown mouth badly drawn on my face.

I, Ann Lyken, belonged somewhere else, somewhere I will find when I grow up and leave all this behind me.

I will fly through them diamonds up there and maybe find one or two of my own.

It was also exciting to be out at night because it was the first time I'd gone past the burial ground in the pitch blackness of the night. Ghosts lived in the graves, you know. You shouldn't look at them when you walk past. Put your head straight and walk by quick. I reckoned you couldn't see bad things on the side of you if you got your head pinned forward.

Because my eye was covered, I had to turn all the way around to see Theresa walking behind me, and I remember Mammy telling me that I wanted everyone to see my big towel bandage. I didn't really understand how more people could see it if I turned around than if I walked straight ahead, but I wasn't meant to understand stuff like that. I was only about seven at the time.

Mammy told me to tell the nurses that I fell down the stairs on my face, and that a rusty nail on the bottom step caught me on the nose. She said, "Mek sure you say *rusty*."

They seemed to believe me and were very nice. They gave me a tetra-nust injection because they said rusty nails were 'sssss' bad. They made this snake sound, inhaled loudly, and shook their heads from side to side when they said, 'sssss bad.'

"This a bad one you got here," the older of the two nurses said. "That nail must have been very big to cut yuh up like this."

She was the one who smelled all fresh-like, not the way Mammy smelled, and she must've been older than Mammy. Maybe Mammy's smell is not oldness; maybe it's hate or something else.

"You fall down, you did?" the younger nurse with the cornrows asked again. Then she looked at the older one and smiled.

I was surprised they believed me so easily.

"Yeah, on the step."

I settled my bottom on the hard stool.

They then told me to close my eyes. They were busy doing all sorts on my nose. They had sprayed it first, but after that I didn't feel anything except their hands moving about up there. The older nurse was now standing in front of me. I could feel her soft middle close to my face.

"You must have really long stairs."

"Yeah, long."

"And the nail? Where was it?"

"At the bottom. Right at the bottom."

I thought that I should try lying more often because maybe I was good at it. Only thing is, I forget to lie when I'm scared.

At last they were finished and I was told to open my eyes.

"Don't touch it."

I stopped my hand in mid-air and brought it down again.

"The rip is close to your eye," said the older nurse. "But I have a feeling that when you get bigger, and your nose gets longer, that it will grow down, and away from it."

She had a look of Theresa in her eyes.

* * *

My exams have finally finished today. Marleen and Marla and I, and the rest of us in the two fourth years have answered – at least tried to – six hundred and fifty points worth of questions each.

"Wouldn't it be cool," Marla began. "If we got 625 points each?"

"The questions were hard, Marleen answered. "I doan think anyone will get over 550."

"Hmmm, 625 out of 650," Marla went on, as if her sister had said nothing.

Maybe it was Marleen who was right though, some of the questions, especially the Maths ones confused me stupid. They wrapped my brain around their little finger, spun it silly, then let go.

Theresa said that I had to try my hardest to do well, because if I failed, Mammy would say, "See ah told you so," to everyone who she'd told that I was a no-good, including myself.

This morning we got a letter from my uncle Daniel. He's the one who Mammy used to make kneel on the grater. Mammy said he was really bright but that he was ashamed of his family. Maybe that was why he never contacted us or came to see us.

I was the letter reader in the house, and also wrote all the ones we sent, coz Mammy couldn't do that sort of thing without her glasses.

Uncle Daniel's letter wasn't a very enjoyable one to read.

"Yet again," I read aloud, "Christopher has not been keeping the rules of the army."

Mammy was paying keen attention. She liked to listen to me read while sniffing on her special piece of cloth, soaked with mentholated spirits. She did this smelly-ritual at least once a day.

"I thought he would appreciate the break I've given him, but yet again my family has chosen to embarrass me. He has been running riot here and disrespecting his superiors. It has now gotten to the point where he's being inves,- inves, - tee, - gay, - ted, investigated for theft…"

"So he not on leave," Mammy mumbled. "He lie to meh." I stopped for a while, unsure of what to do next.

"Read on, nah."

"As a lee, - you, - ten, - ant, lieutenant, I will vouch for him, but this is the last time I will bail him out. I want him to return to Georgetown this instant, so that we can start to fix this mess in which he's now involved me. As you may or may not know, I am in the middle of studying for my bar exam . . ."

That very afternoon my uncle Christopher spent ages cleaning his shoes and clothes. He said he learned to do that in the army.

"Ah glad ah going back at the weekend and not tomorrow, because there's going to be a freak storm tonight," I heard him tell Theresa while he pressed his uniforms, taking time to iron the crease in his green trouser uniform until they were knife-sharp. I was sitting on the floor just outside the kitchen door, picking the paddy, weevils and stones out of the rice to prepare it for cooking.

"What?" she asked.

"A freak storm."

"What's that, now?" Theresa asked him, turning to look at his face as he spoke. He looked down at her, standing opposite him on the other side of the old, rusty ironing board. She looked small, standing so close to him, smaller than I have ever seen her look.

"Well, the weather people called it *'freak'* coz it will be a stronger storm than we ever had."

"Don't sound good at all," Theresa said. She scratched her head, and my eyes were drawn as always to the little muscle above her elbow, on the inside of her arm. There was something about her muscles that made my eyes follow them whenever they beckoned.

"Sshhh," Christopher said. This made me smile, especially when Theresa 'sshhed' herself as well. She laughed at herself whenever someone sshhed her. You see, she'd sometimes forget how loud her voice gets.

I didn't understand fully what Christopher really meant, but I think he was talking about the stuff we hear on the radio, about those faraway places in the Caribbean where high winds whip away houses. I would like to see that. It must be really exciting.

When I went to bed later, Christopher was busy polishing his shoes.

Curled up in the corner of Mammy's bed, I heard him ask, "Why you hanging round? What you want me to say?"

"Nothing," came a small voice, but it wasn't Theresa's.

CHAPTER 10

THE FREAK STORM

"Wha happening!" Mammy screamed.

At first I thought I was dreaming, because I often had nightmares about people shouting and waving cutlasses around.

It took me a second to realise that the house was shaking, and that there was loud wind and clapping thunder outside.

"Wake Theresa up!" Mammy shouted at me, tapping me heavily on the shoulder.

I threw the thin, torn sheet off my legs and stepped off the bed.

I walked, still in a sort of daze, through the door separating the two bedrooms and to the bed where Theresa slept with Franc.

"The house shaking. You got to get up."

"Huh?"

The house rattled, starting with a little belly rumble at first.

"What . . ." she began, then in one movement, she tore the sheet off her middle and pitched her legs to the side of the bed. She stood up, but then looked behind her, pulled the covers over Franc's naked chest, and left the room.

I followed.

In the living room, Christopher was up from his mattress on the floor looking out the front window. It seemed like all the neighbours were getting up, too. Lights kept going on all down the street.

"Wha going on?" Mammy asked.

This time Christopher answered and said that it was a hurricane, but this was just the tail end of a big one that was happening in one of those other countries.

Someone in my class once said if you were not prepared for a hurricane and one suddenly crept up on you, you should open all your windows so that the winds could pass through the house instead of blowing it down. I didn't say this though. Suddenly, there was a noise in the roof. We could hear what sounded like zinc sheets - being pulled out by a giant with his daddy's hammer.

"The roof's going!" Theresa shouted, gathering her old tee-shirt about her body.

"Nah," said Christopher. "Is only a few zinc sheets, mon."

Theresa and I stood on opposite sides of the living room, she by the front windows, and I towards the entrance into our tiny kitchen. Mammy and Christopher paced up and down the polished floor.

Several times a year, we bought a tub of floor polish. It came in a similar tub to the one Christopher used to polish his shoes with, only bigger. On our hands and knees (well, on mine and Theresa's hands and knees), we rubbed the polish on every little bit of the raw wood in the living room after clearing it of the three blue chairs with the silver legs, the coffee table with one of its legs tacked on, the cabinet where we kept the dishes we never used, and the doll which stood next to it.

We would leave the polish to 'soak' in overnight, and in the morning we would get down on hands and knees again to shine the entire floor, just like Christopher shined his army boots until they squeaked.

After this exercise, one of my jobs every morning was to shine the living room floor until it was spotless. If Mammy wasn't looking, I would put the old polishing rag under my feet and slide from corner to corner. This did the job just as well, but with Mammy, it's best to look like you're working when you are.

Christopher went to the back door and started to open it.

"You crazy?" Mammy shouted at him. "What yuh doing that for?"

"Ah want to see if the mango tree still standing," he answered. "Ah think I heard it crack."

He opened the bolt on the back door and pushed. Nothing happened.

He put his tree-cutter shoulder against the door and pushed. Still nothing happened. Just then we heard a giant wrench, a thunderous screech and a whip-like buzz. My feet became one with the hard floor and my eyes shot upwards. I was horrified to see one of the unpainted zinc sheets that made up our roof, suddenly sprint off the wooden planks, and go whizzing through the air.

I pulled Mammy's old tee-shirt, my nightgown, close to my body, but my feet refused to leave the spot. I really wanted to go over to where Theresa stood staring upward for a hug, just a little one, but Mammy said that when you hug children, you spoil them. So I just stood and watched the rain instead.

"The rain coming in," Theresa said finally, and looked at her brother with questioning eyes.

It was now raining in our living room and the big blue chair with the silver legs was getting wet, not to mention the shiny, polished floor.

"We got to move everything and put them up against the walls," Christopher said. "Ah think we about to lose another zinc sheet."

When I finally moved from my spot to help him, the lights suddenly went on strike. In the deep darkness, I saw a swift movement – white wings.

The angels had come for me at last!

They had come in the storm, through the roof.

Swish!

Cottony, soft wings brushed my outstretched hand. I took a sharp breath in – almost a hiccough.

A match was struck.

"Keep the matches and lamp nearby fuh when the blackout come," Mammy always said.

The kerosene lamp coughed, spluttered, then became alive. A little flame at first, then – blaze!

Someone turned it down.

Mammy was covering Aunty Meena's mirror with my torn sheet. Lightning strikes on mirrors, you know. You can't leave them uncovered in a storm.

No angels.

Not this time.

We spent the rest of the night sitting on the floor looking at the storm. I must have gone to sleep a couple of times because soon it was morning and the winds and thunder had stopped. It was still raining in our living room when Franc woke up for her breakfast.

"Ky, Ky, Sissy," she said to Christopher, pointing upwards.

"When yuh gon learn to say Christopher and stop calling me Sissy?" he asked, picking her up.

"Stop kicking me," he told her, and put her down instantly.

"Yuh got a bad habit of kicking people when they pick you up," Mammy told her. "I got to teach you a lesson for that. Come here to meh." Mammy beckoned to Franc.

Franc looked at her but stood still, forefinger in her mouth – nibbling her nail.

"Come here, ah said!" Mammy shouted.

Franc looked on, glanced behind her, flexed her fat baby-knees, but did not move.

"Don't mek me come and get yuh!" Mammy took a step in her direction.

Franc took a step back, her little chubby legs set for action.

Mammy took a sudden lurch forward, but those little legs were too quick for her.

What now? My brain raced. What now?

Then Mammy laughed.

Christopher later went looking for our zinc sheets and found them in Islington and Glasgow.

"Good thing you here," Theresa said to him while he was washing his hands at the kitchen sink. "It would've been worse without you."

"No problem, no problem at all, big sister," Christopher said, licking his lips. "Someone's got to keep she . . ." he nodded towards the living room at the tower of cigarette smoke, ". . . In she place." Then he laughed.

Theresa laughed too, but she put her hand in front of her mouth and hunched her galloping shoulders when she did.

I smiled and wished he could stay.

As Christopher packed that day, after he had put our zinc sheets back on the roof, he was playing Bob Marley on the little portable record player:

"Sun is shining..." (and by then it was)

"You playing that black people reggae music again, Christopher?" Mammy asked him.

"When you get a chance, Mammy," he answered, "You should tek a look at yourself in the mirror. I sure yuh will get a big shock." Then he chuckled, a little laugh with that clicking sound.

I thought I'd save this to tell to Theresa later on. She didn't always get jokes, so I would hold onto it in my head like a priceless little jewel to share with my most precious person.

Mammy made a kissing sound with her teeth and walked away.

"Ah gon glad to see the back of you," she mumbled, but by then Christopher was singing, *". . . Scooby doop scoop scoop."*

CHAPTER 11

SLINKY AND THE DOGS

"I have two announcements children," Mr. Williams said. "One of them, very sad."

He waited in his usual manner, the one that gave us the impression that he felt like shouting but wasn't going to utter a word until we were all very quiet, and if we weren't, there would be serious reckoning after.

A sort of hush settled, but there was a slight bit of giggling coming from the boys in the back benches. I could hear Ravi behind me, drawing his pencil for the hundredth and seventy nought time through the line on the bench between himself and Leroy. We all did that, but some of us used chalk on the long wooden benches which came with matching desks.

Each person shared their bench and desk with someone else, usually someone they didn't care for very much. The teachers tried to trick us into not chattering too much by making us sit far away from our friends, but that didn't matter to us too much, what with all the paper we could pass around the class and all that. I think we spent more time writing notes to our friends across the room than we would've spent talking with them if they were sitting next to us.

"Firstly, I am glad you all made it through the storm," Mr. Williams continued. "I have never seen a storm like that all my life, so it was something very rare in this country. You may never see one like it again."

One hand in his pocket, the other on his beard, Mr. Williams was getting ready for one of his speeches. Though he sometimes looked up to the galvanised, zinc sheets in the ceiling, he managed to keep his eyes on all of us, all at the same time.

"Apparently," he continued, "It was extremely small by comparison to what happens elsewhere in the world, so we are very lucky."

"Secondly," he said, leaving his beard alone and pressing his thumb and forefinger into his eye sockets, "We've lost one of the boys in the other year four. Most of you know him as Slinky."

We *did* know Slinky. He was our age, and was one of the boys who used to put little mirrors on their shoes then sneak up behind you. Once they had succeeded in getting close to you without you realising, they would put their foot beside yours, so that they could see the colour of your underwear from under your skirt. They would then sing, "Blue, blue, (insert name) loves you (if you were wearing blue). If you're wearing red, they sang, "Red, you peed your bed." White meant you were a blight. The worse one was, "Pink, you stink."

Slinky was also the one of the boys who had a lot of fun rubbing out our hopscotch when we drew them in the dust. He was really popular in school, so when we stood on one side with a little stone we'd found in the school yard drawing the little square boxes, he would get belly laughs from the crowd as he used his foot to rub out the lines on the other side. The quicker we drew, the faster he erased. Marleen, Marla and I would hop around drawing lines, but it would only take a skip and a quick succession of dragging steps for him to erase them all.

"You will, I am sure, find out the details later," Mr. Williams was saying. "But it's not very good at all. I don't want you to be shocked, but I should say that Slinky was beaten to death by someone. Again, don't be alarmed or scared, this is all very unusual," he said, showing us both his palms in a sort of push-push motion, his head cocked slightly sideways.

"We were all knocked for six at how someone could beat another person to death," he continued.

Actually sir, I'm sure it could happen very easily if someone is very big and very angry, and the other person is very little and scared.

"It is alleged," Mr. Williams continued, "– and this means that it's not been proven yet – that Slinky climbed up the man's guava tree, swung onto his window sill, and into his bedroom. He was caught as he tried to climb back out, and in his hurry he fell out of the window. The man then ran outside, untied his dogs, and then proceeded to beat Slinky. No one knows what really happened, but apparently when he was found, he had bite marks on him as well."

I glanced at The Honourable Comrade Leader's picture on the wall to see if he was taking all this in, but he had his usual 'I'm-watching-you-but-not-really-caring look.' A sort of look I once saw (in a book) on a painting my uncle said was world famous. He said that the picture was so famous that Nat King Cole once sang a song about it.

Mammy sings Nat King Cole when she's in a good mood. Her favourite one is *Smile*, when he says you gotta put a smile on your face even though your heart's in pain.

It always felt uncomfortable to look directly into the Comrade's eyes. The grown-ups thought that he knew everything, so they'd lower their voices every time they said something bad about him (which is a lot, I can tell you), even in their own homes. They dared not say anything ratty about him or the PNC party to anyone but family or close friends because of all the stories and legends of his spies. I thought maybe he'd somehow managed to work out a way to make himself see stuff through the pictures that hang in all the public buildings and schools. How else could he have known of some people's secret dislike of him?

"The man who allegedly killed Slinky is now in the lockups," Mr. Williams continued. "I don't want you all to worry, but I am sure it will be all over the news later on. If anyone has any questions or wants to talk, I am here always. You all have some time to now work quietly. Remember you have your end of term tests soon. And also, don't forget that the deadline to pay for your final tour is today. Lyken, are you sure you don't want to go?"

"Yes, sir," I answered.

"This trip is for the whole class, you all worked really hard in your Common Entrance Exams."

"I know, sir."

"Everyone else is going. This is your last chance."

I put my head down and didn't answer him. He wouldn't understand. I am not allowed to go on trips and things. Mammy said she didn't have the money, *or* the time. I couldn't tell him that. I was too embarrassed, so I closed my eyes, bit down on my back teeth, and waited for him to just go away.

* * *

Two days later the newspaper printed the story about Slinky. Mammy heard about the incident from Edwards. She was one of the teachers at Mammy's old school, before she transferred to the one in the scheme near to where we used to live. She was nice, but I didn't know her first name. Mammy always called her Edwards. She was one of those grown-ups who you never saw on their feet, because she always travelled around on her bicycle. I think her legs must feel very strange when they're asked to walk around her house.

Mammy bought the papers and made me read Slinky's story to her. The reporters and police didn't seem to know exactly what had happened, but the papers said that the 'suspect allegedly accused Slinky of repeatedly climbing into his house and stealing his possessions.' It said that the man was so annoyed that he decided to catch Slinky and scare him. When he caught him that day, he set his dogs on him to trap him, then he hit him. The papers said he must've hit him several times and really hard, because he had lots of broken bones.

Poor Slinky, I thought, but I didn't say nothing.

* * *

"My gosh!" said my friend, Marla. "You seen that?"

She was talking about Slinky in his coffin. Our class was taken to the funeral, along with lots of other people from the village.

"Did you see?" I asked her. "He had cotton wool in his nose."

"I hear the funeral home had to fill up bits of his head and face with cotton wool, coz he had holes everywhere from the beating," Marla said.

"Poor Slinky," we moaned together.

We saw his mother cling to three of her daughters and weep for her only son. Somebody in the crowd fainted, then animal-like moaning and shrill weeping filled our heads. The cries made the little hairs on my arms stand out straight. It was all so awful and confusing that it made us feel like helpless sacks of air.

Somebody said that Slinky's dad wanted to kill this man who had taken his son away, but I don't think he got his wish because the beater died by his own hands before he could even get to him.

CHAPTER 12

RESULTS

The day before the other kids in my class went on the tour, Marleen, Marla, Dianne and I discovered what a prostitute was. We had heard the word before. Mammy said red girls like to be prostitutes. I knew it had to do something with women who look and smell really nice on the outside, but who're not so sweet on the inside, so I knew this wasn't something good at all.

"Look, look," whispered Carmalita in a sort of loud, quiet voice.

She was walking home with us today. She was bigger than all of us and lived in Islington, but she was visiting her dad in Stanleytown.

"Prostitutes in that taxi!" she squealed, jerking a half-hidden thumb towards the car that had stopped beside us in the street to pick up a woman.

"What?" Dianne asked, baffled.

"You know, *prostitutes.* They go up to Everton where the ships come in, kiss the sailors on the ships, and then get paid for it," Carmalita said.

She was talking about the port where the Bauxite mines are, the place where foreign ships come in to collect the Bauxite for export. *Or is that import? Nah, import is the stuff you buy, isn't it?* The way I remembered it is because 'im' sounded like 'in' (the stuff you bring in).

Anyway, we learned at school that the foreign people make all kind of stuff like pots and things with Bauxite. That must be very hard to do, because Bauxite is simply red dust.

"How can you tell though?" Marla asked.

"Coz they wearing short dresses and they smoking," Carmalita answered. "My big sister said that they all dress up nice, and then have a special taxi come and pick them all up to take them down to Everton."

"They get paid for kissin'?" Marla asked.

"Uh, huh," Carmalita answered. "That's wot my sister said, and she knows everything. She's got a boyfriend, you know."

"No one knows everythin'," Marleen piped up.

"Some grown-ups do," Carmalita said.

"Some grown-ups *say* they do," I offered. "I doan think they really do."

The thing I left out, though, was the fact that both my mother and grandmother smoked.

Did that make them bad women?

In our town it was a shame for a woman to smoke. It meant something, but I don't quite know what. This is why I didn't want anyone to out that they do. Not that they ever do it in the street, though.

* * *

Today was the big day! I was going to pick up my exam results and I couldn't decide *how* I felt. It was a mixture of ants in my belly, needles in my feet, and buzzing inside the soft bits of my brain.

Marleen and Marla and I met at the front of the school as planned. We met up with Ricardo, one of the bright boys, who was just coming out. He said he was going in and out of the gate because he didn't know what else to do. He walked back in with us, across the wooden slats of the bridge, which lay over the tiny trench that ran the length of the road outside Overwinning Primary School, and told us that Mr. Williams had a big pile of blue and white papers in his hands.

He ran his hand through his long, straight, black hair, then shook it all back into his forehead.

Why do people do that?

Hearing about the pile of papers made us more nervous because we were now sure we were going to get the results today. We were hoping that somehow they could go lost or something.

"Listen up, everyone," Mr. Williams said.

By this time I was shaking real bad. I wanted to go to the toilet but didn't dare. My hands were sweating worse than usual. I wiped them on my skirt yet again, on the dark green circles now getting larger and larger. I was chewing on my nails as usual, and so was Dianne.

"I have the future of all sixty-two of you in my hands. I've left the papers in the order they came. That means that they are in order of the least points out of 650, to the greatest points out of 650. Understand?"

There was no answer.

Silence.

Wipe, wipe, my hands went on the sides of my skirt. My stomach did a few flutters to remind me it was still there, still empty.

He started to call out names. On and on he went. I heard Carmalita's name and she went to get her paper. I was getting nervouser. I kept listening for Lyken. At one point I did hear Lynch and started to go up, but Hazel went up instead.

Ricardo was still standing with us and he kept wringing his hands and shifting from leg to leg. He mumbled something about getting a new bike.

A tiny bit of nail and a bigger bit of finger-tip skin fell to the ground beside me.

"Dianne Abrams," Mr. Williams said, when he got to about half way through the pile of papers. Dianne went up to get her paper and when she opened it she whispered, 'Tutorial Academy.' This was one of the schools the twins and I didn't want to go to.

Ricardo kept mumbling, "One more, one more, one more."

"What yuh talking about?" I asked.

"The more papers he give out, the better marks I get," he said.

That made sense, I thought, but it did make me think that maybe I did so badly that there was no paper for me.

"Marleen Mercy," Mr. Williams said.

"Ohhh," Marleen groaned. She came back and tore open her paper.

The tiny classroom got hotter and hotter, my hands dripped with water I couldn't even remember drinking.

"B.E.I!" Marleen shouted, happily waving her paper in the air. She was quickly sshhed.

I could see that Marla was beginning to cry, she really wanted to go to same school as her big sister. Well, I say *big*.

Marleen said that, Bibi, their old friend, a girl I always identified as 'the girl with long hair up to her bottom,' passed for B.E.I last year, so she already had a friend there.

I sort of knew Bibi. She lived opposite the Persaud's corner shop on the Main Road. I saw her a lot because that was the shop I ran to all the time.

Mr. Williams went on and Jan's, his daughter, name was called. My heart had switched up gears on me without asking, and I wiped my hands on the front of my skirt. It turned entirely bright green and almost dripping with sweat.

"Marla Mercy."

Up gear.

Up gear.

Aren't there only four or five gears in a car?

Marla ran up and tore open her paper. "B.E.I!" she shouted, and she and her twin jumped up together.

"SShhh!

More names, and dozens of sshhhs later. I still had no paper in my hand.

A lot of jumping and screaming were going on, as Mr. Williams was now well into the blue uniforms pile. The hall was now almost half empty because quite a few of the kids who'd had their results had left. Mr. Williams had only about five papers left in his hands, which made Ricardo as troubled as I was. He went over to where Mr. Williams was standing and looked at the very last paper from under his hand.

"Geff Williams," Mr. Williams said beaming, handing his son his paper.

Ricardo came back to stand next to me and sort of whispered in a shout, "I see your paper!"

"Where?" I demanded.

"It's the last paper in his hand," he said.

It didn't register in my mind what this meant at the time. I was too busy eating my nails. I was rooted to the spot and could not go over to see for myself. I was sure there was no paper for me, that I was the worse pupil of all.

"Ricardo Singh."

Ricardo rushed over and took his paper.

"B.H.S!" he shouted at me, waving his paper in my face.

I was now breaking down. There were no more gears left.

His was the second to last paper and Mr. Williams still hadn't called my name. The pressure in my heart was like going under water and not coming up for air.

Ever!

Then Mr. Williams opened his mouth. And smiled.

And showing all his perfectly white teeth, he chanted, "And now! Our top student! We are all so proud of her!

"With 599 out of six hundred and fifty points!

"Ann Lyken!"

Breathe.

When I got home a bit later, after talking to my teacher, Theresa was hanging halfway out the window waiting for me, smiling. She said that some kids from nearby had passed by the house and shouted, "Ann Lyken, 599! Ann Lyken, 599!"

She was really, really happy for me.

"So is not a repeat of yuh end of term tests results," was all Mammy said.

Only *Mammy* could think of my worst report ever, at a time like this.

Mammy said that now I had to write Esther to tell her what colour material to bring so I could get my uniform made for secondary school.

CHAPTER 13

GREAT-AUNT HYACINTH

It was the end of the first week of the eight-week long summer holiday.

I never got anything planned to do, and I hated holidays. Somehow, this one has been especially bad. The strain of my exams collided with my ant of a body in a bang so big that something was bound to get smashed.

My body might have been wrecked, but getting into B.H.S. meant I was a little closer to the diamonds winking at me from the open, free sky. I reckoned when you're hurting, you've just got to move faster to get the job done quicker so you could sit down and rest.

* * *

On Monday I got off the end of Mammy's bed to go to the bathroom and must've made it half-way there. When I came to, I was lying on the floor looking up at Theresa, with Franc and Mammy staring down at me.

"What kind 'a trouble yuh going to put me in now?" Mammy asked.

I blinked.

Theresa took me by the arms and pulled me up. Her muscles curled, then unfolded again.

Fainting, for me was a regular, not to mention restful 'exercise.' Sometimes when I was standing by the wall waiting for instructions, especially if it was early in the morning, my head would go light, the room would spin around and I'd end up on the floor. Theresa said Mammy should have me checked out because I must be sick or stressed.

"Yuh stupid, na," Mammy had told her back then. "Children doan get stressed, and she not sick, just lazy."

"Ah say, what trouble you gon put me in now?" Mammy repeated.

I blinked again. I couldn't remember what I had done before I fainted. Had I been bad? Had I said something? How much time had passed?

"You!" Mammy pointed a strict finger at me. "You dare ignore me?"

"I doan know," I said, hoping that it would end there because my head felt empty-like. But I could feel one of Mammy's long question-arias coming on.

"What you mean you doan know?" Mammy asked again. This time the finger had left the pointing to her forehead crease. "You falling down like that, and you doan know?"

"I feel bad."

"Bad, how?"

"Sick," I said, and really didn't want to stand there answering any more questions. I squeezed my eyes so that those red and black polka dot spots could go away.

"Explain to me what *sick* mean."

"My head hurt, like."

"What you saying, I hurting you head. You dare be rude to me?"

"No . . . but . . ."

"Doan answer me back, or ah will punch you in the face!"

Just then Theresa came in with some green tea and handed it to me. You always had to mind what you said to Mammy. Theresa said she could turn anything you said the wrong way. It was worse when it happened during ordinary conversations, when you'd end up trying to juggle your confusion with one of these long question-aria thingies.

I stayed in bed all week drifting in and out of con-chos-ness. One time I woke up and found Mammy covering my body with a thick paste of flour and water to make me sweat because the fever was so high. I'd always remember that moment for as long as I lived because that was the first time in my life I saw her look at me with concern. I passed out again right after. I don't know if it was out of shock or because of my illness.

On Friday morning I woke up soaking wet with two or three sheets stuck to my damp, numb body. Disturbed flies buzzed around me in the heavy air coming through the bedroom window as I threw off the coverings and swung my legs to the floor. This movement brought on the sense of faintness again, so I plumped back down.

I called for Franc, because Theresa wouldn't hear from a distance. After a while she came running in armed with the cat.

"Yook, cat," she said.

Theresa came in straight after, felt my forehead and said, "Yuh fever broke. Good. We wrapped you up so you would sweat out the fever. Ah glad it worked."

* * *

Dear Aunty or Mister,

I know why Theresa was so worried. You see, when I was a little baby I caught new-monia. I know you don't spell it like that, but it's a very difficult word for me, even though I'm improving with my writing and speaking all the time in preparation for secondary school.

Esther said that I was extremely ill by the time they took me to the hospital. The doctors, seeing that I was in such a bad way, gave me an awful amount of injections quite quickly, so many that I developed a big abscess at the injection spot, on the back of my hip.

While the new-monia was improving, the abscess grew much worse, so the doctors had to operate and cut it out. Esther said I had a big hole there, as big as a ping pong ball. I've still got a hole, only, not so big now.

Anyway, when I was seven, I got new-monia again and got really sick, which meant that I had to stay home from school a lot. That, I think was the worst part of being ill. The 'having to stay at home' bit.

"Three times," Mammy had told me once. "Three times is all it takes for new-monia to kill you."

It feels wrong to wonder, 'What if?'

Best wishes, xxx

* * *

It was Monday again.

The morning greeted us with, *knock, knock.*

"Open the door." Mammy threw some irritated words at me. "I wonder who that can be so early in the morning."

At the door, my face was caressed with weighted, warm August air. It felt as if I had just stepped out of a hot shower under an open sky.

I looked right into the bosom of a short, old woman – a woman I was sure I had never seen before.

"Hello child," she said. Her voice had a song and a smile in it. There was a small, brown travelling bag beside her on the landing. This was strange. No one ever visited us, especially people we didn't know.

"Mata living here?" she asked.

Almost at the same time Mammy fretted, "Who is it?" and put her head round the door.

The woman answered before I could say anything.

"Is me, yuh sister," she said, stepping into the house and kicking her bag in. "You, a hard person to catch, mon," the woman said, slipping off her shoes at the door. "Ah went to yuh old address, but that big-foot neighbour said you moved. Why you moving so much?"

"Ah not like you, with me own house and fancy riches, you know, Hyacinth," Mammy replied. "Come in and tek a seat."

"Oh, Mata, you call everything riches," Mammy's sister answered, moaning as she took a seat in the old rocking chair. "You'd know ah not rich if you come to see me sometimes."

And this is how they started and continued for a bit. No, *'Nice to see you.'* Not even, *'So how d'ou do?'* None of that pleasant-istic stuff.

Mammy's sister, Great Aunt Hyacinth, had come all the way from the Corentyne to give her some bad news.

"So this is Esther's oldest," she said after a while, looking at me. "Last time, she was this high."

She stretched out her hand about three inches off the floor. Surely, no one is ever that small.

"What yuh name child?"

"Ann," I replied.

"How come yuh so fine? Don't you grandmother feed you or something?"

"That is what she want people to say 'bout me," Mammy said from behind me. "She starve she-self to give me bad name."

"Ow Mata, ah did only joking."

"Doan call me Mata," Mammy said crossly. "Me name is Elizabeth now."

"Relax. It's me you talking to, remember? Yuh sister, Hyacinth. Don't come to me with all that hoity-toity nonsense." Great Aunt Hyacinth waved her hand in front of her face, almost hitting the fly that buzzed around her nose.

She was the opposite of Mammy in the way she looked. She was short and tubby, and instead of an exclamation point, the crease in her forehead made a friendly wave, going from one side to the next. She was also very dark and spoke in a rough country accent, unlike Mammy, who was very city-fied. Not that we lived in a city, mind.

"You can't talk to me like that, I am a married woman," Mammy pouted.

"*Was* a married woman," came the reply. "How long did you keep the man?"

Great Aunt Hyacinth had come to say that Mammy's husband Arthur had died, and that she should go to the funeral, even if it was only because she had come all this way to tell her. Mammy said she wasn't going.

"Let the woman he lived with go to the funeral," she said. "I left him donkey's years ago. He was a good-for-nothing."

"But he always had a good job, and he took good care of you and the children," Great Aunt Hyacinth protested. "He provided for yuh and all dat, you never had to work."

I wondered how this wavy-crease woman could be related to my stiff, exclamation-mark grandmother.

"Yeah, but he was lazy, all the children I had for him, come out as a waste of space. Look at Albert and Eve and Melly."

"Yeah, but Mata, you doan even know where poor Melly is, if she dead or alive."

"Dead or alive, no matter to me at all," Mammy said.

"What about the last two you had for that married man?" Great Aunt Hyacinth asked. "Christopher's no good. Yuh spoil him rotten, yuh said so yourself. He's not Arthur's and he's no good. What he doing now anyway?" Having filled her pipe, she began to set it alight.

"He in the army and doing fine, thank you," Mammy replied.

"You know, Mata, you should really tek these picknin' to see they grandfather. They never seen him before, and not likely to see him again. You should really think 'bout it. He you husband still, yuh know. Yuh never divorced, did you?"

"No," answered Mammy. "But ah not coming, and that's final. And stop talking in them Hindi words."

"They not Hindi words anymore, they Guyanese words now, ever'body says *picknin* where I come from. Besides, I live in the country, so ah can say what ah like."

Later, Mammy said she had to go to the market and left, holding her head way up high. Theresa and I were told to finish up the housework before she came back.

We went downstairs to do the washing. Theresa did it bent over our big blue tub, washing everything carefully, one at a time, between her long, lean fingers.

"Scrissh, scrissh, it went – cloth between folded, gripping fingers, again and again, bit by dripping bit.

I helped her with the rinsing when she was finally finished. All the clothes had to be checked for stains and smells, using our threading-needle eyes, because Mammy likes her clothes to come out of the wash alive with freshness.

Theresa hung them out on the line because I had to go back to the front gate to look out for Mammy.

She didn't like it if you didn't see her as soon as she came into the street with the bags. We lived on the end of the street but one, and the passenger hire car would drop her off at the other end of the street, on the Main Road about 200 yards away.

We would time it so that we were peering up the road, hand shading eyes, after every three minutes. As soon as we saw something that looked like her shadow, I'd start racing up the street as fast as my two wobbly legs would let me so I could take her shopping bags and bring them home. I started looking out early today because I didn't want to get licks in front of a stranger.

"What yuh doing, pickny?" Great Aunt Hyacinth asked after a while, hanging her head out of the window as she looked down at me.

"I looking out for Mammy," I said, "To help her with the bags."

"Ah, Mata can bring in her own bags," she said, waving her hand in front of her face again. She really didn't like those flies.

I didn't say anything to that. I was sure that she wouldn't understand.

"So, I sure yuh got you uniform ready and crisp, waiting to turn out to yuh posh, new school," she said to me, after Theresa and I had finished the washing and had gone upstairs again. I knew it was rude to leave her on her own upstairs, but she had Franc to keep her company. Besides, politeness wasn't a reason for not finishing the washing.

"No, I'm waiting for Esther to bring the material so I can take it to the seamstress," I answered.

"Is already near the middle of the holiday. Yuh can't just march into the seamstress and get it made in one day, child. You got to first go and get measured to see how much material you need. Then you got to go and buy the cloth, thread, and zips and things. *Then* go back to her to get it all made. All this gon take a while. When is Esther coming?"

"I doan know," I answered. "She never says, she just surprises us."

"All the seamstresses usually busy round this time of year, you know. They making new uniforms for ever'body. You grandmother should just buy material from the market. She tell me yuh wearing blue, right?"

"Yes, a blue skirt and a white top, with a smart blue tie. I also have to get a white skirt, and a white tee shirt for P.E. days."

"That's nice, child. How 'bout yuh father? Can't he get your uniform? After all, yuh did very well at yuh exams."

"Mammy told Mr. Charles that I passed for B.H.S. He lives up the road and he works at Bermine with m' father. He said he'll tell him, and that he will be proud."

"You granny says that he got other children now. Yuh know them?"

"No," I said. I could've added *I'm not allowed to meet them*, but Mammy would beat me if she knew I was telling people about what she was not allowing me to do.

"So yuh got other brothers and sisters that yuh don't know?"

"'Bout ten of them," I said, and she laughed.

My skin nearly abandoned me at the sound of her laughter. It was really strange to have a grown-up laugh at something I'd said. Theresa wasn't really a grown-up. Not really.

"I really like how yuh trying to talk proper, child," Great Aunt said, nodding her head. "We country people can't talk proper, yuh know. But you got to practice for your big-shot high school, mon."

"Yes," I agreed. "I got to start talking proper and stop using slang and stuff. My teacher told me that they'll expect that at my new school."

I was trying really hard. I had to try to remember the big words I learned to use at Open Day, which is at my new school very soon. I hope Esther comes by then so she could come with me. That would be nice. I know she will come. She wouldn't leave me without a uniform. I know she wouldn't. Yes, that will be extremely nice. Everything will be just fine.

"By the way, me child," Great Aunt said as I made yet another trip to the forbidden window to look for Mammy (it was alright if you were looking out for her).

"Ah know yuh granny doan want you to call her 'Granny,' coz it will make her feel too old, but you really shouldn't call your mother full-mouth. Esther never say anything to you?"

"No, I doan feel right calling her *Esther*, but I think she wants me to, coz she never said for me or Franc to call her *Mammy*."

At that moment I could make out a tall, thin, very upright figure cat-walking into the street. I ran to the door and yanked it open. I took a quick glance back and I saw Great Aunt looking at me with a great, big circle plastered on her face at the spot where her mouth used to be. I didn't stop to explain.

CHAPTER 14

BLOOD SUCKING OL'HIGUES

Mammy and her sister talked or argued what felt like all night long. I heard them talking about all the banned stuff that people were getting into trouble trying to smuggle into the country: split peas, tomato ketchup, wheat flour, cooking oil, and all that.

My sleep was splattered with their voices roaming in the secret parts of my head as I half-slept at the side of Mammy's bed.

"The Honourable Comrade so powerful, why don't he do something about all them foreign countries who put 'Demerara' on their sugar? I seen 'Demerara' written on all kinds of sugar not made here when I go abroad. 'Demerara' is in Guyana, not anywhere else."

Great Aunt lives near to the Stelling on the Corentyne. The Corentyne River is the border between Guyana and Suriname. It's the river the two governments are struggling to decide who should own.

I mean, who's ever heard of people fighting to own a river? What exactly do you own? The mud at the bottom? The fish that swim in it? The actual water?

"Ah was so glad when ah left she and she Obeah ways. Ah didn't care that ah hardly knew Arthur, I just wanted to get outta there and live me own life."

Great Aunt said that she sees lots of new traders every day, and that the Corentyne is packed with them going over to Suriname to get contraband food stuff.

"Mostly Indian women," she said, "because the Indian people feel that The Honourable Comrade had a particular spite for them when he banned wheat flour."

"After all, the Indian people have to make their roti every day. It's a good thing we make Madras curry powder right here in Guyana, or The Comrade and the PNC wudda banned that, too."

I stirred and turned over, but always kept on that one tiny spot where my body had made a sort of Ann-shape. I didn't mind falling off the bed in the night, just as long as I didn't touch her, nor she, me.

"I going abroad to live soon. Me and me husband so glad we sent them kids abroad before it got so hard to leave the country. Ah can't stand all the murderin' and robbin' going on nowadays, and it's not just the criminals doing that, mind."

It may have been only a couple of minutes, or a few hours later, but when I pulled the sheet over my feet to stop them being bled dry by the mosquitoes who came every night to feed on my blood, the voices were still floating from the creaking chairs in the living room.

"Ah went to visit Daniel. He and he wife live like big-shots. Imagine that, I live like a pauper and he got his wife and children all uppity-like. Ah seen she put butter on both slices of bread when she make a sandwich for the little boy. Imagine that! Butterin' both slices of bread! No one does that."

Later that night Great Aunty Hyacinth snored, snored, and snored some more.

The next morning she looked all bright and fresh, the opposite of what I was feeling.

"So what yuh neighbours like, Mata?" she asked at breakfast.

"There's this family up the road," Mammy said, jutting out her chin in the direction of the fancy house nearby. "The daughter is a nurse, and the mother, she so hoity-toity, she doan talk to me at all. The husband got a big position at Bermine, so she think she too good for me."

"Maybe she just doan like you," Great Aunt said, a bit of the bread she was chewing flew out of her mouth and landed on the larger piece in her hand.

"No, not that," Mammy answered. "I think she is an Ol'Higue. Her eyes really red and she can't look you in the face. I always put garlic and raw rice at the side window. Ah doan want the likes of her sucking me blood."

"Oh Mata, get over you'self. Even if that was true, why would she want stale, washed up, old blood when she got a fresh young, virgin girl in she prime, and two nice little red children?"

Great Aunt Hyacinth had her breakfast, toasted it to, "Arthur, a very good and pleasant man," and left.

Before Great Aunt Hyacinth had said this, I almost believed the lady up the road was an Ol'Higue.

This was where I bought ice from these days, and every day when I have to look into her face and ask, "Can I have a pan of ice please?" I think, *'And please don't fly over and suck me tonight,'* but no matter how hard I try, I can't look away from her eyes, her red, weepy eyes.

Ol'Higues are meant to be women who look normal in the day time, but at night, they shed their skin – just like taking off a wet suit – and turn into creatures that ignite into a ball of fire. They then fly out to suck their neighbours' blood, getting into their houses through little creases and open windows.

The key to their life and death is the mystery of where they hide their skin. As the story goes, if you wish to expose someone as being an Ol'Higue, you have to sneak into their home, sit still and keep watch, making sure you never fall asleep. If they find your hiding place, they'll know exactly what you were doing and bleed you dry. The moment you see them fly out, you have to quickly get their skin and pour salt all over it, on the inside.

"But yuh got to mek sure that they never catch you doing it," Mammy had told us once.

"If yuh in the middle of salting the skin when they come home from sucking, woe is you. They strike you down there and then. Dat's why yuh got to keep careful watch."

When they'd return after the sucking rampage, they'd find it impossible to put on a skin that had salt in it. They'd holler and scream for days, as anyone who didn't have a skin to wear would, then eventually they'd die.

It is said the way to spot an Ol'Higue in the day time is to look for red eyes, fidgety fingers, and a bad case of garlic intolerance. At night, the best thing to fend them off is a handful of raw rice.

"They got to stay there and count them grains of rice," Mammy told us. "They can't cross over your window sill or doorway until they finished counting every grain. If they mek a mistake, they gotta start all over again. Soon daylight will catch them there, and they have to hurry home before sunrise."

I'd never seen Ol'Higues in flight so I couldn't really say if all this is made up or not, but Mammy said that she had.

One thing I knew for sure was that if I got a choice between being sucked by that nice red-eyed woman up the road or being hit by Mammy, I would choose the blood sacrifice any day.

After all, how is losing a little bit of blood going to hurt me? The mosquitoes come out at night and have their fair share of me as it is. A little more couldn't hurt that much.

* * *

"I hear the sound of distant drums . . ."

Jim Reeves sang on the record player while Mammy informed us that she was going to take us to see *Sholay* tomorrow. Her favourite actor, Amitha Bachan, the star of this Indian movie, never fails to put her in a good mood. Theresa and I would have to wake up early so we could finish all the house work before we set out.

I figured that Mammy and I would be friends tonight because tomorrow I would be reading her three hours' worth of subtitles.

CHAPTER 15

A BRIEF TASTE OF VICTORY

It was Sunday again, one day and one week exactly from the day I would start my new school, so I started keeping a *special* diary of the next seven days. Writing gave me choco-listic flutters inside my chest. Usually, in the school term, I pretended to have more homework than I really did so I could write poems and read books.

I did this coz (I'd have to say 'because' now that I was about to go to high school) homework time was the only time I was left alone. I didn't have any books of my own, so I used to secretly borrow some from my friends at school and smuggle them in. I would hide them inside a school book while I read them, and this was how I've learned lots of big words.

I borrowed a dictionary, concealed (another word for hide, I learned) it inside one of my school books and read it all up – this is why I think I like to make up words. Sometimes, when I didn't have any other book, I read (strike that) consumed one of Esther's Mills and Boons novels that she'd left - *just* for something to read. I'd better not get caught though. I didn't get to write much now because there was no school, so I wrote a brief diary of this week.

<u>Monday</u>:

This morning I went with Mammy to my new school. They made us sign forms and important papers, then we had to go to the auditorium to be placed. The letters of the forms, like 1B, 1C, etc., corresponded with the various houses we were put into. Mine was 'B' for Beharry, and so was Ricardo's from my old primary school.

He wasn't sitting near to us, but I heard his name when the teacher read out the list. I was praying that he didn't speak to me, because I get licks if I speak to boys.

Throughout the lists and greetings, I heard almost nothing. My focus was only to hope and pray with a churning sort of watery belly ache that he would be too taken up with all the new things to see me. He was talking to a boy I didn't know, a boy wearing a name tag that said 'Steve,' who was also in 'B' house. I saw all the kids who I'll share at least three years of my life with, until we are all streamed off. This is what you're meant to do in your third year.

I also saw a girl I knew. We only go to church on special occasions like at Lent and Advent, but this is a girl I've seen at church and recognise. She wasn't going to be in my class though, I think her name was Joanne, but I couldn't see her name tag.

Ricardo didn't come over to me at all. He was busy with Steve. He did smile and wave but Mammy didn't see because I didn't wave back. Good old Ricardo.

The huge school, peppered across a former colonial estate, was grander than I'd dreamed. Some of the classrooms, like the Home Economics department and the staff room, had all been houses lived in by foreigners. The library and music rooms were once servants' quarters. There were two new buildings, but we would have to wait to get to form five before we could use them.

It was time to go up to the teacher and register individually. His name was Mr. Jake Paltoo. Being tall, dark and muscular, he looked too young and sporty to be a teacher. He took my birth certificate and placed it in front of him, then asked me my name.

"Ann Lyken," I said.

"And that is Anne with an *e*," he stated, glancing at my birth certificate and writing at the same time. I was just about to interrupt when I too looked at the certificate and noticed that *indeed* my name was spelt with an *e*.

Ever since I could write and spell my name, it was without an *e*. Theresa taught me to spell my name, but I suppose she never had any reason to look at my birth certificate. I wonder why the two people who gave me the name didn't bother to see that I spelt it right. Mr. Paltoo took all of the details he needed, swept his hand through his thick, curly hair, and said he was going to be my P.E. teacher.

The film 'Sholay' was exciting, way too long, but exciting.

* * *

Tuesday:

Today I have made a decision to remember to do two things: one, to spell my name with the *e* and two, to stop biting my nails. I was now growing up, nearly eleven, and I should spell my name properly and not bite my nails anymore. My mother has fiery, long nails, she paints them in super red nail polish and decorates them nicely. Maybe if I can manage to stop biting mine, I could grow them like hers.

Mammy said that we have to go and stray the cat again. This was because earlier, when Theresa was preparing to wipe the kitchen floor, she left the bucket of water in a corner while she strained the rice in the little zinc sink. While she was busy, Franc took the cat and dunked him in the bucket of water.

After she had soaked him, she pulled him out, wrung him, then went to wipe the floor with him. His black and white fur almost for an instant resembled the old grey rag Theresa used on the kitchen floor.

Mammy came in from the living room to see about lunch and caught Franc red-handed. There was no way we could hide it from her this time.

"Ah want ya'll to tek this cat and stray it. I ain't putting up with this no more."

"She don't know better. It's alright, the cat ain't hurt," Theresa answered.

She turned down the one-burner kerosene stove, put her lips together, took a huge breath, and blew out the fire. Nothing happened, so she put her hand into the bowl of water in the sink, collected a bit in the palm of her hand and whipped it on the stove in one swift movement. "Ssssssss" it went, and dark, smelly smoke filled the air.

"Lunch finished," she mumbled.

"Ah doan want she to end up killing the cat," Mammy said to her. "You and that other one got to tek him far away this time, then run away so he don't follow yuh."

Mammy had spoken and there was no way we could get out of doing it. Last time she sent us to stray the cat after Franc had tried to drown him, he followed us all the way back home. Theresa and I *did* see him walking behind us and every time he stopped, we whistled him to keep coming.

When we got home, Theresa said we should pretend we didn't know how he got there. I knew that we couldn't repeat that this time because Mammy was really spit-flying angry and one, or both of us, would get licks if he came back home with us again.

After lunch we took him far away on the Back Dam road, where we left him on his own and ran away until we couldn't see him anymore.

We didn't like doing this one bit, but Theresa said it was better for him, because someone good would surely take him in. I think she was right, because sometimes Mammy kicks him out of the way when he tries to rub himself on her legs. When he comes back and does it again, she bends over, picks him up and throws him with all her might way across the room.

Thud!

He lands on the polished floor, then slides across the smooth surface until he connects with something to make him stop. He gets up, licks his thin fur, and scrambles across the floor, again making his way towards Mammy's legs.

Maybe someone good will take him in, poor thing.

I think he was a very stupid cat though, because he should at least remember all the hard skids and kicks and stay away, but he always, always comes back for more.

I was only about three and I still remember my kick. I even remember what Esther was wearing when it happened. We were living at Fifty-seven, Stanleytown. This is the first place we lived in after we moved to this village from the Corentyne. I know I was three then, because I was four when we moved into the house opposite the one we now live in.

I was sitting on the floor at the time. Mammy wanted to get past, so she said, "Why yuh sitting in the middle of the floor, eh, when I got to get by?" Then without warning, I was skidding across to the other side of the room.

"Stupid," she had said under her breath as she went on. Esther and her friend were standing on the veranda. She was wearing a yellow dress. When I went outside afterward to cry, Esther's friend said, "Esther, you should really tek yuh child away."

I always run out of Mammy's way now. When I see her coming, I get out of the area fast. This is why I think the cat is stupid, because I am not very smart, and if I could learn from my kick, so could he.

Today Theresa and I also went to line up for kerosene oil to put in the stove, but it was all gone by the time we got up to the front of the queue.

* * *

Wednesday:

Still no school uniform.

Mammy says I have to go and see Mr. Charles. He lives a few doors up from us and works with my father. I am told that my father is one of the head men of the Security at Bermine (the Bauxite mines, where the foreign ships come in). Mr. Charles also works in security, and he's got lots of stripes on the shoulder of his uniform. He's not a man I know, but the magic of him is that he works in the same department as my father. We're not sure if they're friends, or even speak to each other.

My stomach bent over and my spirit felt very small on the inside, but I had no choice. I had to go.

Going to high school is the only way that I will be able to climb up and pick at those diamonds in the sky. If I have no uniform, I can't go. If I can't go, what will become of me?

If I can't go, I'll never be able to inhale completely.

Please Lord, I don't want to take shallow breaths forever.

Mammy says I have to go and tell Mr. Charles about what's happening (not happening), and ask him to see my father at work tomorrow and tell him to buy my uniform and school bag and shoes and stuff.

I walked to Mr. Charles' house, all nearly eleven years of me, in a compact little ball.

I knocked on the stranger's door, a man I had only ever said, 'Good Morning, Mister' to, even though he passed our house almost every single day on his way to work.

His wife came to the door, and looked down at me. "Yes?" she asked. She knew who I was. I was not like her kids, I was of the pack they called the 'bastards.'

She turned away to get her husband when my bastard's voice said, "Good afternoon, Aunty. Can I speak to Mr. Charles, please?"

My knees shook from the marrow, and my palms tingled on the insides as I waited for him. I had practised what I was going to say on my way over. How did it start? How *did* it start?

A towering, black man stood in front of me. He was chewing. I had caught him during his dinner.

I don't know if I told him my name, or if he already knew it. If he did, he probably did not know that it ended with an *e*.

Words came tumbling out of my mouth. My mother was meant to bring my uniform and we wrote her twice but we didn't hear from her. I didn't have anything to start school with, *nothing*. I was meant to start secondary school in five days but had nothing to wear and we had no money. Not a single penny to buy anything.

When I eventually opened my eyes, his mouth was empty and his brow was creased. Confusion flashed in electric signs inside his skull. I knew this because I could see the reflection of it in his eyes.

"I'll tell yuh father," he said.

"Thanks," I answered, then turned my back, slimed down his stairs, and walked away.

His house was next door to Parmanand's bar on the Back Dam Road, a convenient place to do my cigarette and rum shopping these days, being a stone's throw away from our house. I stopped on my way home to buy some cigarettes. It's lucky that we happen to live near bars, or else I would be spending half my life walking to get cigarettes.

We're running out of kerosene fast, and Mammy said we might have to cook on the fireside. She said that Comrade Leader and his PNC party ration all the kerosene so that families could only get a small amount to cook. She said that a lot of her friends cheat because they send their teenage children in the line separately, so they get two, or even three portions.

Yesterday when Theresa and I went to Esso petrol station, we were nearly two hundredth in the enormous anaconda-shaped line in the hot sun. When we got up to about fourth position after more than two hours, the pumps had all gone dry (or so they said). This happens often, and to lots of people. Mammy said that tomorrow, we'd have to get up at four in the morning so that we could be first in the line.

Thursday:

I woke up and got dressed by the light that was always left on in the living room. I took the kero jar that I carry (this is the two gallon one; I usually have to change hands often to walk home with it, but I can carry it okay), went to the back door and opened it.

"What on earth you doing, stupid? Is the middle of the night."

"Buying kero," I said, but before the words had come out of my mouth, I realised that I was sleep walking again.

"Go back to bed," Mammy said. It was only 11 p.m. after all. The first time I sleep walked was just after we had the break-in, back when we lived in the scheme. Like then, I tried to open the back door and escape outside. Good thing Mammy woke me up.

I was woken up – properly this time – at about 3:30 a.m. Mammy stayed with Franc, and Theresa and I prepared to go out into the warm morning air. The crickets were noisily chirping, as the birds still seem to be sound asleep. It was very dark, but it was all right.

Theresa said that there was no need to be scared because people would look out for us, seeing that we were two girls in the street on our own. It was a long walk into the town to the petrol station. When we got there, the line of people waiting was already poking its way into the main road. There were about fifty people who'd gotten there before us, but in the end, we got our kero. In the afternoon I went back to see Mr. Charles to see if he had any good news for me.

"Me child," he said, and I knew from the look on his face what he was about to say. "Yuh father said that if yuh want him to buy your uniform, yuh have to ask him yourself, not come through me."

I felt my eyes looking up to his, but can't remember seeing his face. I had dreamed of Mr. Charles bringing me parcels wrapped in golden paper, parcels with notes scrawled on top of them saying, *'To my loving daughter. I'm so proud of you.'*

I'd had visions of walking home and trying to peek into the packages, opening them at the side, just a small bit where Mammy wouldn't notice.

I would see blue, and I'd smile to myself. He would make me guess what was inside the parcels, but I would know. His trick wouldn't work, but I'd pretend I hadn't looked. I'd go home and wonder out loud about what would be so beautifully wrapped. I would open them and gasp in surprise, then I would smile and begin to try them on.

"Sorry child, I can't help you. You did very well and you father proud of you," Mr. Charles said. I waited for a second, but he didn't bring out any parcels.

When the tears fell, I saw Mr. Charles scratch his head. Once again, I walked down his steps hands, empty.

What have I done for nobody to want me? Is that why Mammy hated me? Was she the person tricked into taking care of the girl nobody could love? I'm tired trying to be so good and perfect all the time. I don't know what's happening with Esther. I wrote her twice, no reply. I can't call, because even if we had a phone, I have no phone number for her, nor for my father.

I wiped my eyes dry before I went inside because I'd have some explaining to do if I was crying. The child nobody wanted should know that you can only feel hard-done-by if you're worthy of having something in the first place.

"Mr. Charles said that m' father won't help," I said when I returned home.

Then I tried to block out the flies buzzing inside and around my head – everything that Mammy was saying. My brain couldn't take in anything anymore. I felt like I would faint but I didn't.

Maybe I should have.

Please make it stop.

* * *

Friday was the last working day before I start high school on Monday, with no school uniform. Theresa woke up with a brilliant idea. She asked Mammy if she could spare the old blue skirt she used to wear to work. Theresa said that she would take the skirt apart and then cut it, pleat it, and make it into a skirt for my new uniform.

She said she learned enough sewing to make a pleated skirt, and that she should have enough material left over to make my tie.

The shade was lighter than what I should have, and the cloth was old and worn, but at least it was blue. She said that although I needed a white shirt, I could wear my old cream shirt from primary school for the time being. Mammy thought it was a good idea. I thought so too, but was still feeling raw about yesterday and everything else.

"Instead of sewing it with yuh hand, I could send she to Barry's wife in the scheme to ask if you could use her sewing machine," Mammy said, flicking her thumb in my direction. 'She' 'You,' and 'That One' had always been Mammy's names for me. There was no question that she meant me.

Theresa said that that would be even better, and that we had to do something now. We couldn't wait any longer for my mother to show up.

I went up to the scheme to Mr. Barry's wife with a note that Mammy had dictated for me to write, asking if we could come on Saturday morning to sew my skirt. She said, "Of course, why not?"

I took my time walking back home. I knew this could be bad, but it was nice being out of the house after eight weeks of 'school holidays' being locked up indoors and feeling watched all the time. I felt good and free, even if it was just a walk back home past the smelly Back Dam trench.

I looked for the cat but I didn't see him. Maybe someone took him in like Theresa had said.

When I got close to the house, I noticed Mammy's head pop out of the window. I saw her face and knew straight away that I was in big trouble. When I walked through the door, she said to me, "Go take off yuh clothes, you getting licks."

The projector coughed, the desolate screen stumbled to life, and this scene played:

My heart is pounding and my head feels like it's been wrapped with new elastic bands. I'm chewing on my finger nails to keep from fainting. I walk into Mammy's bedroom and start to take off my clothes. When she's getting ready to do a nasty beating, Mammy insists I get naked – completely. I don't know why, since the licks are really painful even with my clothes on.

I take my tee shirt partly off, but I leave it hanging round my neck to cover my chest because I have a tiny little pip growing out there. Just the one so far and I don't want anyone to see it.

Mammy comes into the room with the stick and she's screaming at me because I'm still wearing my clothes. She rips the tee shirt off me, so hard it bruises my face, and I'm left standing there with my little, tiny pip pointing at her.

I start to cry, but it's more from my shame than from fright. I need to cover up my body, so I put my arm on my chest, partly shielding the sharp ribs which are barely covered by my stretched skin. She hits my arm with the wood and commands me to take the rest off. She stands there and waits. I am crying as I take my shorts off but I don't want to lose my underwear too. It's the lone piece of the precious rags left to cover up my cowering frame. I'm growing up you see, and don't want anyone to look at me.

I break down.

I can't take my underwear off. I can't.

But by then I'm crying too much to do anything else. She gets really angry. She doesn't like to wait.

Mammy never waits, not for anyone.

Now she can't wait for me to undress anymore so she starts to beat me all over, the only place on my body that escape without licks, is my head.

In all the riot and pain, I keep holding on to the thought that keeping my underpants on means that I've achieved my only, precious, towering moment of victory.

I feel like a chewed up, spat out cherry. I know I'm bleeding somewhere but I can't look now, the licks are too bad.

Much, much too bad.

She sees the blood, too. Some of it spills on the wall and she glances at it. I think she'll stop. I know she can't bear to have any stain on her bedroom wall. I cry, but I can't scream. I'll get more licks if I do, and I'm ashamed of the children next door hearing. She stops and now she is dragging me by my hair into the kitchen, the pain of each strand etching her fury into my scalp through to my brain. She imprisons me by the hair while she takes down the jar of salt from the shelf next to the kitchen window.

Salt!

Blood rushes fast to my head and I feel my throbbing belly suddenly knot inside me, protecting itself, waiting . . .

I wriggle to get away but she's very strong and very powerful – stronger and more powerful when she is angry. She opens the jar with her mouth and pours salt into my cut, which I then realise is on my leg. Five million grains of salt feel like ten million angry bees stinging! Stinging!

Stinging!

I hear her grind her teeth as she rubs the salt in.

I scream. Once.

"Next time," she hollers, releasing me, "I'll pepper you parts!"

But does she know I won?

Does she?

Does she!

As I limp away, arm protecting the growth on my chest, I see her pick up some salt and throw it over her shoulder. It brings quarrels into the house, you see, if you don't throw a little bit of salt over your shoulder when you spill it.

I am beginning to not believe that one. Nor the one about when the inside of your hand itches, you get good luck. Or the one about when your eyes twitch, you see someone you haven't seen in a while. Or the one about . . .

"Wipe up that blood in me bedroom and clean up this salt!" she shouts after me, heading for her cigarette chair. I don't know why I got the licks today but it must be because I took a long time to get home. That's the only thing I did wrong. I must not do that again. I must not be like the cat.

CHAPTER 16

HIGH SCHOOL AND THE DARK POWER STATION

Two days until I start secondary school.

Saturday. We had an early, brisk start today. We had to get going on my uniform, so we had a quick breakfast and cleaned up. Mammy said she would look after Franc if Theresa made some lunch and left it for her to reheat. I didn't have to go, she said. I could stay and help her with Franc. However, Theresa insisted that she needed me to get the fitting right, since we didn't have a tape measure.

"If she wasn't so stupid, she would've thought of borrowing a tape measure from Shirley when she was there yesterday," Mammy moaned.

"Yuh can't expect someone who isn't even eleven to think about something like that all on their own," Theresa told her.

I didn't know who was more right since I wasn't even aware that you needed a tape measure to sew things.

"Go buy two Bristols before you go, then," Mammy conceded, handing me thirty-five cents.

I opened the door and had actually walked down the steps before I saw her. She was stepping out of the car when she looked up at me and smiled, not the twinkle-on-teeth kind of smile, just a total, honest-to-goodness one.

My eyes fell on her, and breathing – suddenly, after months of spluttering and hiccoughing – became easy. The late August air weighed moist and heavy on my skin. The butterflies sailed by onto the hibiscus flowers in the neighbour's front garden, while the mechanic across the road scrubbed and sanded on his latest Morris Oxford project in the pot-holed street.

Her hair was longer now, shiny and pressed as straight as I imagined the hot comb could possibly get it. She was fatter too, round and pie-like. Her eyes were two slits in her dark, heart-shaped face, reminding me of how they disappeared when she smiled, or how her eyes watered when she laughed out loud.

I didn't know if I should race back inside to tell the others, or run to her and never go back inside again (I liked it out here for the few minutes where my breath was able to butterfly-wing out of my nostril without me having to heave it out). I didn't do either because Mammy saw her too. She must've been looking out the window, because she came running downstairs in an overcoat of excitement.

Franc came out too and Theresa followed. I finally ran down after her, when everyone was smiling and laughing and generally breathing huge sighs of relief. I felt like crying, but laughter surprised itself out of me.

My belly untied itself.

We carried bags and bags of stuff inside the house, an abundance of things. Esther always brought tons of things. Foodstuff like milk, banned things like potatoes, onions, garlic, tomato ketchup, cigarettes, and money. She didn't bother too much about bringing clothes though, but I suppose food was more important.

I hoped she *did* bother this time, because I only had two going out outfits: two tee shirts and two pairs of shorts. I'd had the shorts since I was six and a bit. I remembered because I got them when we lived in that house across the street. By now they were very short and rode up to the very top of my thighs, but because they were stretchy, I could just manage to hitch them up.

I used to have my First Communion white dress to wear to church but that was too small now, so it had become a grey mop for the kitchen floor.

Esther brought the material for my uniform. She said that she was on her way since yesterday but was pulled in by the police because she had the contraband foodstuff. She said they made her sleep at the police station on the Corentyne, but let her go early this morning when she pleaded with them and explained that she was away for two years and hadn't seen her children. She even had to show them the uniform material as proof she did have kids, and give them some peace money to cool things off.

Theresa and I still had to go into the scheme to do the sewing, but instead of taking an old faded used-to-be-skirt, we got some nice new, navy blue material. Theresa said that we now had enough to make two skirts and two ties. I also got two white shirts to wear with my blue skirts.

That night I had milk with my tea, and it was really good.

* * *

Mammy had diarrhoea. Esther said that was because she drank too much milk. She said that when you haven't had milk for a long time, you should take it easy at first. Mammy took pleasure in mixing the milk powder into the tea, until it was as thick as cement in water. This makes little white lumps float up to the top of her cup.

The cement tea went down well, but it only took one night for it to start rattle-snaking out of her. The loud noises made me giggle every time I heard them. Esther laughed and said she always gets caught like that.

Me, I thought she was like the cat, but perhaps she could afford to be like him because she only had to sit on the toilet and holler for more paper. She didn't have to run over to ask the mechanic's wife for more old newspaper, race up the back steps, tear them up into strips, and soak them in the kitchen sink before rushing them to the whiffy toilet.

Esther showed me the rest of the things she brought, and while Mammy was off producing her fresh concrete in the toilet, Theresa told her that Mammy had hidden some of the foodstuff and the cod liver oil tablets.

"She hides them until yuh gone, so that she can have them all for herself," Theresa whispered to Esther. "She likes to eat the cod liver oil tablets because she said they make your skin look fresh and young, and the more you eat, the younger you look."

Esther laughed.

I've got a new pink cat-suit. I wasn't sure if I liked it because it fitted a bit tight. Esther said that her friend from French Guyane didn't want it anymore, so she kindly sent it for me. At last I got something else to wear other than shorts. Esther said we were going to see Khabi Khabi, the new Indian movie, at lunch time, and even though it was my special outfit, I'd be allowed to wear it then.

It wasn't jeans, the only clothes in the world I'd ever wished for (even someone else's old ones), but it was different.

I got together everything I needed for school – again – and didn't feel the stiffness in the back of my neck, for the first time maybe in years, as I lay my clothes out on the bed. I looked at them again and a rush of breath escaped me. It was not a sad sigh, it was one of those long, smiley, dreamy ones.

It was always nicer going to the cinema with Esther because we got to sit in 'house' (the middle floor of the cinema). I'd never been to balcony because this was the expensive bit at the top with the soft seats and fewer rats. We usually went to the cheapest section at the bottom of the divide – the pit – where all the drunks would go.

Theresa didn't like it in the pit, not only because you had to be careful not to step on the wet bits on the concrete floor, but because she said her neck hurt from having to watch the whole movie looking upwards. Also, the drunks snored pretty loudly, and when they'd get up to have a wee, you'd just have to hope that at least they were sober enough to turn their backs to you. Pit was where a lot of them went to sober up before going home to face their wives. This was after they had chucked wings to their wages and let them go in the time it took them to walk from their work places to their homes.

I always wondered about this. I wondered if it wouldn't be better for them to go home drunk after squandering their money on rum. I didn't see any reason to sober up if your wife was going to fly into a rage with you anyway.

That was the good thing about watching Indian films, though, because you didn't really have to hear anything, just read the subtitles, then whisper the important bits to Mammy. She can't really read from a distance, you see. Her eyes let her down sometimes.

* * *

Monday was the perfect day for the start of a new school.

I met all my teachers (including my P.E. teacher again), and talked to a girl called Roma Singh, whom I'd be sitting next to. I met that girl from church, the one I saw with her mother on Open Day, and found that her name was actually Sita, and that she lived on the Main Road, on the edge of Stanleytown, not too far from the burial ground, just before you got into New Amsterdam, the town.

"How'd you get to school today?" she asked me. "My mother said I should look for someone who lives in Stanleytown to come home with."

I told her where I lived and that it was impossible for me to walk to school because it was too far away, that I got a passenger hire car to take me halfway here, and then walked the rest of the way.

* * *

I now lived almost at the end of the village of Stanleytown. There was the long Main Road I told you about, which went all the way into the town called New Amsterdam, thus named a long, long time ago by Dutch settlers. This was at the time when *they* were bullying the natives. That, of course, was before the British came and chased them out so that they could bully us instead. The British must've been a lot better at bullying than the Dutch, I thought.

The passenger hire cars that I'd be taking to school through New Amsterdam are mainly Morris Oxfords. You had to flag them down when you spotted them coming from a distance if you wanted them to pick you up.

I'd been told there was never any danger of them not stopping to pick you up, because no matter how many people they already had mortared in the back seat, your fare was still attractive enough for the drivers to cannon you into the pile. They could get as many as twenty-five children in one Morris Oxford, and that was the non-exaggeratistic truth. Some of the hire cars went specifically to B.H.S. because it was the school in the remotest bit of the town.

This morning, on my way to school, in the back seat of the old, rusting, used-to-be-black Morris Oxford, I had one girl sitting on my lap.

When the car chugged to a stop on the side of the narrow Main Road, there were already about ten of us folded up together on the torn, plastic-covered seats.

"You going to B.H.S?" the girl who'd flagged the driver down, asked.

"Yeah, mon. Jump in the back," the driver said. He was big and gruff, and already smelling of tonight's drinks and sweat.

We shifted down, but there was nowhere else to go.

The driver checked his gear stick which had disappeared under the legs of the boy sitting next to him in the front, eased himself out of the black, iron, rusting turtle of a car, and inspected the scarce empty air in the back seat, for a place to slip the girl in.

"You," he said to me, pointing a chubby finger at my face. "Lean back."

I pressed my back into the plastic.

"Go back a bit, no," he told the girl sitting on my lap.

She leaned back and the side of my face made one with her back.

"Jump in," he signalled to the girl in the street, taking her back pack and disappearing around the back of the car.

By the time he had slammed the car boot door, the new arrival had one foot firmly placed on mine.

After some ouching (on my part) and crouching, she'd managed to crumple herself in half and sit on the lap of the girl whose back I cushioned with the side of my face.

I didn't know who was worse off – me, the very bottom, the cheese pressed in the middle, or the folded, scrunched up girl at the top, trying her very best not to sit down too hard (and how does one do that?).

The driver eventually slammed the door, but it couldn't shut. Someone's hip was usually in the way in these situations (I'd been in cars like these before – but with adults in them).

"One of you got to hold the door, mon," he said, giving up after three or four tries. "I can't get it to shut."

The girl on my lap volunteered, but when the engine vomited to life, the car jumped forward, her hand slipped, and the door sprung open suddenly. The only reason the girl on the top of the pile did not fall out was because of my help.

Well, I say *my help* – but that only applies if the process of 'help' can be described as someone stepping on both your feet with all their weight, forcing you to jump up with pain, which results in that person being caught between the back of the driver's seat and the children sitting behind them, making it impossible to fall out of a moving car.

This would've been scary except for the fact this wasn't the first time someone had threatened to fall out of a moving car which was too packed to have its door shut.

In the afternoon, Sita and I had to do it all over again, the opposite way around. We flagged down a Morris Oxford which took us from school to High Bridge (near the burial ground), the street that marks the end of Stanleytown and the beginning of New Amsterdam. She lived just a stone's throw from here, so we walked to her street together, and then I hurried home the rest of the way.

It took me about forty-five minutes to get home after dropping Sita off, but I was accustomed to walking long distances, so that wasn't too bad.

* * *

Two months later:

My new school was excellent, and we were learning lots of new things, but there were also some changes going on.

Our English teacher, Mr. Pegg, was leaving to go back to University. He wanted to become a writer and producer of stage plays.

Acting on stage was not something I'd thought of doing. Surely that kind of thing was beyond my reach.

Of course I couldn't know it then, but Mr. Pegg would become my director in my first stage play, and the role he would write, would make me a local star.

This afternoon when I got home, Mammy told me that our pipes weren't working any more. This was not like when all the pipes in the village fail, and everyone has to fetch water from the pumping station. This was just *our* pipes. Something was wrong with the connections. Anyway, since we lived near to the Back Dam road where the pumping station pipes were, it wasn't that bad.

"Go and ask the men at the pumping station if we could fetch some water from there," Mammy told me. I was scared of the big noisy station and all the dirty, oily men who worked there, but I couldn't say so.

My heart was throbbing when I got to the guard hut at the pumping station. Before me stood a big, strapping, black man, dressed in a black beret, and a khaki uniform suit, with a broad, black belt. The little sweat on his upper lip looked like a liquid moustache. When he leaned close to me to hear what I was saying in my shaky, rustling voice, I got a waft of Irish Breeze soap, which was Mammy's favourite soap to buy when we had money. The smell was heavenly, compared to the oily one Zex clothes-washing soap left on my skin.

"Can we fetch some water, please?" I mumbled. "Our pipes stopped workin'."

"You have to ask the super," he said to me. His smile was framed with perfectly white teeth, with a small space right down the middle of the two front ones. Perfectly black skin, perfectly white teeth, perfectly pressed uniform – this is how he could be described in three short sentences. Well, Mr. Pegg would say, "They're really phrases, not complete sentences, Lyken."

You know how picky English teachers can be.

"Who?" I asked the guard.

"The supervisor," he said. "Inside the pumping station."

I was sure I didn't want to do that. Going to the pipes outside in bright daylight was one story. Going *into* the pumping station, inside a cave, was that story told in the horror version.

I eyed the station every day, tomb-like and soot-dark even from a distance. I didn't know what to expect when I got inside, but it had to be better than going back home to Mammy and saying I was too chicken.

The first thing I noticed was that inside the cave (horror version) looked deserted. There were pipes and engines crawling all over the walls and ceilings, with their arms and necks separated from their bodies at the slimy junctions. The greenish slippery floor vibrated with the humming coming from the square, robot-like stations plugged into the sides of the walls.

The low tones filled the pumping station with moans and groans from a beast trying to hide its footsteps - running footsteps - as it approached you from behind.

The last thing you'd hear before you opened your mouth to scream was your own head exploding, but never his footsteps.

"Hello! Hello!" I shouted.

But of course no one could hear me. I itched to turn around and go back outside, but just then the security guard shouted in my ear. I hadn't even heard him come up behind me, but maybe this was a good thing, because I got really scared when I heard footsteps behind me, especially running ones.

"I came to see if yuh alright," he shouted above the beast. "I was just going off duty and my replacement took over. You want me help you find the super?"

I nodded and swallowed my stomach back into place.

We walked deep into the beast's belly, and came to a small windpipe passageway, where there was a little sweating man looking thoughtfully at some large pipes. He was probably wearing ear plugs or something because the guard tapped him on the shoulder and signalled him to come outside.

"This girl want to ask if she could fetch some water," the guard said to the man he called his super. "They pipes not working."

"Yeah, why not child," the super said, scraping sweat off his forehead with his forefinger and flicking it to the ground.

"There's a tap there," he said, pointing towards the guard hut. "You could use that one. It's more quiet than inside there, and the guards are there all day and all night."

"Thanks, Mister," I said.

The guard told me his name was Richard as he walked me back to the gate. I went one way, he, the other.

When Mammy heard that we'd got the okay, she said that Theresa and I should go right away since there was hardly a drop of water left in the house.

That afternoon, Theresa and I filled up the blue tub that was half the size of a barrel, a few buckets, all the pots and pans, and even some jars. We had to have enough to flush the toilet, wash everyone, do the washing and the cooking and everything else you need water for.

We didn't mind doing this though. It got us out of the house. After all, who would think that this was to be our routine every day for the next two years.

* * *

At school we have a new, young English teacher to replace Mr. Pegg. Maureen is her name. I remembered her from when we lived at Fifty-seven Stanleytown. I was very little and she was just finishing secondary school. She and her family lived just a few houses away from ours.

Every afternoon, she would pass by our house wearing her B.H.S uniform and her fancy tie. She used to talk very proper, not like her younger siblings who all went to my primary school while I was there.

Because she was young, the kids in my class didn't pay her any attention. One day she came into the classroom holding a stack of marked homework in both hands.

"Now, quiet, class," she said. No one looked around. Not many people even noticed her, or the anger that darted across her eyes for a moment.

"Quiet, everyone!" she said, louder this time. I, and a few others stood up as we were meant to, when a teacher entered the classroom.

"What is the matter with you people!" she shouted, punctuating the very end of the sentence by slamming the pile of books onto the hard floor. Books and pages spilt in all directions. The Comrade Leader's face hit the floor several times with the books that hadn't been papered. A hush hovered in the classroom, so silent you could hear the voice of the teacher in the next classroom.

"Right," she said, after everyone had gotten to their feet. "Good afternoon, class."

"Good afternoon, Miss."

"Take your seats, and you two," she said, pointing to the two students closest to her, "Pick up these books."

It only took a second after we'd all sat down in our seats for some of the kids to start sniggering. Me, I'd never seen a teacher behave like that before, so I didn't know how to react, even though I liked her.

I looked at my friend, Roma, who sat next to me, and I could see she was thinking the same thing I was. In that moment, we shared something that made me think of Marla and Marleen – who I hadn't seen since that day we got our exam results. That *something* reminded me I had started not to miss them so much.

CHAPTER 17

THE TRUTH IS FINALLY OUT

As I was walking home from school this afternoon, I ran into Marleen and Marla. We all had *so* much to say that we tried to marketplace-talk about everything.

"You heard the news?" Marla asked me.

"What news?" I said.

"Mr. Williams and his family are leaving the country soon. He's leaving Overwinning."

"Ricardo's leaving, too," I told them. He hadn't been at our new school for long before he told us that he was going abroad. He said his family wanted him to have better chances than he would have here.

"Everyone's saying the country's getting worse, and soon you won't be allowed to leave. That's why everyone with money's escaping now," Marla told me.

We all agreed how bad it was that friends were leaving, but the other stuff didn't really affect us much, which is why everyone calls children our age 'The Comrade's children.' They say we don't know any better, so we don't know what to miss.

As I walked home, the meeting made me think of things we'd done and the games we'd played. It was a nice feeling to be reminded of the only good memories I had about my life. I had new friends now but it wasn't the same, because we'd only just begun making those memories.

Roma and Steve, the boy I saw on open day, had both now become my friends. However, Renee, the big girl in my class, thought I was only friends with the Indian girls, which made me stupid in her eyes.

I didn't get along with Edward either, and this wasn't only because he made it his business to pull my hair.

"I'll tell Sir," I said to him.

"If you think I'll let you do that, you got another think coming," he replied. He has this roundabout way of speaking. I would've thought that a bully as big and as fat as himself would just say stuff like, 'move,' 'sit,' 'get me that.' Now, if I were a bully, *I* wouldn't bother with words like, *if you think I'll let you do that, you got another think coming*. I would say something like, *shut up or I'll beat you up,* which is what he came around to at the end of his speech. Idiot.

Rosie, the bright girl, told me that Edward's dad beats him up at home. But why would you want to beat up on other people if you know how first-hand how terrible a beating makes a person feel? I asked her this question, but instead of answering it, she asked me if I'd finished my homework.

Rosie is always very interested in every mark I get for every quiz we do. If I didn't know better, I'd have thought she was keeping a record of all my marks in a secret notebook somewhere. Some people took the first position in class a bit too seriously. You see, as soon as you went into a new class, you'd sort of identify the person who was as good as you in each subject and try to do better than them. I don't know why it was like this, but that was the way it'd always been at our school. Rosie was my person, I'd picked her out, and I knew she had her eyes on me as well. Some people might say that this was why I was so suspicious of her, but I suppose we'd see what happened at the end of the term when we were all given our final positions in the class.

When I got home, Esther said she was leaving soon. I was hoping she was going to stay for Christmas. The last time we spent the holidays together was when I was six and a bit. I remember because this was the first and only time in my life I'd been to visit Santa, and the last time I got a Christmas present.

Christmas Eve day had trundled along, and I was wearing my brand new stretchy shorts. I had gotten two of them a few months earlier. One was black and yellow with a lace-up front and the other was red and blue, also with a lace-up front.

Little did I know then, that I would be made to wear them until I was nearly twelve, when they would then become the 'hot pants' I was ridiculed by my classmates for parading in public.

I can't remember which ones I was sporting that day when we got down to where Santa was supposed to be. It was on Water Street near to the big shops – Wrefords and J.P Santos, (whose names were changed into something national or the other, names nobody bothered to call them anyway). We had stood in the line with some other people, sweating and steaming in the heat.

It was midday, right when the December heat was just about a nice, frying temperature. The continual fresh breeze was trapped somewhere far above our heads because of the tall, two story buildings in that shopping part of town. The only rustling you could hear was from the wings of the black flies as they rushed past your face on their way to sample the freshly caught cockles and shark meat they could smell in the market about two hundred yards away.

Santa came out of his hut to have a cigarette, but some of the parents in the line started shouting at him about not showing a good example to kids and all that.

"What you want from me?" Santa asked. "It hot in that place, and this suit's killing me in this heat, mon."

"You bad Santa," one man told him. "You really bad. Me daughter think you's this great, good person and look at yourself."

Lots of people joined in. The woman behind us was telling her daughter (who was wearing a tenth 'Happy Birthday' badge) in a real panicky voice that this is not the 'real' Santa who comes through the window they leave open for him every Christmas Eve night.

At six, I wasn't really bothered. I was never told that Santa came through the window. He never brought me anything, so I guess there was no need to make him up for me.

Santa suddenly lashed out at the guy standing next to him, who was pointing a finger in his face.

"Get outta my space, you moron!" Santa said, as he cuffed the guy on his face with a really heavy hand. The man didn't take this lightly. He grabbed Santa's beard and pulled. It became unstuck, held on only by the stretchy elastic around Santa's head. Oddly, the guy looked surprised at this, but recovered enough to shopping-bag whack Santa on the back. Santa was bent over you see, trying not to lose his beard, so he sort of went with the pull.

Little children were screaming and some babies started crying and dribbling. Me, I just stood there feeling guilty. Could it have been my fault? When bad things happen at home it's always my fault. But surely this couldn't be, could it?

Santa had somehow managed to hold on to his cigarette until now. He chucked it down and gave a good shake of his fist at everyone. He then gave us all a good cursing, pulled his red trousers up and went back into his hut. Some people went away, but we stayed, and a good thing too, since this was my only ever Santa visit and Christmas present ever.

We eventually got to the top of the line, Esther paid at the door and I went in and got my present. It was a pack of colouring pencils. Some of them got taken away when I went back to school and took them out to do drawing, which made me weep all the way home.

I didn't have colouring pencils at all, and they were probably the only ones I had while I was in primary school. Pencils are very expensive, you see.

That was a long time ago though, the pencils have been gone for ages.

I'm not sure that was a *'good old days'* story, but Christmas always makes me think of it.

At dinner time this evening, after I'd swallowed Esther announcement, Mammy had one of her own. She was going to Georgetown for a night, because she said she hadn't been in years and it was time to see Daniel and find out what his 'dark-spirits-Obeah-working wife' was up to now.

"Hettie is the real reason he doan like me," she said. "She work her Obeah on him to keep me away, so she could have him to herself. She put the Obeah under her arm, and when she sit down next to him, she lifts her arm up to mek him smell the Obeah."

"That's all lies and yuh know it," Esther said. "Daniel got his own reasons."

"Why you siding with him, anyway?" Mammy asked her. "He was the one who said he was going to move out when he heard you were pregnant with Anne and wanted to come back home. He was shamed 'a you."

"That's all in the past. Why you like to bring these hurtful things up for? He doan want to talk to you, and it's not because of Hettie. You always picking on her, and lying about her. She is your daughter-in-law and mother of your grandchildren."

Of course now Theresa and I, and even Franc looked at Mammy to see what she was going to say. She wasn't going to be outdone by anyone. It was the same as watching ping pong matches in school. The only difference was that tongues were used to rally the object back and forth. I suspected that the object was not Uncle Daniel or his wife.

"What you mean is something else?" Mammy said. "Wha' he tell you now?"

"You went and tell him that Arthur wasn't his father, that his father is some dentist, that's why he not stupid like the rest of us. You think that would make him respect you and be glad he is not Arthur's child? Me father was a good man. You shouldn't do him that way. No wonder he never use the name Daniel anymore. You tell him that you name him after the dentist."

"I had twelve babies when I was with your father," Mammy shouted. "He never disowned any one of them."

"Like yuh said, and you probably right, he was stupid. I surprised he didn't claim Theresa and Christopher too," Esther answered.

"Yuh talking nonsense as usual," Mammy said finally, claiming twenty-one points and the game.

* * *

"You know anything about this library card we have to get?" Roma asked me at school, days later.

She always kept her jet black hair long and shiny. Coconut oil was good for your hair, she'd told me. It seemed like the longer her hair got, the shorter she became. Or perhaps it was me who was growing taller.

"Not really," I answered. "Maureen just said we have to join the library for our Literature assignment. I'm sure we'll hear later."

"Good. I don't want to hear about that now, I feel really lazy and ill today," Roma said, rubbing the bottom of her tummy. "My time of the month you know."

"What yuh mean?" I asked.

"Oh, yuh joking," she said, looking at me intently with a broad smile on her round face. I noticed, not for the first time, how rich her smile made me feel. Her mouth shortened, her black eyes blinked twice, and she turned all serious like and said, "Tell me yuh joking."

I was completely baffled. What was I joking about?

"You know 'bout periods right?" she asked me.

"Not really," I said. "Just a bit." I was embarrassed that she'd ask me which bit, but instead, she gave me girlie lecture on the subject.

"Yuh understand?" she asked when she was finished.

"Yes. But how come you know so much?"

"I get them every month," she answered. "And besides, my mammy tells me stuff. And now *you* know."

I'd had a brief, regular sexual-health lesson from Mammy and this was it:

"If you ever get pregnant, I'll pepper your parts."

At last it was good to know that periods aren't actually directly related to how many boyfriends you've got. This meant that I didn't have to worry that I was a bad girl when mine showed up – if it ever did.

"Thanks, Roma."

"No worries," she said. "It's what you come to school for."

Indeed, learning is what I came to school for. I had learnt the basics about sex from kids at my primary school. I'm not sure they understood much though, because everyone said different things that, when put together, made as much sense as a duck with a water bottle.

"We have to go," Roma said. "What's our first period?"

"Home Ec.," I smiled, and she smiled back. After that, I smiled every time someone said something about our class periods.

Home Economics was always enjoyable, but this afternoon's class was slightly different. Just after registration with Mrs. Singh, while we were getting ready to go to the Home Ec department – which was actually a well made-up, old colonial house in our school compound – Steve said that he wasn't feeling very well. He put his head down on his desk for a bit, but after just a tick of a moment we knew something wasn't right.

Mrs. Singh, our Guidance teacher (and Form Mistress) called him aside to talk to him. His back was turned to the wall and he seemed to be hiding something. Renee, the big girl in our class, was sent to get his cousin Anita who was in form four. She was a Prefect.

If you have excellent behaviour and do well in class work you get to be sub-prefect when you get to the third form. You then get to wear a green badge, which is the exclamation mark, warning everyone of your deserving respect. If you, wearing that green badge, came across another student doing something against school rules and pulled them up on it, they had to listen to you or get into more trouble with a teacher.

Usually, if they have to choose, they'd rather listen to you than have to face a teacher and whatever discipline they would set out. It made perfect sense.

A year later, in form four, if you've served well, you became a full-fledged prefect and got to wear a special red badge - the one thing no one has ever lost or misplaced in our school. Prefect badges do not come cheap.

Steve lived with his aunt and uncle and their two children, Anita being one of them, you see, because his parents lived abroad. When Anita walked into our class, there was a pan of silence across the ceiling of the room. Red badges only came to see us to make us do our work when the teacher had to step out.

She spoke to Steve for a bit, and after a while, he put his bag around his neck. He had one of those bags with one long handle and two short ones, so you could either put it round your shoulder or hold it in your hand. It was blue, and had two little straps with buckly knobs at the very ends. Steve had put the long handle of the bag round his neck, so that the entire thing was covering his bum. You could only see the bottom of his shorts when he turned his back. I watched him walk away and go home, his shoulder-length hair samba-ing in the warm breeze.

When we finally got to the Home Ec. department, a whisper flitted around that Steve had pooed himself. Renee proclaimed loudly that my 'boyfriend' had messed himself and hitched a finger in my direction, laughing with her mouth wide open. He wasn't my boyfriend, though. She had it wrong, as usual. I hoped I could tell him not to be too embarrassed when he returned, and that he was still my friend.

Mrs. Kerry, the Home Ec. teacher, wasn't very pleased with all the laughing and mumbling. She was very strict, but she was alright. She was the person who introduced me to my first cooking experience and piqued my interest in stitching and embroidery.

"We're doing bedrooms today!" she snapped, then marched us up to the third floor of the large colonial house.

When I got home later, Mammy was still at her school, and Theresa and Esther were talking. They weren't just talking though, *they were talking*.

Theresa was sitting with her back to the wall of the small landing on the top of the back steps, cleaning the stone-and-paddy-filled rice. Esther was sitting at the open door, which allowed warm air to blow into the house, while the blue-sakie birds chirped in the mango tree. I'd never before known that it was possible to talk about Mammy behind her back.

"She hides everything," Theresa was saying. "She stuffs herself and then we run out of food and have nothing."

"Well, I paid Shop Lady, so she's owing nothing at the moment," Esther replied.

"She beats Anne mercilessly and calls her 'ugly' and 'lazy,' then sends her to bars to buy cigarettes. And when I say bars, I doan mean them ones that normal people drink at in the evenings," Theresa continued. She stopped for a minute to fan the bowl of rice, then to blow the chaff into the air. When she started to speak again, she looked at Esther directly in the face. "Ah mean Rum shops that open from eight o'clock in the morning, that smell of pee and vomit, where men who drink mentholated spirits go when they got no more money to buy rum."

She took a deep breath and began to pick at the paddies again. "So far she leaves Franc alone, but who knows when she gon start on her, too," Theresa continued with a tone that sounded like she couldn't stop. "You know how she used to beat you and Daniel and all of us when we . . ."

"Yeah," Esther cut in. "But I thought she'd changed."

"Well, yuh wrong. It doan look like she will ever change."

At last! Esther knew what happened when she was not here with me, so she was going to do all she could to save me. Maybe she wouldn't go back, maybe she'll stay and we could have a normal life. I didn't care that we were poor. It will all be perfect! Just me and Theresa and Franc and Esther.

I'd have to tell Franc that we have to start calling her 'Mum.' She'll have to unpack the clothes she's already packed. If I was still biting my nails, this would be the perfect time to do so, but I'd given up that habit. Instead, I let the air rush out of my lungs and allow the smile to weave all the way across my face.

Why didn't I think of telling her before? Maybe Mammy *was* right. I was such a stupid coward because I always thought that if I told Esther anything, she would repeat it all to Mammy and I would get the beating of my life. I was so wrong, as Esther even seemed to be agreeing with Theresa. They weren't paying any attention to me, and Franc was having her nap, so I could sit and listen to them, and their conversation – the best one I'd ever heard.

Suddenly, there was a crash and splintering noise in the bedroom. I felt my stomach coil up inside me. *Splinters! Don't Walk! Don't Walk!* appeared on the insides of my eyelids for a second before I realised where – where in *time* – I was.

Everyone ran towards the sound. We were confronted by a beaming two-year old with face cream all over her sheet, her face and hands, her whole body. As if by an afterthought, she had poured talcum powder over her naked tummy and had rubbed bright red lipstick all over her face. The look in her eyes when she looked up from her design was one that should be stored in a glass jar and displayed for comedy. Even the empty, broken face cream jar on the floor was extremely funny.

We all burst out laughing. And Franc, with a sheepish grin on her red and white face, said "Yook, bewtiful."

Beautiful indeed! We were finally free! I wondered when we were going to move.

Looked like very soon.

CHAPTER 18

THERESA IN LOVE

So, I was in trouble again.

Theresa and I had just finished fetching several loads of water and we were frayed at the edges. Shop Lady had sold the house with us in it, and she wasn't fixing anything. The new owner wanted us out so he wasn't fixing anything either. Esther was away again, food was in short supply, and so were cigarettes.

No, we hadn't moved.

We had dreamed of change after all that had happened. In fact, we were so close that we would sniff the air and detect a faint tinge of sweet freedom. But it was not to be.

Esther had returned to French Guyane again, as usual, and Theresa was left at home with Franc, as usual. Mammy got angry with me this morning (I won't say 'as usual' again) and I had a feeling she was still vexed.

It was my turn to button up the cuffs on her shirt. I used to think that it was impossible for someone to do up their own cuffs until I had my own long sleeve shirts for school and realised, even though I was really awkward, I could do it easily on my own.

Neither Theresa nor I were crazy about doing it when it was our turn, because if you weren't fast enough you got a smack on the side of the face. Theresa taught me how to keep my shoulders rounded and my head bowed while engaged in cuff-tasking, so if Mammy wanted to swing at me, she would get me on the shoulder and not right smack on the face.

I was just getting ready to hunch my shoulders, but because I was so close to her soft, cold, untouchable body, the nervousness overtook me. My hands wouldn't stop shaking, and of course that meant that I took longer to button the cuff – not good.

She swung at me and missed. Luckily, the button went into the hole at that instant and I didn't have to go near to her again. This was why she was angry.

Maybe it would've been better to just let her hit me. After all, having her build up rage because she missed my face is a lot worse. But you don't think of things like that when you're trying to escape pain, do you?

Late this afternoon, while I was sitting in the rocker after we'd lugged in all the water, Mammy walked into the room and screamed, "Yuh trekked mud in the house!" Her face twisted with hate. "How many times ah told you to take your slippers off when you come back from the pumping station?"

"I did take them off."

"Well, yuh didn't, coz there's nasties in me house now. And for that, you'll pay."

She took hold of my wrist, bent my arm at the elbow and started pounding it on the wooden arm of the rocker. She said between pounds, "When you . . ." *pound*

"grow up . . ." *pound*

"you will remember this . . ." *pound*

"and you will . . ." *pound*

"get arthritis . . ." *pound*

"in your elbows and knees . . ." *pound*

"and water in . . ." *pound*

"your joints."

Then she took hold of my other arm.

It surprised me, though I shouldn't have been surprised by Mammy's cruelty, but I used to think her punishments were all about now, you know, to satisfy the throbbing ache of anger and hate she feels here and now. What was this awful sin I'd committed that she wanted to punish me for - even in my old age?

I tried to stiffen my arm but it only took a sudden chop on the inside of my elbow to make my arm collapse. She kept pounding and pounding and just when I thought she would never stop, she did.

I tried to cover my face in my hands but my elbows refused to react. My face found my shoulder and I started to shed my silent tears in it. My heart pulsed into my mouth when a sharp pain caught me in the knee. Mammy had gone to the kitchen and had brought in the beating wood.

She started to hit me on the knees, both knees. I heard, 'knock, knock' as she beat me on my knees to ensure my future arthritis, and through the blinding pain I cried, *why, why, why*.

She commanded me to put my hands on the arms of the rocker and to my disgust, I saw my hands responding, and my elbows reacting to the terror of her, dredged inside my head. Was I mad, was I crazy, or simply a coward?

And in the tornado of my little mind all I could think was, *What's this beating for?*

What's this beating for?

Was it for the mud on the floor, for missing the hit in the face this morning, or just for being me?

She'd begun pounding my hands with the evil wood when Theresa came in and yanked it from her. Theresa had a deathly look on her face, and for the first time in my life, I was scared of her.

"Enough," she shouted with tears in her eyes. "Enough!"

Mammy saw the look I did, because she walked away without even trying to get the wood back, and more surprisingly, not even trying to finish off by beating Theresa like yesterday, when she hit her with the big, white enamel cup.

"Get up," she spat. "Get outta me sight!"

I did.

* * *

Later that week:

Theresa had found a boyfriend. Richard, the *Irish Breeze* man who helped me when I went to ask if we could fetch water from the pumping station, likes Theresa and she likes him. We couldn't let Mammy know though. Theresa said she would like to marry him, and that me and Franc could go with her when she becomes her own woman and has her own money.

"Aren't you your own woman now?" I asked on our short walk over to the pumping station, after I had come home from school.

"No," Theresa replied. "I never have any money. No one even thinks that I might need a snack, or a sweet or something. I'm twenty and Mammy still treats me like a little servant girl. I've never ever had a boyfriend or been kissed in all me life."

"Remember that one time when we lived in that house opposite us, and you had ten cents?" I asked, looking up to her dark face. "You threw it out the window to me so I could buy some sweets at school."

"Yeah," she giggled. "And you were so frightened Mammy would see you standing there, that yuh ran away before I threw all the change out."

"Yeah," I replied. "And I cried all the way to school, coz I didn't wait. I wanted to come back for the rest, but was too scared she would look out the window and catch me."

"She was nowhere near."

"Yeah, but she was around, somewhere," I answered. "And once she's around, she would find where *I* was."

Richard wasn't on duty until later that night, but he was at the hut chatting with the guard who was on the afternoon shift. As soon as we got in and placed our bucket under the tap, he came over with a smile on his face.

I stood a bit apart, by the gate so that I could watch for Mammy. We had been doing that journey for months now, making at least twenty trips every day.

"How come it tek you so long to get the water?" Mammy constantly asked.

"Is the tap," Theresa would tell her, not looking her in the eye. "It's really slow."

We each carried two buckets at every trip so we could have enough water to last until the next day.

"One day, I might just drop 'round to see what taking yuh so long," Mammy had threatened once, so that was why I stood guard. Sometimes Richard and Theresa chatted for so long while the buckets ran over I could almost imagine seeing Mammy coming over.

Today she did.

I screamed at them as soon as I spotted her proud head. Richard bolted upright, then darted towards the engine house.

He stopped so suddenly in mid-track, that he skidded on the gravelled pathway. He scooted back, dumped a bucket of warm, fresh water into the ground, and turned the tap off.

There was no time to say anything, and as I stood, heart in open mouth, he turned the tap back on, to where it dripped into our now-empty bucket.

In less than a second, he disappeared round the back of the engine house, all before Mammy was near enough to have seen his shadow.

Mammy approached us wearing the face of someone who'd just eaten a jarful of pickled lime. She glared at us, looked at the filling bucket, and opened her mouth to speak.

But there was nothing to say, even though she didn't seem satisfied with what she saw.

She walked back home without saying a word. However, her action had said enough. It had opened up a surprising new world for me, one in which Mammy was *not* all-knowing.

Theresa said later that it was a good thing she had told Richard about Mammy, or we would've been in the frying pan with scarcely any hot oil to grease our bottoms. But all I could think of was, *If I were her, I would've checked the tap!*

***

"Ah could really do with a smoke," Mammy said, with eyes that looked far away, into a world only she knew. "But I ain't got no money, even for half a' one."

I looked into her tomb-like eyes, something I hadn't done very often. This was my chance to make her happy, to do something to get her on my side, especially after the guilt I felt in finding out that she could be tricked.

"I got some," I said quietly. Just in case, you know . . .

"Where on earth *you* get money from?"

"Great Aunt Hyacinth gave me some change when she was here that time."

"And yuh save it, all this time?"

"Yeah," I said a bit louder – growing more confident. "And 'member that time Esther came back, and I was going to the shop to get cigarettes?"

"No," Mammy said, dismissing the question with a wave of her left hand. "Ah can't 'member so far back."

"Well," I continued, braver still. "I didn't have to go no more, so I kept the money."

"Let me see?" Mammy asked quietly. Asked, not said.

I went to the bedroom, pulled the tattered grip in which my clothes were kept, from under the bed and fished out an old match box. With a rapidly beating pump trying to climb out of my chest, I walked back into the living room and placed the tiny, open box into Mammy's well-marked palm.

"Ah surprised," she said, looking over my head. "Ah surprised yuh kept all this money."

"I found a few cents on the floor too," I announced proudly, pleased that I was the lucky one to help Mammy.

"Count it up," Mammy told me. Said, not asked this time.

I spread the copper and silver change in the palm of my hand and counted more than one dollar. I noticed for the first time that even though my palm was pink, to her brown one, we had the same markings, the crazy train-tracks running up and down inside our hands. I would worry about that later on, now I wanted to gloat.

"Yuh will be a kind person when yuh grow up," Mammy said to the space above my head.

Parmanand's Rum Shop, where I went to get cigarettes, was always dark and smelled of stale rum and urine, especially at the damp corner just outside the door marked '*TOI ET.*' It was a heaven for drunkies who lay around regardless of the time.

There was a red jukebox in the left hand corner near the bar, the kind of portable disco that played three songs for you if you fed it twenty-five cents.

At Grimmond's bar in the scheme, most people used to wait until it got dark to drink. There was no such luck at Parmanand's. There was this particular rummie man, short, thin with spiky grey hair, who always paid lots of attention to me and said things – bad things I didn't like.

Today as I walked into the rum shop with the usual bitter-sick taste in my mouth, this man and two of his friends were crookedly scattered on some of the slimy stools, singing along to Lata Mangeskhar on the jukebox.

The bar was darker than usual. Parmanand had long since swapped the glass panes for wooden windows, on account of the drunken, glass-breaking brawls the bar was famous for. The heat of the day had already cooked up a mighty mixture of all kinds of stink, and the noise from the pumping station directly across the road only added to the rum shop's unpleasantness.

I could tell that rummie man was drunk even from a distance, but this didn't stop him from noticing me as soon as I entered the door. He heaved himself shakily off the stool and staggered towards me. Then he held out his thin, old arms.

"I doan care wat yuh say today, mon," he said, trying hard to keep a mouthful of watery, slimy spit from rolling out of his mouth. "You gon dance wid me to this number."

I backed away, but he kept smiling as if I was his friend, and as if I'd danced with him before. This is what scared me most. He behaved as though everything was fine between us because we knew and liked each other.

I kept backing away, and he kept bumbling forward. It didn't take many steps for me to back into one of the groups of tables and chairs scrubbed and placed around the concrete floor of the bar. This stopped me, but he kept coming with his arms outstretched. His two friends were laughing, and he was, too, as Lata kept whining on the jukebox. He came closer to me and started to sway to the dreamy music, cigarette in one hand, while he twirled the other in dance. The smell of rum and cigarettes on his breath and clothes lay like a sombrero around the top of his head – and mine.

I couldn't get away from the side because he was there, so I started to push the chairs and table back with my bottom, anything to escape.

"Wot?" came a booming voice from behind the bar. The noise of the moving chairs had brought Parmanand from behind the paint-flaked door marked, '*Private.*'

"Raj, yuh fool, behave yuhself, no!"

Parmanand was a big man, maybe 6 foot tall, with a humungous belly. I remember when Esther came to visit us when she was six or seven months pregnant with Franc. By the time she returned to French Guyane, she was about eight months pregnant, and her tummy stuck out like a sack of rice, but Parmanand's belly was bigger.

He came up to us and took the drunk away. I got the cigarettes and left. Lata was still singing that song that seemed to never end. My heart was still racing, and I had a bile taste in my mouth. A sort of bitterness which reminded me of a series of events which happened at school.

It started just after we'd heard that our new English teacher was going to stay, despite rumours she was going to marry and become a housewife. She would continue to teach us English and

Literature. Being the one who introduced me to Shakespeare, Naipaul, Braithwaite and Lee Harper, she was responsible for so many of the things I loved about school. I didn't want to lose her, and had just swallowed my satisfaction of this news when Steve announced that he was leaving the country to join his parents abroad.

That's when the first taste of bitterness presented itself. This surprise was yet another tiny thrust by the invisible hand; a thrust which was threatening to send me free-falling over the cliff of pain I felt in my heart about losing the few people in my life that I'd grown close to.

I didn't see Marleen and Marla anymore. Ricardo, the boy who came to secondary school with me was gone. Mr. Williams has left, and now Steve.

I couldn't know that in the matter of months, I would lose Theresa, Roma and the house we lived in as well.

The bitter taste persisted when Edward pulled my lunch out of my bag and showed it to everyone who cared to look. Some people bought lunch at the school canteen, but the majority of children brought theirs to school because we only had a forty-minute lunch break. Only kids like Ross Ferreira, the Mayor's son, went home because he lived in the big house right next door to the school.

I was one of the children who always brought her lunch to school. Brought it, but didn't eat it. It wasn't that I didn't like food. It was because, well, I was afraid of the teasing I'd get if someone saw me eating the kind of meals (if I could call them meals) I brought to school.

Yesterday, when I emptied the rice with a sprinkling of salt out in the corner of the school yard by the fence, I was happy to see a stray dog wandering by because I thought he would eat up all the evidence before anyone could see it.

Wrong!

He merely smelt it and waltzed away.

Today's packed meal was rice with a drop of cooking oil, topped with a sprinkle of Maggie chicken cube. I don't suppose it was anyone's fault, it was just the way it was, but Edward obviously thought I brought it in for fun. He got into my bag, opened it up, and displayed it like a piece of fine art. I wasn't even in class when he did, but when I arrived, groups of people were sniggering and whispering.

"Mar-got bare rice," Renee sang and squealed in delight, repeating my middle name over and over again, waving it in the air like a piece of filthy, stained rag.

"Just for the fun of it," she said to me. "Just for the fun of it, Mar-got, you could let me beat you up after school."

But Sita, the girl I walk home with, said Renee would get into loads of trouble with Mr. Beharry, our head master, if she *did* try to beat me up. Mr. Beharry threatened that if anyone brought a bad name to the school, especially while wearing the uniform, they would be in serious trouble.

"After all," he'd said, "the founders meant for our school to be the best at everything, including respect and uprightness."

Edward boasted earlier in the term, that he was going abroad before we got to form two. I hoped so, and maybe Renee could go with him. Maybe I wouldn't have been so scared of Renee if she wasn't so much bigger than me.

"Ah could snap you in two," she says, and then shows me a breaking motion with her hands over her knees so that I could see how it was done – as if I wanted to know.

Roma's solution to the bullying was that I should eat more. I generally tried to leave the classroom at lunch time so that she, and everyone else, wouldn't see that I wasn't eating. Many times I'd go into the canteen to pretend I was buying lunch with the rest of the children in there, so that when I came back, the kids eating their lunches in classroom could think that I'd already had a canteen treat. I made a big deal of licking my lips and pretending I had something delicious.

Roma sometimes shared her lunch money with me. She usually bought her lunch, so sometimes I couldn't avoid her if I was in the canteen. If she saw me, she'd insist on buying me lunch, but I didn't like that leechy feeling I'd get when she offered. I was often walking to and from school as well, but Sita sometimes paid my twenty-five cents' fare so we could go home together. I didn't want Roma to know about this because I felt so ashamed.

My friends Roma and Sita were very good to me, but they didn't know my secret of the way things were at home. It wasn't something you'd tell, was it? They knew I lived with my grandmother, so I told them she was very strict. To tell the truth, I wouldn't be able to explain *what* she was even if I'd wanted to.

A couple of days ago, we got a letter saying Mammy has got to go to court as the new owner wants the house for himself. We also got a letter from Christopher telling us he was coming home on leave. This time he says that he is really on leave, with a bunch of other soldiers, because he was stationed in Jonestown, where that American preacher killed all those people.

"Ah hope he bring some money," is what Mammy said between sniffs of mentholated spirit, when I read this to her. "I doan want him here if he gon come with he bare hands. I owe Shop Lady lots of money for goods." Then she dismissed me and the letter with a wave of her hand before she stuffed a piece of the sniffing cloth right up her nose.

Later she told us that Christopher could help us to go and line up for kerosene, because he knew how to push people standing in front of him in a queue. Theresa and I often get pushed around in food and kero lines because we didn't know how to fight, which is exactly what happened last week when we went to J.P. Santos – that big shop that used to be owned by the British, which was now the property of The Comrade Leader.

The Leader said he didn't want to see anything in the country still owned by foreigners, which is why he was going to nationalize everything bit by bit. Me, I didn't know why he wanted to do that. The shops all seemed a lot fuller when they were not called names like 'Guyana Stores' and all that. Even Bermine where my father works will be nationalized and called 'Guymine.'

All the schools will have to phase out their uniforms and wear colours that The Comrade chooses. The nursery school children around the country will wear orange, polka dot uniforms. The dress code for primary schools around the country will be brown and cream, and the high schools, green and cream.

The two highest secondary schools weren't too keen on the change because of status reasons, of having to dress like everyone else. Mr. Beharry said that the change was a must, but that we would wait until the very end when we absolutely had to. He said that the first formers – that's us, would have to change by the time we got to the third form. I wasn't looking forward to it.

CHAPTER 19

THE HAUNTED TOWN

"Is this love
Is this love
Is this love . . . ."

Bob Marley on the record player meant that Christopher was here.

"That place haunted as hell, mon," he told us, meaning Jonestown, where almost a thousand people died not so long ago.

"What you see?" Theresa asked him.

"When I went in first, before ah came home last time, we saw all them dead bodies. Some people still had their arms wrapped 'round they babies."

He took a deep breath. His brown eyes had a sort of empty, lost look in them, but he continued. "Other people were hugging they wife and husband. Yuh could see the sadness and terror in the dead faces. They smelled really, really bad. You had to cover your nose . . ."

He turned down his big lips and put his hand over his mouth and nose.

". . . But yuh could still smell the stench of rotten flesh and dead people's pee."

"Dead people's pee?" Theresa questioned.

"Yeah, they peed themselves, mon," he answered.

"Did you see the Kool-aid?" I asked.

"Yeah. There was still some left in these huge buckets." He made a large circle with his long, black arms.

"Talk about food and jewellery – Jim Jones had nuff things locked away. Ah tell yuh," he leaned close to us and whispered, "Some 'a them soldiers helped themselves, mon."

He leaned back, sniffling a bit, massaging the bulb of his tangerine-shaped nose, little finger pointing upwards, and continued.

"Remember the man who got shot coz he won't take the poison?"

We didn't, but we both nodded in quick succession.

"Well, they found he body sprawled out by the plane. Sad situation."

Christopher shifted his bottom around in his chair. He sat on one cheek, then on the other, then back on the first side again. He went quiet, but we kept listening, listening. He was sure to keep talking for as long as we kept listening. I had learned some time ago that he loved an audience.

"Nowadays you think everything would be back to normal," he said finally. "But even after all this time, yuh can still hear sounds and screams, and people talkin' and whisperin.'"

"Really," I whispered. I didn't know if all this was true, and really didn't care because it was one of the best stories I'd heard in all my life – and Mammy tells some great ones. The little hairs on my arms were standing to attention, the way we have to do in the cinema and at school when we sing the national anthem. I swapped looks with Theresa and I could see that she, too, was well taken in.

"One of them boys said he saw a ghost, and he not the only one, mon. A white man in a long, grey gown, went floating by the guard-hut on his watch. He said he nearly peed himself." Christopher chuckled at this, his shoulders hiccoughing up and down.

"Ah heard Meena saw a ghost in this house once," Theresa said.

Four eyes turned to her face, and it was Christopher's turn to ask, "Really?"

"Yeah, really."

"You two ever seen one?" Christopher asked us.

"No," I answered. "But I always feel someone's around 'specially if I'm home alone. That's why I never go in the storeroom downstairs, I always feel someone watching me from that window."

I didn't tell them though, that when I was home alone, I spent every second standing by the front window with my back against it so I could keep an eye on 'whatever' was in the house with me. I'd get dreadfully scared because I felt this crawly thing on my skin and heard whispering voices, which could have been the mango tree's leaves, mind. But I shouldn't take any chances, right?

I didn't confess that the real reason I stood so close against the window sill was so I could quickly jump out of the window if I *did* see what it was, because I was so scared of 'it.'

"You 'member when we used to live opposite, the old man used to stay all day in that store room while he wife run the shop in the market," Christopher asked. "Didn't people say he was poisoned or something, that's why he was always sick?"

"I doan know," Theresa answered. "But you must feel *something* if you know somebody died in the house you living in."

"I thought he died in the hospital," I said.

"No," Christopher said. "The ambulance picked him up from this house when he was already dead."

". . . Is this love
Is this love
Is this love . . . ."

Bob Marley continued.

* * *

On Saturday, Mammy said we were going to The Strand cinema to see this new film with Rishi Kapoor. I liked him, but Christopher wasn't convinced.

"I ain't going to watch no coolie picture, coz they all the same," he told her. "They all got lots of dancin' and singin,' and hidin' behind trees."

"What you Indian girlfriend say 'bout that?" Mammy asked.

"You know I not a racist, I just doan like coolie pictures, that's all. All the mothers get consumption, cough, spit out blood, and then the bad man gets beat up. Star boy and girl dance, marry – no kissin', mind – the end," he answered, and chuckled.

I was to wear one of my shorts, and I was praying that I wouldn't be seen by anyone at my school or my teachers. But of course, I *was* spotted. Prakash, a boy in my year, was at the cinema. I was sure he got to pick the clothes he went out in, so he must've thought that I did, too. Why would he guess that the vulgar girl wearing hot pants to the cinema and being ogled by the drunks in the pit was anything different from the prostitutes in the street who jump the ships at Bermine when she was dressed in exactly the same way as they were?

I tried to steel myself in preparation of what was going to happen when I went to school on Monday. At the moment I had bigger fish (of *Jaws* descriptions - dum, dum, dum, dum) to fry. Prakash wasn't even in my class but he had to see me, and worse, he had to say, "Hi, Anne."

Mammy said she would deal with me when we got home for having boys talking to me. "I not sending yuh to school to have boyfriends," she told me.

Even worse than that, this new picture was exactly like Christopher said it would be, so all that for nothing.

When we got home, things were different from what I expected them to be. I was sent into the bedroom to take my clothes off to be beaten.

Christopher shook his head as I oozed past him and said, "Doan know why Esther left she children with you. Look at this one," he smiled and nodded in my direction.

Mammy called me 'that one' or 'this headache' too, but never by my name unless she was shouting for me when I was in another room. So at first I thought he was siding with her, but then I looked at him, saw that he was smiling and became even more confused. You never knew exactly what to expect with Christopher, he had very big lips, so smiling, snarling, snickering – they all sort of rolled into one when they reached his lips.

"She locked up in the house all day," he continued. "Bony, malnourished and pale, she is. She don't go nowhere, don't do nothing, don't even smile."

He turned to me. "When was the last time you smiled, girl?"

I started to answer even though I had nothing to say. I'd learned that you always answered. Always.

"No?" he asked. "When was the last time you laughed, eh?"

Again, I started to answer with no words in my mouth."

"No?" he asked again. "Do you *ever* laugh, eh?"

By this time, I'd realised he was asking what my English teacher called rhetorical questions, so I made no attempt to say the answer my brain held captive.

No! No! No!

"See," he turned back to Mammy. "She waiting to escape just like we all waited to get away."

"You don't dare get on my nerves now," Mammy replied.

"Look at the neighbours' kids - all runnin' 'round and playin'," Christopher continued as if Mammy had said nothing.

"I doan believe in keeping neighbours close," Mammy cut in. "I like keeping them at arm's length."

"Maybe they keeping *you* at arm's length," Christopher said. "Ever thought 'a that?"

The two of them could never live in a house together and not argue. Theresa said that they were too much alike to ever get along. She said that Mammy let Christopher get away with lots of bad things, so he runs wild sometimes.

I had a feeling he wasn't making things better for me, but for the time being, I was thankful I could put off the shame of taking my clothes off. He seemed to be baiting her just to get her angry. I wasn't sure why.

"You destroy us. That not enough for you, so now you destroying yuh grandchildren," Christopher continued, "Turning them into mad people."

"I hope when *you* get yuh children, they talk to you the same way yuh talk to me. I am yuh mother. I had fourteen of you. Yuh shouldn't talk to me like that."

"You always talk 'bout having fourteen children. How many us alive? Eh? Seven! Only seven!"

"I sorry I had yuh!" Mammy shouted back. "You bad seed!"

"I didn't tell you to get pregnant again for the married man. He tek you to court and disowned Theresa when you ask him for child support, and a year later, you had me. Not my fault. Blame you self!"

"I want you outta my house tomorrow," Mammy barked at him.

But why didn't she hit him?

"Yeah, use me money out then chase me away. See if you can get rid of me. I staying until I want to go."

Mammy suddenly looked at me and shouted, "You like this, no, people blaming me for you?"

I was keeping my distance because I knew that there was always a way for the blame to find its way to me. I didn't want to be like the cat, so I put my head down and moved towards the wall by the front window.

"This is what you like, no, me getting blame for you!" Mammy said, stomping over to where I stood willing my body to become invisible, but before I knew it, she had slammed my head into the wall. Part of my head hit the wall but my forehead met the window frame and the room went dark for a minute. Christopher put on his shoes and left, slamming the door.

"Wait till he get his children," Mammy said.

Little did any of us know, he would die child-less.

Christopher came back in the early hours of the morning and peed in the wardrobe. He was drunk. I woke up and saw him at the cupboard. I heard the wet noise but it didn't register. Mammy woke up, too, but not in time to stop him. At least he had got a cup from the kitchen and held it under the pee. That might have helped, except it was a tiny cup, and he peed lots of pee.

From that night on I felt like he was my friend, because even though I went to bed with a sore head, he had saved me from the shame of once again having to strip down to my bare skin in order to take my beating.

He didn't know – or did he? – that although the beating hurt, taking it naked steadily swept my eroding soul into a sea of dry, aching dust.

Flying away . . .

Sailing away . . .

Light as a feather . . . .

* * *

School this week wasn't good at all. I had to wait until something bigger than my too-short shorts happened.

It kindly did.

Somehow, everyone was talking about Maureen, the English teacher being pregnant and leaving teaching for good - again. Oh, and finally, Edward is leaving the country! My new friend Frank, who's befriended me since Steve left, said, "Good riddance."

He said he didn't know what it meant exactly, but his mother says it when she gets rid of something bad, like his dad for example. She works at the asylum which is just a stone's throw away from our school.

The mental hospital here in this town was the only one in Guyana. Mad people from all over the country were sent here because there was nowhere else to go. Frank said they were overcrowded, which was probably why the less mad ones sometimes came out for a little walk around.

The B.H.S crowd were the first set of sane (ish) people they saw when they strolled out, because they lived so close to the school. Maybe it was because we, their neighbours, were children, that the mad men thought it was okay to sometimes take a walk in their birthday suits. We encountered them more often during the sports week, which we had at the end of each term, because we paid daily visits to the President's Park situated smack bang halfway between the two institutions.

During sports week, the different houses competed with each other in a number of games for house points. At the end of it all, we competed with the other schools in the town for the big inter-school show down.

I said 'we' but I didn't mean me, because I was really bad at games. I always got picked last for any sport. We played netball and volleyball sometimes for P.E. and no one picked me until the end when there was no one else left. Frank usually got picked first. Mr. Paltoo, our P.E. teacher, would get one boy and one girl to pick two teams.

The girls always picked Frank first, because he was really strong and popular with all of us. The boys said he ran like a girl, but that never stopped him from scoring points in any of the games, especially Rounders.

Well, actually, I did get picked first sometimes, but that was in debate and spelling teams and stuff like that.

Our sports finals had started, and before the cycle races, we stood proudly and sang 'Onward Upward,' one of our national songs.

Renee and her friends got into trouble because when we got to the chorus, they sang the wrong words. Wrong, but funny.

"Onward, upward, Mary had a goat,
Day by day she tied it with a rope,
Till at length,
The goat bust the rope and Miss Mary had to run behind it."

We were *all* involved in the word swap, but Sir must have thought it was only them, because they were the ones who always got into trouble. To be honest, it was a really good substitute for the real thing:

Onward, upward, may we ever go,
Day by day in strength and beauty show,
Till at length,
Each of us will show what Guyana's sons and daughters can be.

And then there is the verse about Kaiteur, the highest single drop water fall in the world. Sir said we should be respectful to our country's national songs, so Roma and I kept quiet in case we got found out and got into trouble as well. The two of us went as spectators because we weren't good enough to take part in any of the games.

Roma bought two crushed ices and we sat and watched our classmates sweating in the sun, running and cycling on the dusty track. I looked at my nails and felt a sense of great achievement. They were pretty long. I was filing them now with the nail file Esther had left for me. Roma said they looked nice. I thought so too.

CHAPTER 20

THE BREAKDOWN

Christopher went back to the G.D.F and I passed my end of term exams for smooth entrance into form two. I didn't beat Rosie this time. She overtook me in Maths and Science. In order to feel better, I told myself that her older sister in the school must have helped her. That wasn't really true though. She was really smart and extremely hard to beat.

Mammy went to court, and the magistrate gave us three months to find another house or face eviction. Mammy said the man who bought the house we live in isn't allowed to take rent anymore. That meant we had an extra thirty-five dollars every month.

I hoped that having this extra money to spend would take her mind off her expanding suspicions about the water fetching. Richard wrote constantly to Theresa, but after she read the letters, she had to throw them away. Mammy searched everything, and she kept asking me about stuff at the pumping station. If she caught me lying, I'd be in big trouble, but what was I supposed to do?

Mammy left earlier one night to go to her friend's house. As soon as she was out the door, Theresa, Franc and I stole our rare chance to play and sing songs. Because of Theresa's hearing problems, she needed to make up her own tunes to the songs we'd sing. You see, she couldn't possibly know what the right tune was since she couldn't ever hear them like people with normal hearing could.

We had a little book that Rafza, Aunty Meena's daughter, had left for us. It was an old book with a picture on the cover of a little blonde girl and her toddler brother looking up into a star-lit, peaceful sky. We usually looked at the pictures of the children in the book and wondered at their lovely, new shoes and white socks, things we could only hope we'd have some day. The book was filled with poems and a few children's songs. One of my favourites was, *"Jesus loves the little children, all the children of the world . . ."*

Theresa opened it to *"Twinkle, Twinkle Little Star"* her own favourite, and started to sing, in her own tune, to Franc and me. I tried to sing it in the way it was meant to be sung, but that was hard for Theresa to follow, so I joined in with her way, that special way she sang every single song she ever sang. It put a smile on her face, and I liked that.

Suddenly she got up, looked around as if she was listening to someone in another room, then slowly got a chair from the kitchen. She put it in the middle of the polished living room floor, pointed to it and said to Franc and me, "Sit there."

Franc was only two or so. She thought it was a game so she climbed on it, sat down, looked up at us and asked, "Wot nex?"

I didn't sit down.

I knew something wasn't right, but all the time Theresa seemed to be listening, listening. Listening to what?

This made me a little scared of Theresa, but I didn't know why.

She picked Franc up off the chair, her lean, muscular arms wrapped themselves gently around her chest, then she sat down herself. Her eyes were two still, dark marbles in her slightly cocked head. Listening…

She turned the book quickly, too quickly for me to see the nice pictures of the children in their pretty shoes, in their big houses. But she seemed to know what to do, because she was singing lots of different songs – all of the songs in the book. One tune. Her tune.

"Sit here," she said to me again, placing the baby on one knee. This time she pointed to her lap. I didn't want to, but how could I refuse her? I sat down and she hugged us both.

And rocked. And rocked. And sang.

All the songs, her tune.

I felt very uncomfortable because she was never allowed to hug us. Mammy said that you spoil children if you hug them.

"I'll come back," I said, and got up to open the front window to look out for Mammy. It was very dark outside and I couldn't see very far.

I didn't know what to do. I walked back and forth to the window and to Theresa's lap. She started to cry.

"My children, my children," she cried. "I will protect you and keep you. I will protect you from evil and keep you safe."

And she rocked. And Franc rocked.

And I was a little scared of Theresa, but I didn't know why.

She started to wail as the tears streamed down her face. I knew that something was very wrong. I didn't know what, though. I was only a child, but I knew that whatever was wrong was something big and terrible, something I couldn't fix. Franc started to cry and me too, but I had to keep strong to save Franc if something worse happened.

We all cried. And we rocked.

Rocked.

We cried abundant tears, all leaking out from tiny holes in the corners of our young, aged, tired eyes.

I was a little scared of Theresa, but I wasn't sure why.

Maybe it was because of that marble look in her eyes. I kept praying for Mammy to come home. She'd know what to do because she was a grown-up. I kept looking at the clock, but then remembered that it was telling the wrong time because we'd run out of batteries for it ages ago, and didn't have any money to replace them.

I tried to sing with Theresa. She was praying a lot, too. I tried to say the prayers with her and when she cried again, Franc and I cried with her.

And we rocked, too.

I was a bit scared to leave Franc on her lap. Again, I didn't know why. She would never hurt us, but I was still scared, so I tried not to go to the window anymore. I stayed and rocked and cried and prayed.

More than an hour later Mammy came back. She made sure that Theresa wasn't just putting on and then she sent me to get Cecil's mother. She called this lady 'Cecil's mother' because she has a son named Cecil who came to her nursery school a long time ago. Cecil's family had four dogs, and one time when Mammy had sent me over there to get ice, all four of them jumped on me and mauled my skinny little frame. That wasn't because they were bad though. Dogs always jumped me. Theresa said it was because they could smell that I was scared of them. They never tied the dogs up. No one ever did. But it was late now so maybe the dogs would be asleep.

It took about five minutes for me to walk to Cecil's mother's house. I walked alone, shivering in the total darkness. No, it wasn't cold. I was quite warm in fact, warm and humid.

I shivered from the fear of knowing that something was desperately wrong with my auntie. I wished, I wished upon that twinkle, twinkle little star, that it would all be fine when I got back home.

For my sake.

For the first time in my short life of eleven years, I was a little scared of Theresa, but I didn't know why.

I knew that if something bad happened to Theresa, I would die of the fright of us being left alone with 'Her.'

When I got to Cecil's house, his dad was on the veranda. He had a good job at Bermine. He was a foreman or something because he wore one of those big, important white helmets to work. He sent down two of his four sons to hold the dogs so I could go upstairs.

Cecil's mother and I walked quickly back home. She was short and fat and was puffing by the time we got up the long stairs to our house. We could hear Theresa crying from the front yard, through our house, which was made of thin slats of timber just like all the other houses in the street.

Between them, Mammy and Cecil's mother decided Theresa needed to go to the hospital. Cecil's mother volunteered to stay with us so Mammy could take Theresa there, but first she had to go home to call an ambulance (which she paid for) because we didn't have a phone.

* * *

The next day, Mammy said I should go to school to keep out of her way. Poor Franc had nowhere to go. I found out later that Theresa had a nervous breakdown and would spend a long time in the hospital. On my way home from school every day, I would meet Franc and Mammy at the hospital and we would visit Theresa. There I would rock, and sing and pray in the silence of my mind.

Mammy said she didn't want to take Theresa to the mental hospital because it would be bad for her if she had a mad certificate. I didn't understand what this was, but that's what Mammy said. Theresa spent about a month in the public hospital and Franc had to go to school in the scheme every day with Mammy. I felt really sorry for her. She had to pedal her little legs all that way, and Mammy didn't wait for anyone.

After she was discharged, Mammy took Theresa across the river to stay with her friend Mayleen for a while (she had Theresa's real name and ran a typing school in the enclosure under her house). Everyone said it would be a good break for her. Mammy made me write a letter to Esther today to tell her what had happened.

"Tell she," Mammy dictated, "Come back to help out with yuh children, or tek Franc away to French Guyane with yuh. Ah can't deal with dem, and now ah got no help."

I translated all this into writing language and wrote it down.

"Read it back to meh," Mammy said when I was all finished.

Meanwhile, there was nothing to eat again . . .

Earlier that week, Roma told me her parents were taking her out of school by the end of the term to get her married off.

"They doan like the boy I prefer, so they want to see me get married to somebody they choose before I shame them," she said to me.

"And you agree with this?" I asked. This kind of thing happens every day but I never thought it would happen to Roma.

"Not really," she replied. "But you know, it's how we Indian people do things."

"You know this boy they chose for you?"

"Yeah, but not to talk to," Roma shrugged. "He seems alright. They're my parents and they very good to me. I have to do what they say."

I knew she was right. I was glad *I* wasn't getting married. I never wanted a boyfriend, let alone marry. Some boys were nice, like Steve and Ricardo, but most of them were like Edward used to be.

My mind didn't know what to focus on: Theresa being away, having to fetch water on my own, Mammy in a worse-than-bad mood, or Roma leaving me. I didn't even know where she was going to live, but at least she wasn't going abroad.

* * *

"We going out," Mammy said to me. "Edwards hear about me plight and invite me over to her house for dinner. Doan you embarrass me. I doan know why God punish me and give me you two, so I doan want no embarrassment."

Edwards is a nursery school supervisor of some sort. Before her promotion, she worked at Mammy's old school, so they still see each other sometimes. She had a large, black Raleigh bicycle, which seemed like an extension of herself. She lived with her aged mother and looked after her. Mammy said that because Edwards was old and dried up, no one would ever want to marry her. I thought she was at least twenty years younger than Mammy's fifty-something, so she couldn't be that old.

Mammy said that Edwards had a bacoo and this was why her house was always dark, and why she was lucky enough to own property.

I was told that a bacoo was a sort of spirit/human thing. It was supposed to be short, with a big fat head and large mouth that goes 'whhoo, whhoo'. If you had one, you were meant to feed it with bananas and milk, and if it was pleased with you, it would give you riches and do nasty things to your enemies.

This invitation thing was new to us. We'd never been invited to dinner, ever. I hoped I didn't do anything I wasn't supposed to do. Mammy said I was going to wear one of my shorts, because the pink cat suit was for special occasions.

"Things changing, Elizabeth," Edwards said to Mammy after we'd eaten. "You hear about the new laws Comrade Leader bringing in?"

"What new laws?" Mammy asked.

"Oh, you know the one that says that all teachers that aren't trained have to attend teachers' training twice a week after school hours," Edwards answered.

"What you mean?" Mammy asked again. In normal circumstances she would've said, "You mean *me*, ain't you? What you saying, I ain't got training?"

I was sure this is what Edwards heard, because she frowned, and changed her relaxed tone when she said, "Well, we *all* have to go to that training hall up by B.H.S road and basically listen to lectures and take notes and things like that. I went to one before, just to see what it involved. It's not too bad, the only thing is that you have to take tons of notes."

Mammy was certainly not pleased about this news. She never wrote anything, and spelling got on her nerves a little bit. How was she going to do it, I worried. But Mammy had her ideas already.

"So," Edwards said in a voice that suggested she was about to change the subject. "How's the house hunting coming along?"

"You won't believe how hard it is to find a house to rent these days," Mammy moaned, "Especially if you got children. Nobody wants to rent their house to people with children, and since I got these two headaches on me hands, I can't get nowhere."

"I heard," Edwards said uncomfortably, like - as she glanced at me and Franc. "Of course, this is Mother's own house, so thank God we don't have to rent. How the children coping? They seem like very good children."

"Them?" Mammy spat. "They give me worries, no end."

Then she looked at me, with narrow eyes, lifted her finger, and pointed at my face. "This one really sly."

We left finally and walked home in painful silence, Franc and I holding hands. When she got tired, Mammy said she was old enough to walk and she wasn't going to carry her. It was a long way so I offered to, but Mammy said I wanted to break my back so that she could get the blame. Nearing the end of the journey, I was almost dragging Franc by the hand, and when she refused to go any further, Mammy had to give in and let me carry her.

CHAPTER 21

EVICTION DAY

Dear Aunty or Mister,

At the weekend we went to see Theresa at Mayleen's house across the river. Mammy had to take us with her because there was no one to leave us with. Theresa was looking well. She told me she had seen Judith, her sister who was now married. She said that Judith – an aunt I've only met once - was sent to do domestic work at this woman who lives nearby. This woman treated her well and even found her a husband. Theresa said that if Judith hadn't left home, she would have never married.

When we lived in the house opposite the one we now live in, Aunty Judith came for a visit with her baby Michelle. The baby kept screaming at the top of her voice, a sound which made me very uncomfortable, as I felt I must've had something to do with her obvious pain.

Aunty Judith repeatedly put the bottle at the side of Michelle's mouth where she couldn't get it, and then laughed heartily when she stretched out her little pink tongue to reach it. I thought it was a game at first, but when the baby kept crying, I realised that Aunty Judith probably didn't like her very much. I don't know much about what mothers are supposed to do, but I know that I have never seen Theresa do that to Franc. She always gets the bottle in a hurry before Franc gets really hungry.

Maybe it's stuff like this that make Mammy say that Aunty Judith and Uncle Albert are really Grandfather Arthur's children. "Judith is stupid and Albert can't stop stammering," she complains.

"So I hear your oldest boy studying to become a lawyer," Mayleen said, when she and Mammy finally sat down to talk. "He's so bright."

"Daniel not so bright when it come to his family," Mammy replied. "He's shamed of us and never even send any money for me."

"Well, you know what it's like when kids marry out and leave home. He has his own family now."

"Well I doan think he should forget his mother," Mammy told her, shaking her head. "He can't be sure that the children are his, but you always sure of yuh mother."

"Who is older, Esther or Daniel?" Mayleen asked.

"Esther is the oldest, then Daniel. They used to be so close when they little, you know. Now he shamed of Esther too. Being Lieutenant in the army not enough for him, nothing enough for him. Now he's becoming a lawyer."

Mammy went on and on. Finally when she'd had enough she said it was time to go. She said she would come for Theresa when she found a new house. Franc looked at Theresa with tears in her eyes when Mammy told me to put her shoes on. I could only imagine how she was feeling because Theresa was like a mother to her. She really didn't know anyone else.

Best wishes xxx

We got home late and found a letter under the door. There was no stamp on it, so it was clear that someone other than the postman had put it there. I bent over to pick it up, as is my duty when Mammy wanted something that was lower than her arm's reach. As I took the sheet of paper out of the envelope, I noticed a drawing of a love heart coloured in red. Mammy saw it, too.

"Who is this Richard?" Mammy mumbled. She looked at the top of the letter and saw that it was addressed to Theresa.

The ball of spit I'd named blit gathered on her lips. The little white bubble transferred from the bottom to the top in a fascinating sort of kiss. Up and down, faster and faster it went, as I pretended to listen to what she had to say. My concentration on the little blit was a clever tool I'd only recently dared to use.

I escaped the beating that night because she was hungry and had to cook. She was just getting used to cooking again after having Theresa to do it for years. That didn't really stop her from questioning me. Mammy's questioning – and I learned the word for it – interrogation would last for an hour sometimes. Earlier this week when I spoke to Richard at the pumping station, I'd told him that Theresa had been sent away. He knew she wasn't there. Why did he leave the letter?

I could see that she was extremely angry because as she was fretting at me while trying to get information, a mouthful of angry spit flew into the pot she stirred. What she got out of me that night was that this guy used to see us at the pumping station and tried to talk to Theresa but she wouldn't ever talk to him and didn't like him at all. Of course, none of this was true, but I felt like I had to sacrifice someone to appease Mammy's anger. What if I'd read out loud *all* of what he'd actually said? The next day she went to see the supervisor at the pumping station.

The next day Richard was gone for good.

* * *

The magistrate gave us three extra months to move, on top of all the extra time we'd gotten before that.

That was three months ago.

We hadn't heard from Esther in a long time. We were managing somehow. I was still fetching water, Richard was still missing, and Theresa was still living with Mayleen. The only thing that was different was Mammy said she wasn't able to take Franc to school anymore.

"Ask the curly hair girl's mother to keep Franc," she said to me one day. Sita had long, curly hair, which her mother always put in lots of ringlet curls. I'd only ever said 'hello' to Sita's mother, so I didn't know how she would react to me asking her to keep my sister while we were at school, especially me being newly twelve and not grown up and all.

Well, she did say yes, and every morning I dropped Franc off, and then stopped by to collect her on my way home from school. She didn't like walking all that way, so sometimes I carried her.

That was three weeks ago.

Yesterday, Sita's mother said that it was too hard for her to look after Franc, and she couldn't do it anymore. Maybe it was because Franc kept wetting herself, but it wasn't her fault you know, she only did that when she was nervous. This morning she had to go to school again with Mammy.

I wondered about her all day at school, even when my class was playing netball, the only game I'd even remotely liked. During the game, Renee and her friends had fun teasing me because I kept dropping the ball.

"Ochro, ochro, Mar-got got ochro hands!" they cried, laughing at the invisible slime that seemed to coat my hands – my entire body.

Mr. Paltoo, our P.E teacher, heard their song.

"If you all are so clever and witty," he said to them, "How come you don't know that Margot is pronounced 'Margo' and not 'Mar-got.' Who wants to tell me?"

No one answered.

"Anyone?"

Silence.

I didn't say a word because I didn't know either. I thought it was a baffling coincidence that Mr. Paltoo was the one who was responsible for making me spell my first name correctly. Now I knew what my middle really sounded like, I liked it better. Ironically, when later someone said, "Margo isn't Mar-got without the 't.' It's Mar-goat without the 'a'," it made me laugh.

An announcement was made today at general assembly that we had until the end of the school year to change our privatised blue uniforms for the plain, national green ones. All the girls were to wear green pinafores made with an inverted front pleat, with a cream shirt. The boys were to wear green shorts (forms one and two) or long green trousers (forms three to five) and cream shirts. I tried to imagine all the high school kids in the whole country dressed the same way, but had to shake my head vigorously to clear it quickly. This was the law, though, except for 'The President's College' pupils in Georgetown (these kids wore purple, The Leader's favourite colour). The Comrade said he was tired of the British-founded high school, Queen's College in Georgetown, being the best in the country. He was going to build this new school called 'The President's College' after him, which would be the new highest school in the whole of the country.

He also built a new one here in this town to take over the position of our school. But everyone knew that our school still had the better teachers and the advantage of more than a century of good name and teaching.

I began to worry, not about the state of the schools, but because of what it took for me to get my blue uniform. I had a feeling it would be harder the second time around.

After this horrible day at school, I got to the top of our street, and noticed that something huge was blocking it towards the other end. There were bulky things laid out in the middle of the street. As I got nearer, I noticed that some of the items on public display looked quite familiar, very familiar in fact. As familiar as the mirror Aunty Meena gave us, and the bed I slept in.

Those were our things!

But how did they get there? Why were they there?

When I got closer, I realised in horror and confusion that there were men emptying our entire house, and slowly putting the contents in the middle of the tiny street.

I hurried into what used to be our yard, but before I could get in the gate, one of the boys who worked at the mechanic's shop opposite our house came up to meet me.

"Y'all being evicted, girl," he said.

"Why?" I asked him, but I already knew the reason.

"The man want he house," he answered. So *he* knew too. "Yuh grandmother say to tell you that she gone to get a moving cart."

I nodded and pushed past him, but there were men coming down the stairs, bringing out clothes, shoes, pots and pans, dishes. They walked past me, and I turned around and watched as some of Mammy's bras fell to the ground, but the men still kept dumping item after item of our belongings in the middle of the street.

The doll I wasn't allowed to play with came out next. The man was holding her upside down, showing her pants to everyone. As he came down the stairs she fell out of his hand, and into the dirt at the bottom of the stairs. So even the doll could not escape the humiliation.

"Them went to get yuh grandmother from school because the new owner brought a bailiff with he," the apprentice said knowingly from behind me.

I didn't answer. I didn't look back.

I stood in my spot at the bottom of the stairs.

Nothing was packed in boxes. Everything was being brought out and stacked.

They brought out some glasses and put them on the mattress lying in the street. At least *they* weren't going to get broken. Next came the desk I did my homework on. One drawer escaped as they brought it down the steps. Lots of books and papers fell out. Some flew away into the dirt in the backyard. I went to get them but the man wearing the white shirt and black trousers carrying the note book said we weren't "allowed to step on the premises."

But I was on the premises, wasn't I?

At last they said they were finished, but we weren't allowed to go back in the house to see if everything was removed.

What were we going to do? Where were we going to go?

Mammy came back with Edwards, dragging Franc behind her. I walked out to meet them. Mammy said she had met Edwards in the street while on her way to get the cart. Edwards leaned her big, black Raleigh bicycle against the mechanic's fence, put her arm on my shoulder and told me not to worry.

"I inherited an old house from a relative," she said. "It's unsound and broken but it's somewhere to stay. You can't live on the street."

It was then that I started to cry all the tears that had been piling up in my eyes. I cried a lot in secret usually, but not like this. My eyes seemed to be made of heavy grey clouds that just had to break loose.

Edwards wasn't joking about the house. It was literally in pieces. The front steps were broken down, but were still surprisingly hanging onto the house like a very loose front tooth. Some of the window panes were gone and the toilet wasn't usable. Thank God there was an outside latrine in the neighbours' yard that they kindly let us use. We were all thankful. This wasn't a dream house, but it was shelter. And best of all, it was in New Amsterdam. My journey to and from school was cut down by more than two-thirds.

My Dear God,

You know how Mammy says that you're punishing her by making her take care of us? Well I know that is not fair. I know you do take care of us. When that man threw us out, you provided this place for us. I dread to think what would've happened if Edwards didn't have this house, or even if she wasn't on the road at that very time Mammy was. I know you always take care of me and Franc and keep us safe. Every day, I read the plaques Mammy keeps on wall. They say, "In all thy ways, acknowledge Him and He shall direct thy path." And "God is thy refuge and strength, a very present help in trouble." I feel like they talk to me and will never forget them, no matter where I go. I promise.

Don't ever let me not believe this, because if I do that I will surely die.

Amen.

CHAPTER 22

OFFICER JOHN

"Papa was a rollin' stone . . . ."

The Temptations were belting out as I stood in front of the mirror brushing my hair, getting ready to go off to school. With every brush stroke, I could see the muscle I was always so fascinated with on Theresa's arm curl up and down on mine. I didn't know when it had happened, but I had – suddenly, it seemed to me – developed little tennis balls in my arms, just like the ones that hypnotised me in Theresa's.

Up and down they went as I brushed, relaxed, brushed, relaxed.

I'd learned the name for Theresa's body shape. There was a boy in my class. He was tall and thin and had what seemed to be solid knots where the muscles under his skin should've been. Lanky was what everyone called him. Lanky Dexter.

"He's never lanky," Mrs. Singh said one day when she heard the chant. "Wiry is what he is – nice and tall and lean, with all the muscles in the right places."

Now his name is, 'Lanky Wire'.

Or 'Wiry Lank', when the bullies are in the mood.

"Wot yuh doing so long?" Mammy startled me out of my trance. "Yuh gotta clean this rice before yuh go to school," she said, chucking a large bowl of rice on the largest of the three chairs we had. The coffee table was now propped up in a corner because its fractured leg had finally fallen off completely. It was awaiting mending when we had enough money to buy some nails to fix it. I would have to borrow the new neighbours' hammer when that time came, as ours was broken.

"Ah don't know what The Comrade give us to eat there," she said pointing to the rice. "He sends all the good stuff away and leaves us with the leftover rice they pick up off the ground."

I turned around and eyed the bowl of rice which was made up of about one-fifth paddy, dust weevils, white worms and stones, and sighed inside. It was my job every morning before I left for school to pick them all out so that the cheap rice would be clean enough to be cooked for dinner. Of course, now that Theresa was back, she was doing all the cooking.

She looked after Franc, too, because she was too young to go to school with Mammy anyway. I'd started going to Teachers' Training twice a week after school, since The Leader made good on his promise to train teachers. When my classes were dismissed, I walked down to where the teachers meet, which wasn't too far from my school. There I copied dozens of pages of notes because Mammy said she couldn't write as fast as the trainer speaks. Trouble was the training started an hour before I finished school so I missed quite a lot of the lectures.

Mammy borrowed Connery's (another teacher) books, and I'd copy all the stuff I missed from her notes when we got home. Sometimes I felt buried in sea of writing. On days when Mammy missed a session, it meant that I had to stay up very late to write it all up. Last night, I had twenty pages of notes and columns of '*Pupils should be able to do this, and pupils should show that*' to copy from Connery's very neat and well-kept books. As I drew the straight lines of the columns with the side of my Science text book, I wondered if Mammy had ever looked at all my hard work.

Connery was a nice lady. I didn't know her first name, but at least Mammy *used* one of her names. She referred to one of the teachers at her school as 'fat bum' and never called her anything else. Connery and Edwards were both from Mammy's old school. They didn't work in the scheme with her, but somehow managed to keep in touch.

Connery was in charge of going to the bank and drawing the salaries for all the teachers at her school. She then brought the cash to their homes so they could sign for it. On pay days, she'd ring her bicycle (not a Raleigh) bell before she leaned it up on the post outside the house. The clear, high-pitched sound always signalled gladness for me because having just over two hundred dollars in her possession never failed to make Mammy happy.

Connery still brought Mammy's salary, so Mammy must have still been getting paid on her old school's pay sheet. I didn't really know.

Edwards sat next to me and Mammy at the Teachers' Training hall, and once in a while, when I couldn't spell some of the big, teacher-speak words the trainer called out, she would spell them for me. She said the process of learning teacher training would go a long way to help in my English and my writing.

Maybe she was right because Maureen, now married to the most handsome male teacher in our school, was convinced I was getting better at my writing and gave me full marks on my book reports – well, almost full-marks, anyhow. She also asked me to write the signs up for the classroom and for house meetings.

Meanwhile, Franc was ill almost all the time now.

"Oh, ah doan trust them Cuban doctors," Mammy said when they diagnosed asthma. "The Comrade flooding them into the country, and ah hear they no good."

"Well," Theresa said, "I heard that they really good. Maybe it's coz the bedroom window's got no pane on it. She must be getting a chill in the night."

"Where could *you* hear 'bout Cuban doctors?" Mammy dismissed with her usual look of disdain. "Yuh talking nonsense."

Me, I didn't know much about doctors. I remember when I was little and we used to go to the hospital, there used to be lots of white, funny-sounding, English-speaking ones. Nowadays, there were only Cuban ones, who sounded even funnier since they couldn't even speak *English.* I supposed that had something to do with the grown-ups saying that The Comrade had agreements with Cuba because he admires their politickings.

I was sad that Franc was ill, but me, I had my own problems which I couldn't share with no one. I meant 'anyone.' Yesterday at school, Mrs. Singh, the Guidance Mistress, sent for me to go to the staff room to see her. I already knew what it was about, so I was more anxious than my usual stress-mania self. I remembered the last time I was anxious like that was when we still lived at Fifty-four Stanleytown.

Mammy was out and Theresa and I had this urge to eat some of the sweet mangoes that were hanging invitingly from the tree in the yard.

I'd carefully, awkwardly climbed up the tree, and eventually got to a very high branch. This (like in the story books with witches and things) was where all the juicy ones were. As I stretched my arm out to pick a particularly ripe mango, I heard a low buzz, a buzz that rose from a faraway muffle, to horror-jaw-dropper in seconds. Now, I was aware there used to be bees living in the tree, but we all knew they were long gone.

A long time ago, Mammy had asked Christopher to knock down the bees' nest because she was afraid that the ones that inhabited that squidgy, holey hive were African ones. She was afraid that during the night they would creep up to her room while she was asleep and sting her to her very death.

"So even the bees after yuh, Queen Elizabeth," he had said, but he had knocked them down anyway.

Before I could withdraw my arm, I felt a rush of pins and needles on my face and neck. For a moment, I forgot I wasn't on the ground and started to wildly lash out at my face, which by this time was performing a fireworks display. As you can guess, I fell out of the tree and onto the ground with a massive thud. I hurt my back and my neck but the stinging was much more painful. Not as painful as the anxiety of waiting for the swelling and then having to explain why I had gone outside. But not only outside, I'd gone *outside*, and stayed there long enough to climb up the mango tree. That was unforgivable!

Theresa gave me some sugar water to drink. She said it would prevent me from getting injured from the fall. We cut up the few mangoes I had managed to get before the ground-drop, and ate them in a delicious mixture of pepper and salt, as fast as we could. Mammy couldn't know that we had them, or that I had fallen down, or that I had been stung by the bees.

So you could understand clearly why the knowledge that my face was about to swell up like a football left me miserably anxious, I had witnessed in amazement Christopher's stupendous swell-by-the-second face when he'd stuck the pole into the bees' nest to evict them at Mammy's request.

I spent that mango-eating, back-aching afternoon waiting for the first sign of the swelling to show up, while planning what I was going to say. I was leaning towards: 'A swarm of bees flew into the house, came straight for me, stung me all over the face and neck and then did an about turn and flew straight back out again.' Yes that was the best explanation.

But the swelling never came.

“Anne,” Mrs. Singh said in her cotton-ball voice when I got to the staff room in my anxious state. There were no bees involved in my anxiety this time - and certainly not a mango in sight.

“I see situations haven’t changed. As I told you the last time, this is very awkward for me to talk about. Yes, I know it’s my job as Guidance Mistress,” she continued quickly, “But as I said before, the other teachers are expressing constant concerns about this matter. Have you told your grandmother yet?”

“Yes,” I said quietly, my arms across my chest. I could feel my face turning red, sweat pouring out of the burning pores.

“What did she say?” Mrs. Singh asked, flicking an invisible piece of dust from her lacquered, hardwood desk.

“Well,” I answered, trying to remember the last time I dared ask her, “She said she can’t afford one, but I wrote my mother a while back to bring one for me.”

“Can’t she just send you one?” Mrs. Singh asked, patting the back of her short, grey hair as was her habit, “Or send you the money to buy one?”

“She doesn’t send anything,” I said, trying to remember to put on my best, polished, English voice. Mrs. Singh didn’t do lingo. “She never sends money. She just brings stuff when she comes, Miss.”

“So when *is* she coming?”

“I don’t know, Miss. She never says. She just surprises us.”

“Look, I know it’s not your fault, but you’re the President of the Junior Inter-School Christian Fellowship. You know, it, it . . . .” Mrs. Singh was thinking how best she could put into words what she was really thinking. “You have to do something about it, apart from holding your arm across your chest all the time.”

“Yes, Miss,” I answered, wrapping my arms even tighter around me.

“Go back to your class now,” she said standing up. “Your new period should start soon.” Her shoulder reached mine when she stood.

“Yes, Miss,” I answered guiltily. However, somewhere in the back of my mind I was starting to think that this thing wasn’t really my fault. It couldn’t be.

I had two school shirts, the ones I got early on that Saturday morning more than two years ago. Wearing just two shirts for more than two years, five days a week in the hot sun, and washing them at weekends makes them nothing short of see-through. The thing was, I was growing up, and even the mole on my chest was visible through the white shirts.

This was my problem.

Not the moles. They weren't a problem. Although, I did often wonder why, out of everyone else, Theresa and I had to have a mole in exactly the same place as Mammy did. We were different from her, weren't we? She once told us that her mole was scraped off completely when she and her husband had a fight.

She said she was hammering grandfather when he sort of grabbed her clothes to push her away. His ring caught the skin on her chest and completely ripped off a small piece. Her mole went with it, but came back when the skin grew over again.

"No matter how much I hit him," she had marvelled, "He would never hit meh back. That used to get me so angry."

But back to me, Mrs. Singh had told me to get some bras some time ago. Mammy wouldn't hear of it.

"Too expensive."

I went down to vests.

"No money."

I wrote to Esther asking her to bring some, but I had to wait and I didn't know how long. Meantime, I walked around with my arms permanently glued across my chest. Renee would've teased me to shreds a year ago, but she had turned nice to me. I didn't know why, but I liked it this way. I often wondered what made her change from a bully to a nice person, but I supposed that wasn't really important, was it?

* * *

We found out after we had packed everything away in our new house that all our valuables were missing. We didn't have much, just one small gold necklace that Christopher had left for safekeeping, and a few one-sided gold earrings that Esther said she was going to take to the goldsmith to be melted down and remade into some nice earrings for us. Mammy also had a watch and a few bits and pieces.

This didn't sound like much, but these were all the earthly valuables we had. Like all other girls, I had my ears pierced when I was three months' old and was given a pair of gold earrings by my God-mother. One got lost along the way, and now the other had been taken.

Mammy said she couldn't recall seeing the bag outside of the house on the street with everything else, but I could. I could still see it resting on the bottom of that big blue tub we used to fill up with water every day. Our pipes here didn't work, but at least the tap downstairs did. That meant my water-fetching was nothing to talk about these days. It took me one minute to get two buckets of water up the steps. When the pipes stopped running, it was usually along with the entire neighbourhood's supply. I knew that this shouldn't make it better, but for some strange reason, it did.

* * *

"Somebody at the door!" Mammy threw the words over her shoulder to me.

She was sitting in her rocking chair, "*The only thing she's ever had from her mother*," smoking a Bristol. I got up from the dining chair we'd brought into the living room (because one of our three blue chairs was dead), where I was preparing for a maths test and went to the back door.

A tiny, grey woman stood at the open door brandishing some Watchtower magazines over the bottom half, which was still bolted shut.

"Hello, child," she said in a voice that sounded like it should be coming from a young man. "Is yuh mother home?"

"Hold on," I told her.

"A Jehovah's Witness at the door, Mammy," I told the circle of smoke above my grandmother's head when I came back to the living room.

Her hair had begun to go white again, as it was a long time since she'd had enough money to buy the hair blackening stuff she used so frequently. She got up and stubbed out her cigarette in the Demerara ashtray. The side of her smooth, brown face still showed signs of the white talcum powder she had polished it with this morning before work. I knew she was very old, mid-to-late-fifties, but she managed to look decades younger than other people in their fifties. If you couldn't smell her, you wouldn't know her age. Or maybe I was right in thinking that the smell had nothing to do with her years. I was sure it wasn't sweat. I knew for certain that even though she only took a bath once a month, she cleaned herself properly and never sweated.

Mammy tutted loudly, patted down her hair, and went to the door. A few minutes later, she came walking in with the boy-voiced woman.

This was a first. Jehovah's Witnesses always got sent away from our door without so much as a '*Good day.*'

"I didn't know this was where yuh lived," the woman was saying.

"We just moved in," Mammy answered. "Tek a seat."

Theresa came out of the bedroom, the one where we had put up cardboards on the missing window panes. We couldn't really use it to sleep in because when it rains, the roof leaks. We kept the desk and a few other things in it.

"Meet me daughter," Mammy continued.

"Hi," the woman said, looking up and stretching out her small hand to Theresa. "Everyone calls me Sister Mac."

"Theresa."

Sister Mac sat down.

"I meet yuh mother on the Back Dam road sometimes in the afternoons," she told Theresa. "These your kids?"

When she said the word, 'kids' she did something very odd with her mouth. I thought that the entire bottom row of her teeth moved slightly outward and to the left, but I wasn't sure.

"No," Mammy cut in, "Me oldest daughter's kids."

Sister Mac's voice rattled on from the time her bottom took refuge in the bigger of our two surviving chairs. Her mouth seemed to have a motor of its own that worked separately from the rest of her body. Her hands moved to rearrange the hat of steel-wool hair she wore on her head, but her mouth never took notice of the change of activity. I kept an eye on my revision, but I watched for the jaw-teeth-movement thing, just to make sure that what I saw wasn't real. I knew about dentures and plates because Mammy had to wear one, on account that she had no teeth left in her gums at the top of her mouth. However, the only time I'd seen them move was when she took them out to give them a wash.

"That makes a lotta sense," Sister Mac was saying the next time I looked at her mouth. Her bottom jaw moved in and out again, and there was a definite click when they fell back into place.

In the end she even managed to leave us a magazine. Mammy said she didn't have any money, but Sister Mac said, "Tek it anyway."

She invited us all to go to the Kingdom Hall, fixed her wig, and left. She did a good job in putting Mammy in a good mood because that evening after dinner, she sat us all down and told us a story.

When Mammy told a story, you had to sit down to listen to it. Not because she made you, but because she puts you in a trance with her perfect words, her fine hand movements, and brain-tickling voice. Nevertheless, you had to be careful when she was like this, because it was easy for you to get the false impression that you were safe, when we all knew that she could snap very easily.

Lots of her stories were about things that had really happened, like tales of her ex-boyfriends, or her life as a maid in the Bhattacharya's household. On rare occasions, when she was in the mood, she treated us to a Brer Anansi story. Not today though. Today's story was a true one.

When Mammy was a teenager, a well-to-do family came to live in her village from the city. The husband, John, a tall, strict man of half Scottish decent, was an officer and had fought in World War II. He was called 'Mussolini' by the locals because he looked like him (but neither Mammy nor I knew who this Mussolini person was). His wife, Elizabeth, had moved as a child with her parents from Madeira to take up land in this country.

This was at a time when the British were inviting white Europeans to come and join the native Amerindians in populating Guyana, along with the Indian and Chinese indentured labourers and the African slaves. I don't know what the Amerindians thought of this, since it would be akin to your guest inviting random strangers to come and live at your house.

Anyway, back to Mammy's story: These two people had seven children, who Mammy said looked different from everyone else in the village. There were three girls and four boys, but the mother had lots of health problems and sometimes found it hard to cope. So she'd asked my grandmother's mother to send Mammy to work for them as a companion for the kids because she was about the same age as a couple of them. Teenaged Mammy – then Martha – went to work for this family and remembered how the mother, Elizabeth, a short, quiet woman, had thick hair down to her bum. Mammy said the kids used to tie it around the bedposts as she lay sleeping so when she woke up she would have to call someone to set her free. This call was used as a signal for the kids to pack up any mischief they were up to.

She told us that this woman, Elizabeth, was a very good cook and that when she was well, she would gladly teach her to make Portuguese dishes and fine drinks. She said the youngest of the seven children's name was Steve, and before he could pronounce his words properly, his older brothers and sisters used to get him to stand on a tall windowsill, and crouch down where they couldn't be seen.

Then they would tell him to repeat all kinds of rude words and odd phrases to people passing in the street.

Mammy said that the older siblings under the windowsill would almost wet themselves with laughter at the shocked responses of the passers-by, and egged Steve on even more when they saw how much fun he was having.

"Say, 'Yuh stinky man', Steve," they would tell him.

"Yuh tinky ma!" he would shout to the next man to walk by their house.

"Say, 'fatty Rasta punk lady'."

"Fa-ee Wasta punk yay-dee!" he would shout to the next man he saw, while the older ones nearly killed themselves laughing.

Decades later, after John and Elizabeth moved back to the city and Mammy had married, and had her own grown-up children, one of the now late John and Elizabeth's daughters came back to the village. They met up, and Esther, my mother then in her twenties, went to stay with them in Georgetown. A couple of years later, she came back pregnant with me. Little Steve, now grown-up, smooth-talking, thirty-three year old Steve was to become my absent father.

CHAPTER 23

THE ARMAGEDDON

"So I hear The Comrade Leader gon ration us electricity now," Mammy said after Sister Mac told us about the upcoming Armageddon which is due to happen in the year 2000. She was a regular visitor now, but her clicking jaw was still a fascinating piece of her that both my mind and my eyes immediately stapled themselves to without my request.

The year 2000 sounded so far away that it was almost a fantasy – something you've heard of but didn't think you'd ever experience. I didn't even know if I would be alive then. Don't get me wrong, I wasn't going to kill myself or anything. I thought that would bring Mammy too much pleasure because she would be able to say, "See, I told you so. She's a no good!"

Although, I *did* sometimes think about being knocked over or something so I could stay somewhere safe, like in hospital, for a while. But then I realised that I could die, and that would mean I would miss out on the good future that I dreamt of, too. I didn't understand why yet, but thinking of myself dying made me feel better, even though I didn't really want to die.

"How they gon do that?" Sister Mac asked, scratching her scalp through her wig.

"Well, I hear that they gon black out certain parts of the town at certain times. So say Stanleytown would be outta electricity in the morning, then New Amsterdam will be outta electricity for the rest of the day and so on."

"I hear over the radio that they can't afford to run the power stations all day," Sister Mac answered. "But I didn't know it would come to this."

"Doan bother me too much," said Mammy. "We got no electricity at all."

"Yeah, but when you send Anne over by me for the ice, I might not have any coz of the blackout," Sister Mac said.

"I didn't think o' that."

"I'm off," said Sister Mac. "Got to go home straight away to the old boy b'fore he start to worry."

"Turn on the radio," Mammy told me after she'd left, twenty minutes later.

". . . It's not unusual. . . ."

"Oooh, I just love him." Mammy did a grown-up sort of giggle. "Tom Jones is so fine. Years ago in Georgetown I saw him on TV and he was so good. All the women throw they underwear at him, and he just picked them up and wipe he face with them."

I tried to picture this Tom Jones in my mind. He sounded a lot like Mr. Williams at my old primary school. Maybe he looked like him as well. I pictured him to be about Mammy's height, a tall, muscular, black man. He would probably be very dark like Mr. Williams, with black afro hair. Yes, this Tom Jones would also definitely have a beard – a thick one, you know, to go with his voice – a thick, rich beard, and a friendly, dark face.

I liked him too, but I didn't say so because Mammy didn't think I was old enough to like music. Theresa said Mammy just doesn't think anyone but herself is important enough to like anything, or to be upset by anything.

Mammy certainly was losing herself in this Tom Jones person. Her stiff neck had relaxed, and even her normally straight back had disrobed itself of its pride. I couldn't help wondering that if Mammy was on the TV thing, she would've been one of the women throwing their underpants at Mr. Tom Jones.

". . . It's not unusual to . . ." Mr. Jones went on and Mammy whistled along with him. She can whistle like a man.

* * *

Dear Aunty or Mister,

Esther came for a short while to take Franc away to French Guyana. I can't even remember what happened, because one day she was here, and before the excitement had worn off, she was gone again. I hope that it wasn't our broken-down house with all our missing windows and dangling, crumpled front steps that made her go.

I mean, the neighbours in the small cottage in the yard where we lived did let us share their latrine with them, but I promise we did keep it all nice and clean and well-scrubbed. Any newspapers left in it were always kept folded and neat, so I really hope it wasn't the conditions. All I remember is that she came, got Franc, and left.

One of the best things about the visit, was that at the ripe old age of twelve, I got two string vests to wear under my shirts, and was finally able to walk with my arms down. Being string vests, they weren't completely girlie-nature proof, but they were the best thing that had happened to me in a long time.

I think it was good for Franc to go because I had a lot of things to do. School work was getting more pressing because with our new library cards, we were expected to do lots of book reports. Plus, we had to go to the laboratory more often.

I had Teachers' Training twice a week and lots of notes to catch up with when I came home. Since we've got no electricity in the house, this has all got to be done before it got really dark. After I help with the water fetching etc., it's late and Franc is too tired to hang around.

Besides, Franc is getting bigger and she needs to go outside to play. Since we're not allowed, it's not fair to her, is it? Plus she is getting really ill. Before she left I was taking her to the hospital, (we now live near to it) almost every week.

Mammy said she was tired of running to the hospital with her all the time. Sometimes we had to wake up in the middle of the night and make Franc sit up to sleep. We didn't get much rest because the three of us were in the same bed. My chest felt tight when she couldn't breathe, because she looked so little and so hurt.

Worse than all this, she had to live in a house with Mammy. My heart felt columns of guilt when I looked into her innocent face, because I knew that, poor thing, she didn't know what was in store for her.

I felt that because I knew, that I should be doing something to warn her, but what? I tried to think, but all I could see in my mind was the spinning face of Theresa and the stranger's eyes she now bore in her head. She had left us – left me – and had gone to this floaty, cloudy place, a place I know she didn't want me to reach. For in getting there, I would be with her, but being with her meant I'd have to **become** her. I wanted to, but she wouldn't let me.

Cruelly, like an evil joke, her body had been returned to me, empty of all the things she had poured into me. Was I now meant to take up from where she'd left off and help save someone else? How could I do that when I still needed someone to save me? I was weak. I couldn't do saving. Not like Theresa does saving.

She has to take the tablets to make her better, but they just make her sleepy. She can't do much these days, but the doctor says that if she doesn't take the tablets she'll be sick again. She's going back over the river to Mayleen soon. It will just be Mammy and me. I don't want her to go, even though I know that she's got to use up the last bit left of herself to save, not me, but herself. Theresa is strong, I tell myself. Can't she do both?

We're going out every evening to search for a house to move to. The safety people said that we can't stay in this place because it could fall over anytime. The way to know if a house is vacant, is to walk down every street at night and look for all the houses that have no lights or lamps turned on. You have to mark them down and then go back in the daytime to check them out for any activity. If it still looks empty, the neighbours would usually know who the owner is.

End of term exams are coming up soon, so even though I joined the nightly search, I was hoping that we didn't have to move while the exams were on. Study revisions were brightened up at school today with a concert which was held in honour of both our headmaster, Mr. Beharry, and our guidance teacher, Mrs. Singh's, farewell treat before they left for the USA.

I said that like they were going together, but that's not the case at all. They were leaving within months of each other, with their separate families. It was just convenient to kill two birds and all that.

It was one of the best concerts we've had, I think. There were Indian dances, songs, skits, and jokes in tubs-full.

The party-before-the-exam-itch was so buoyant in the air it didn't take much convincing from Renee (and this was friendly convincing, mind, not the kind where they make you pay a penalty for not doing stuff) to make me go up with her to sing 'Seasons in the Sun' by Terry Jacks, a song I often heard played on the radio when we have batteries.

It was a song about losing friends, something we thought was happening to us, not only with Mr. Beharry, but with so many of the kids in our school and their parents. 'Brain drain,' a man on the radio had called it. I wondered about 'brain drain' for an entire day because I couldn't understand why someone would want to do that, or how it was done for that matter. Is that what they had to do at the airport – all these rich, educated people who were fleeing the country? Were they leaving drops of their brains before they boarded the Comrade's planes? Did they have to be hooked up before the flight and leave their brain juice behind?

It bothered me when I walked into school the next day, and all through the register. On her way out of the classroom, I'd stopped Mrs. Singh and asked her about this 'brain drain' thing, and she set me straight.

Renee and I got a big applause at the end of 'Seasons in the Sun,' so when I got home my head was still buzzing so loudly I wasn't thinking straight. I went and opened my mouth and leftover, excited stuff came spilling out.

"Mammy, I sang 'Seasons in the Sun' at our farewell concert."

"How'd it go again?" she asked through puffs of smoke.

Usually, I say nothing about school to Mammy because she's not interested, besides I didn't want to make her feel like she had to help with anything. By the time I'd finished the first line, Mammy interjected.

"So that's what you go to school for?" The grey smoke that had travelled from her lungs was still finding its way out of her chest by escaping from the corners of her downturned mouth. "Ya'll talking 'bout girlfriend and boyfriend at this age? Is people like you who grow up and kill themselves. Get outta me sight!"

I walked away. I would never understand, no matter how old I got, why she said this or what she meant. Even for her, this was one of those things that made my brain hide away indoors and pretend not to be there so that it didn't have to figure it out.

'Get outta me sight,' she always says, but that was better than a slap in the face, I suppose. When I was little, I wasn't sure. But now that I am twelve and a bit, I know that this is not normal life. Someday I will have one of those. I hope soon.

Best wishes xxx

* * *

Theresa wasn't going away anymore. She said she was getting better because she didn't have to take the stupid tablets anymore.

"I like how you're awake more often," I told her.

"Yeah, them stupid tablets are a pain to me soul."

"Why you not taking them anymore?"

"Don't have to. I could do more stuff now, and soon I'll be able to help yuh with your hair again." Theresa's eyes flashed across my hair and face, and for the brief moment when she looked at me, I saw a tiny bit of life trying to peek its way from somewhere behind the back of her pupils.

"When I was across the river, I learned lots of new hair styles. Your hair will look nice in them."

"I'm glad, because it's really hard to brush by myself. It gets really tangled."

Ever since Theresa went into hospital that night, I'd been doing mine and Franc's hair, but not very well. Yesterday morning I woke up, determined to make a good go of it for once. I got my comb and placed myself in front of the mirror Aunty Meena had given us, the only one in the house. Not long after I started, Mammy came and stood behind me. My heart skipped a beat and I made extra-long and deliberate strokes so as to impress her with how well I was learning.

"Your hair is awful," she said after a couple of seconds. "Other mixed-race girls like you have far nicer hair. Look at this," she added, reaching out and chucking a few strands of my hair out of the bun I was beginning to make.

But Aunty Meena's mirror said my hair was alright, especially since it was getting darker. I'd been using that mirror for the last few weeks in this house, and it had shown me that I had okay hair. Yes, it did agree with Mammy that my neck was long, and that my waist looked like you could break it with a sudden flip of your wrists. However, when I looked at my hair, my dark, curly hair was fine, maybe even more than fine. I think I was going to believe that – and me. Yes, that's what I *will* do.

After that decision, I went over to get Sita so that we could walk to school together. They'd recently moved into New Amsterdam and now lived only three streets away. We walk to and from school every day and had become best friends.

I asked her about my hair, and she seemed to think that it was quite nice. I decided then I was going to find and use this opposite-to-Mammy approach to become stronger to fight what she puts into my head so it doesn't stick.

We got to school a bit late and could see from the hard court where we played netball, that kids were standing around in groups, chatting excitedly in the classroom. This was unusual from the order that was expected at 8:05 in the morning. Within seconds of entering the buzzing classroom, we found out that Sumatra, a girl who both Sita and I were friends with, had swallowed sleeping pills.

"Why?" Sita asked Chatra, another classmate. "Why would she go and do that?"

"Well, yuh know this boy she liked, right?"

"Which boy?" I asked.

"I don't know the boy," Chatra hurriedly waved away my question. "Just a boy. I don't know him."

"I wonder if it's that boy she told us about, who lived down her street," Sita said, turning to me.

"Yuh want to know or not?" Chatra asked.

"Shhhh," I said to Sita, touching her on the arm.

"Well, she liked this boy, but her parents said that she couldn't see him anymore because they had someone else for her to marry."

"Who told you?" I asked.

"It's all over the place," Chatra replied. "Bibi who lives down her street told me on the bus this morning that Sumatra's parents said that the boy was too dark for her because, well, you know how Sumatra's fair-skinned, right?"

"Yeah."

"Right," Chatra continued. "So she fought with her parents. And she said this and that, but they said no way."

"So she killed herself?" Sita asked.

"Well, no, but what happened was that Sumatra and the boy she liked made plans to kill themselves at the same time."

"I can't hear this," I said, but I couldn't walk away. "This isn't good."

"So," Sita said, and looked at me all worried like. "What happened, did he die too?"

"That's the thing," Chatra hesitated. "They got hold of the sleeping pills, divided them up, and went home. Sumatra took her half and went to bed."

"No," Sita sighed, "And then they found them both in the morning."

"No," Chatra said. "The boy never bothered to take any."

"No?"

"Well, wait," Chatra told us. "Sumatra didn't die, she stayed in hospital overnight and they had to pump her stomach to get all the pills out."

"Get to your seats, everyone," Sir said behind us. "Class Rep, you're not doing your job, are you?"

"Sorry, Sir," I said, then quietly padded to my seat with all the other gossipers and waited for him to say we could sit down.

"Take your seats."

"Thank you, Sir," we all chorused like we did several times every day with all our teachers.

"I'll take the register and then we have to talk about your streaming," he said. "I'm sure your parents have already made their choices for your streams."

It was a busy and stressful time for us all. Stressful for the teachers and for all the parents and students involved. It was the time in secondary school when all the students decided what field they wanted to move into and what suitable subjects to take. This was all a slow and steady build up to the final exams in form five, when most kids are sixteen or seventeen.

Me, I'll be fifteen.

"Right," he said clearing his throat. "I know you are all very young, and as I said before, maybe too young to be making a decision like this one. This is why we ask your parents, teachers, and older siblings to help you in this. In just over two years you'll all be writing your C.X.C exams and what you do there will affect the rest of your lives . . ."

My uncle Daniel did England's G.C.Es, but that was before we teamed up with the Caribbean to do these new C.X.C examinations. We partnered the with Caribbean for lots of things, maybe because we had no neighbours in this continent who spoke English like us, or maybe it was because our other English-speaking friends in the Commonwealth were so far away. I wondered why this was so. I must find out.

". . . So talk to your parents during this month because you all have to give me your answers at the end of the term."

"Which stream are you going in?" Chatra whispered to me from behind.

"Mrs. Kerry wants me to go into the Home Ec. stream but Mr. Barran thinks I'd do well in the Science one," I answered. "I doan know yet. What about you?"

"My Mammy said I should do Business because I can get all sorts of jobs with a good qualification in Business," Chatra replied. "What did your Mammy say?"

"Dunno," I answered. "I think I have to make my own decision."

"At twelve?" She wasn't whispering any more. "This is important. You mad?"

"Chatra!" Sir stood up from his desk. "Stand up and share that with the class."

Chatra stood up, but kept her mouth tightly shut until Sir gave up.

She was right, but there was really no one to ask. Theresa never got to go to high school and neither did Esther, but even if she did, she wasn't here. I'll just have to do it and hope for the best.

"Don't forget to remind your parents about the new green uniforms," Sir said, looking down at the ground. I thought he did that so as not to look like he was accusing me in particular. "Some of you are still wearing the blue ones." Dunno why he used the word 'some.' There was only one person in the class still wearing it.

* * *

And what became of the upsetting story about Sumatra? Sad thing was, she wasn't sent back to school because of all the shame the little sleeping-pills' adventure had brought to her parents. She would soon be married to the boy her parents chose for her in the first place.

A lot of girls attempted suicide. Our new Guidance Mistress said that some girls do that just to scare their parents into letting them do want they want to do, but that none of us should try that because some of the girls do die.

I suppose she was referring to one of the older girls in form four last term. She didn't actually say it was her, but we all knew the story anyway. She'd hanged herself because the boy she liked wanted someone else, and she saw her own death as a way of punishing him.

She died, and he went out with the other girl he wanted anyway, so where was the punishment in that?

CHAPTER 24

LILLAWATTIE AND THE FOOD LINE

Mammy's story tonight was about a true incident that happened a long time ago in Stanleytown. This story occurred three doors away from the house we first lived in, when we came here from the Corentyne.

There was this Indian woman who had a daughter called Lillawattie. This woman was single and poor, so she had to work very hard to give her daughter a good life. Mammy said her family didn't want her, due to the pit of shame she had emptied on them. Maybe she'd done something bad, but the way Mammy said it, made it seem as though this family-dumping split was her daughter's fault. I wondered if this was why Mammy didn't like me. If Lillawattie could bring shame to her mother, maybe I did too. Maybe little girls like me who bring disgrace to their family have to pay for it with their lives like she did.

A well-known lady in the village – a distant relative of Mr. Barry in the scheme – lived two doors from Lillawattie and her mum. This lady indulged in all kinds of Obeah on various things and people. Mammy said she helped folks to become rich, and caused bad things to happen to her enemies.

Alright, maybe 'indulged' is not a strong enough word, considering that people went to her to cast evil spells and to keep their husbands from cheating.

"Small world, eh," Mammy had said when she told us the 'Mr. Barry' part.

Mammy had once told us that women came from all over the county, bringing their husbands' hair and toothbrushes, so that Obeah lady could put a ju-ju on the men to stop them cheating.

Oops! I'm straying a bit. Let's go back to the story I want to tell you.

One night Obeah lady had a dream. In this dream, a Dutchman 'told' her that he had buried fine treasure under the large, old tamarind tree that was standing at the top of the street (it was still there when we lived in that street, right opposite our house). It was the custom of Obeah ladies and people who believed in them to claim dreams about Dutchmen and treasure, but this particular woman believed it with all her might.

Why didn't she just dig up the treasure since she knew where it was? No, no, no, it didn't work like that, you see. As legend has it, if you came across a Dutchman's treasure by chance, without his direct permission and blessing, whatever treasure you found would just be worthless pieces of rusty coins. The magic was in the offering and your gift.

The Dutchman said in order to lay hand on the treasure she had to pour blood on the roots of this tamarind tree.

Now this was a true story, although it sounded unbelievable.

Weird as it seemed, Obeah lady decided it was best to give the Dutchman human blood, even though he didn't really say what kind he liked his tree roots to be soaked in. You would think that sheep's blood would've been an easier option with all the sheep and cattle roaming the main streets all day and night. Besides, the Dutchman was only a spirit. What did he care about whose blood it was? Dead people can't see things. All she had to do was lie and say it was girl's blood when it was really the neighbour's old cow's. But no, she decided that Lillawattie would be a perfect little sacrifice because she was pretty, innocent, and had nice long hair.

Besides, her mother was a maid. Obeah lady would be doing the mother a favour by removing her 'shame.' And she was so poor, she couldn't really cause any problems, right? As a matter of fact, Obeah lady was a powerful person in the area. No one would fancy messing with her.

So the idea came about to have a party in order to get Lillawattie away from her clingy mother for a few hours. Obeah lady threw a nice, big party and invited Lillawattie knowing that her mother always had to be at work. She convinced the mammy to leave the girl with her and to pick her up after work. Lillawattie was dolled up with curls in her hair and a long red dress, and brought to the party. These details were later described in the papers. Her mammy then went off to work.

Obeah lady had lots of children at her party, but she soon sent them home, all apart from Lillawattie, that is. (Mammy said that everyone devoured the long court case afterwards). Obeah lady gave Lillawattie something bad to drink and when she fell asleep, milked all the blood from her tiny body into a bucket. She then folded her limp, lifeless body and dumped it into the latrine in the back yard, poking it so that it sort of got buried under some of the you-know-what, squelchy, mucky stuff in there. In those days, before they built indoor toilets, people had latrines in their yards.

Meanwhile, after a long day at work, when Lillawattie's mammy came over to collect her daughter, Obeah lady told her, "Oh, she's sleeping. Come back later, yeah."

An hour later she comes back again. "Oh, come back later," she was told again.

Yet another hour later, same thing. So Lillawattie's mum ended up at the police station in town.

They searched for days until they finally found Lillawattie's body in the latrine. Obeah woman made all kinds of excuses but was found guilty. The saddest thing was the doctors found poo in the little girl's stomach. They said this meant she was alive when she was put in the latrine. Obeah lady ran out of excuses so she told the judge, "I am a very powerful woman. If you hang me, all the waters in this country will run dry."

Judge said, "Madam, I would like to see this land of many waters run dry." (The word 'Guyana' is an Amerindian word that means land of many waters.) So Obeah lady went down in history as the last woman to lose her neck by hanging. Trouble was, she never banked on Lillawattie's mother's boss spending all that money on their maid's court case to find her daughter's killer.

Roll on about twenty years or so and the Abrams, some new people in the area, bought Obeah lady's house. This was now in my time because we lived three doors away and Mrs. Abrams' grandchild went to Mammy's nursery school, but she also had a grown-up son who had some mental problems. He always cooked and set two places at the dinner table, one for himself and one for a little girl, whom he chatted with, but who no one else could see.

I used to run inside if I was on our veranda when he passed by our house because he was always talking and laughing with himself. He was tall and thin and looked like he should be playing cricket with the other men his age. Mammy said he was maybe just a big teenager but he looked older to me. Anyway, before we moved from that house, he had twice jumped into the latrine in their back yard to try to drown himself. Most people used water when they tried to commit suicide by drowning, but I supposed he thought he had a better idea. People who lived in the street had to come and yank him out. One time, after they took him to the hospital to treat him for poo digestion, he jumped out of his ward's window after the nurses had fallen asleep and killed himself.

What was the point in this story? None, really. I just wanted to tell it to you because it scared me. Even though I'd known of men killing children, this story made me realise that women did too.

* * *

We were in one of the food lines today. Theresa and I were lining up at Wrefords – or I think you have to call it Guyana Stores now – for split peas and cooking oil. We hoped that they didn't run out of them before we got to the top of the line like they did last two times we were here. There were a couple of guys in front of us talking politics, one tall one with a green bag, and the other, wearing Puma jeans. They didn't sound like they knew much, but everyone talked politics these days. Everyone seemed to be an expert. Everywhere I went, there were people whispering about The Comrade and the P.N.C. I hated politics-talk because all I heard was, "Ah hear this" and "Ah hear that."

There was a young man behind us who had a small, transistor radio. I could hear 'The Mighty Sparrow,' one of those Caribbean Calypsonians, singing that song about how you had to beat your wife every day to make her love you. And just when he had you thinking, *What kind of song is that?* he'd say, "Then she'll leave you eternally."

It made me realise 'The Mighty Sparrow' was very clever, and that he wrote a very smart song which used sarcasm to give a very important message. Maureen, our English teacher, was doing satire and sarcasm with us. I''ll try to remember to cite him next time she asked for an example.

"And yuh know wot?" the tall man with the green bag who was standing in front of us said. "Ah hear that they rigged the elections the last time."

The one standing next to him was shorter. He was wearing one of those 'Puma' jeans that were so popular. I would love a pair of those – just one pair.

"Ah ain't votin' this time," Puma Jeans replied. "Is waste of me time, anyway. I hear that they go to the burial grounds and copy all the names off the headstones, write dem down on the votin' list, and then mek them vote P.N.C."

I wondered why 'they' had to go off to the burial ground to get the names of dead people. Couldn't 'they' get them an easier way?

"Yuh know that red stuff 'they' put on yuh finger when yuh done voting," Green Bag continued. "Well, I hear that some o' the P.N.C people go home, dunk they finger in bleach and then go back to vote as someone else."

"But 'they' gat everyone name wrote down on the list," Puma Jeans said. "How can dat happen?"

"Ah doan know for sure," Green Bag confessed. "But ah sure 'they' find a way, mon. Just like they found a way to smuggle that soldier chap off to Suriname, when he done that killing."

"Wot killing?"

"That chap, mon," Green bag said and scratched his head for the answer. "What's his name again? That W.P.A. man they blew up who been running against the P.N.C in elections."

"Ah, yes, the one they killed when they set the bomb in his car. His name on the tip of me tongue, mon."

I knew this could be Walter Rodney, as he was the leader of the Working People's Alliance Party, whose name had been all over the news when a bomb was placed in his car. I wondered how his name could slip Puma Jeans and Green Bag when some radio people had said that he was a hero.

"Ah got it!" Green Bag shouted at last. "Walter Raleigh!"

"Ain't he that English Sir who put his cloak in the puddle so the Queen wouldn't have to step in it?" Puma Jeans asked.

"Is he?"

"Yeah, mon. I learned that in school."

"Rodney!" Green Bag shouted suddenly, and I nearly cheered him for getting it right. "Walter *Rodney*, not Walter Raleigh. Ah doan know why ah getting them two mixed up."

"Alright! We jammin'." Bob Marley told us on the radio.

"Ah doan know, pardner," Puma Jeans continued. "This country getting from bad to worse."

"Last night, me old girl had a party for she sister, right, and in the middle of cuttin' the cake..."

"Black out," they both chorused, laughing like they had just heard a particularly good joke.

"Yeah mon, I tell yuh . . ." Puma Jeans began, but a surge of people came back onto us and knocked Radio Boy's radio off his shoulder.

"Oye!" he shouted.

When you're queued up in these food lines (and some people came every day so they knew all the ins and outs of lining-up-success), you had to push as hard as you could against the person in front of you so that the entire line is literally joined up together. If you didn't do this, you were in danger of allowing a 'poker' to squeeze himself/herself in front of you.

Most of these pokers work in shifts, so Mummy poker would start the four a.m shift, get her stuff when the store finally opened, hide it in a bag or in her frock and stand around to wait for a sign of daylight between any two people in the line. Finding this tiny space, Mummy poker would then plant herself in.

In comes Big Brother poker. He would then take Mummy poker's stolen space in the line, go up and get the two bags of food stuff, be it split peas, flour, oil, or whatever. Brother poker would then hide his ration of whatever item was being rationed that day, and do the same as Mummy did. They would continue this until all of the goods were gone. Obviously, these people have large families to feed, but it was still not fair.

Ahead in the line, someone had caught a poker trying to edge in. They pushed forward to stop Miss or Mr. Poker, and the whole line of people went into the barrier at the front of the queue. Our science teacher told us that for every action, there was an equal and opposite reaction, hence the whole line came back onto us.

"Oye!" Puma Jeans shouted. "You trampling people back here!" He turned back and asked me, "You alright, child?"

"Yes, Mister," I said.

"Yuh know dat dispute wid Venezuela," Green Bag said, as if nothing had happened. He was obviously reminded of this because of the Calypso playing on the radio.

Our music teacher had told us Calysponians took political issues and turned them into lyrics for songs. Ours was the only high school in Berbice that taught steel pan music so far. We had a band room with a set of steel pans. I liked playing bass because you had to stand in the middle of four big pans and manage your way around to play them all at the same time. It was cool and made me feel very talented – even if I wasn't.

"Ah hear that the reason Venezuela want that bit of Guyana is coz they want Mount Roraima," Green Bag continued. "That is we biggest mountain, and they want to tek it 'way. Is like they want to leave us wid nothing."

". . . Not one rice grain
Not one Curass
Not a blade o' grass . . . ."

Sang the Calypsonian, and Green Bag sang along with him.

"Not a blade of grass" was Guyana's slogan and response to the Venezuelan threat of taking a piece of Guyana. The Comrade Leader ended some of his radio broadcasts these days with, "Tell Venezuela, not a blade of grass!"

My friend and I thought since Venezuela was right on the border, if they desperately wanted a blade of grass, they could just walk over and pick it.

Yes, we've already been told, "That attitude is not very patriotic."

Theresa and I got up to the top of the line and got a small bag of split peas and a quarter pint of cooking oil in the little bottle we'd brought with us. The oil was a bit cloudy and Theresa said so.

The woman behind the barrier said we should be thankful because, "Dis young man behind you ain't gettin' none! Oil finished, and we only got four bags of peas left."

As we were leaving, *"Electric Avenue"* by Eddy Grant was playing on the radio. It reminded me of something Christopher had told me when he was here. He said if all the rich and famous Guyanese like Eddy Grant lived in Guyana, spent their money here, and employed people, that it would probably give more of us Guyanese a chance to become rich and famous ourselves.

"Hi, Silver Fox," Margaret, from one of the form fours, said to me as she passed Theresa and me in the street.

"Why she called you Silver Fox?" Theresa asked me.

It was a long story. My one pair of shoes I had when I started high school were no longer alive. I'd worn them for more than two years, every day, everywhere. They saw me through the sun and the rain. I coloured them with black markers I borrowed from Sita when they faded. I nailed them when the soles came off, and then tacked them when the nails got rusty and fell off. I even bent my toes when they didn't fit anymore. Finally, though, footwear can only take so much, and they gave up the ghost.

I didn't get a new pair. Luckily, Esther had left some plimsolls she didn't want any more. Mammy said I should wear them. The only problem was I was a size five and Esther was a solid size ten. Her feet were also about two inches wider than mine. The only solution was to stuff the plimsolls with newspaper.

Apart from two things, this wasn't much of a problem. Number one, when it rained, the newspaper in my shoes got wet and kept my feet slushy and noisy all day. *"Splat, slosh, splat, slosh,"* along the corridors I went.

And number two, I had to walk flatfooted because of my clown-like, big shoes.

My schoolmates said I looked like this very popular Chinese movie star called Silver Fox because he was flat-footed and all he ever wore were plimsolls. I once saw a Chinese movie with Christopher and all *everyone* wore were plimsolls. Christopher said that they wore that type of shoes because they helped them to fight better. He said tightrope walkers wore similar shoes, and so do ballet dancers, except theirs were pink. So now I was called 'Silver Fox' or sometimes even 'Bruce Lee.' Any Chinese star's name would do since they all wore the same shoes.

My shoes were well-known around school since no one can play a serious game of netball if I was around on a wet day. I'd make a quick succession of *'splat-slosh'* noises, and every time I ran for the ball, my shoes lazily slumped off my feet. I didn't know which was worse: that sound and the constant bending over, or the large holes in my one pair of socks.

Next week we had to come back to line up for flour.

". . . Electric Avenue . . . ."

CHAPTER 25

ONE HUNDRED AND FORTY FOUR THOUSAND

Every night since I could walk, I had to help cover up the dishes and tightly wrap up the cutlery with pieces of cloth to store them away. Mammy said that leaving them out meant you were encouraging the germs and cockroaches to crawl all over them during the night. Now, I'd seen the cockroaches play at night. As soon as it got dark they appeared through the cracks in the walls, and covered the surfaces like three-dimensional wallpaper. Sometimes, if you were lucky enough to get picked, they would even land on your head if, on the way to meet their friends across the room, they got tired of flying and needed a rest.

Mammy had given up trying to chase after them with the pointer broom because that never stopped them dropping by. Besides, the white sticky mess she made me clean off the wall when she *did* manage to swat them didn't exactly come off entirely. Mammy had long ago focused cockroach-related energies elsewhere. When she got up in the middle of the night to use the pee bucket, she went to the kitchen to look for dishes and spoons that were left out of the mummy-wrapping we performed on them in the evenings. She checked, not before, but after we'd gone to sleep. Finding any single spoon or plate left unwrapped, Mammy would shake you out of bed, and stand over your shoulder while you washed that spoon and put it away.

Once the spoon was dry and safely wrapped, you were not allowed to go back to bed straight away. Mammy made you stay up so she could interrogate you until she was tired and wanted to go back to sleep herself. Theresa said that Mammy could have easily wrapped up the spoon herself, but she couldn't pass up a perfect opportunity to torture us.

Tonight, after clearing up the kitchen together, Theresa and I put everything away, wrapped and tied the cutlery in their assigned cloths, and went to bed.

* * *

I only knew I'd fallen asleep, when I started to dream:

"Wake up, you!" Mammy was shouting at me in the silence of the dead night. "Yuh left out a knife!"

I scrambled out of bed, but I was going too fast and I lost my footing. I fell over. I can never walk upright in my dreams – *but this dream felt so real.*

"Get up, man!" she shouted again, getting angrier because I'd fallen. I pulled myself up and attempted to take the lamp she was holding out. She chucked it into my hand and it almost slipped onto the floor, but I held onto it, looking down to the floor to gather my footing firmly. I could see ribbons of fading, reflected moonlight from the bottom house coming through the wide gaps of missing floorboards. I walked into the kitchen and began to search all over the surfaces for the knife. I was wide awake. This was *not* a dream!

"Yuh can't find it?" she demanded. "Yuh should know where yuh left it."

I kept looking, but Mammy was not a patient person so she took hold of the back of my neck and squeezed down hard. She then pushed my head under the table with a force that almost made me drop the lamp.

"Look dey!" she shouted.

There it was, under the table. It must've fallen down earlier. I picked it up and scrubbed it by the light of the lamp. I then dried it and put it away with all the other wrapped up dishes.

"Come in here," she called to me, heading to the living room. She took a seat on her rocking chair and got a Bristol out of the almost empty box. I waited while she lit it with the match from the little yellow box and inhaled the burning tobacco deep into her soul. I glanced at the clock on the cabinet. The time was 2:10 a.m.

"Ah tell yuh every day 'bout the cutlery," Mammy said angrily between puffs of smoke. "Why yuh like to tempt me so, eh?" Her eyes, hiding from the smoke, were little raisins in her head, but the lines of warning on her forehead stayed focused on me.

"I didn't know that it fell down," I answered.

"What yuh mean you didn't know that it fell down?" When Mammy asked a question like this, whatever I said wouldn't be an adequate answer.

"If I saw it, I'd put it away," I answered quietly.

"Yuh dare be rude to me, you snake?" Mammy shouted, her voice echoing in the thick, black quietness.

"I . . . I just didn't see it."

I know that you're probably thinking, that this is a very stupid conversation and I must be making it up. I wish.

Now I was up, I needed to use the night bucket, but I never got to bother with such little details like toilet problems during interrogations. My head hurt, and I felt faint. Finally, Mammy seemed ready to go back to bed and she let me go. I glanced at the clock again, and it was 2:50 a.m. Not a record, and sadly, not a dream either.

* * *

Meanwhile, at school, it was time to write down our names on the streaming lists. Sita had already made the Business stream her choice, while I was persuaded by Mrs. Kerry to go into Home Economics, and by Mr. Budan, who thinks I should be in his Science stream.

I'd just come back from my meeting with the two teachers to find that the rest of my class had already left for the art room. I liked art, but I was better at crafts and decorating things than at drawing. Nevertheless, it didn't hurt to do a few sketches.

I'd started to walk to my desk to get my art book, but before I got there, one of the other Science teachers came up behind me. I didn't even know he was there until I felt someone hold my hand. Anyone would be scared. Of course being the coward I am, I was even scareder – make that 'more scared'. Maureen wouldn't let me get away with language like that.

"Don't try to get away," he said softly from behind me, when I tried to wriggle my hand out of his. I felt like I was doing something wrong by trying to get away, but I hated the feel of his hand around mine. It felt like leaking snot that you just *had* to wipe off the tip of your nose or go mad.

"Where are you off to, little lady?"

"Art room," I said.

"No one will miss you."

At this point I semi turned around and gave a half-hearted yank, still scared that I wasn't meant to pull so hard, but he held on. He looked me in the eyes and I looked back at him. What he saw there, I would never know, but whatever it was made him drop my hand.

They never put me in races at school because they say I am not fast enough, but they should've seen me that day. When I got to the art room, I realised I had left my exercise book back in the class, but it would have to wait – along with the Comrade Leader who was still on the cover – until I returned to the classroom with the rest of my friends.

I didn't know why Sir held my hand, or even if he'd thought it through before he did. I didn't think much of that incident at all because as you know, I get scared easily and he could've just been playing with me. Trust me to get things wrong.

I didn't know at that time of course, that nearly a decade later, I would see him on the University of Guyana's campus and he would pretend not to know who I was, even when I looked into his eyes and called him by his name. Maybe he couldn't relate the eyes of a confident woman to those of a fragile puppet, groomed to be fearful to fight even for her own soul.

So, along with the swollen dead body, Slinky's missing nose, Errol's crab-eaten bits, Red Cap, and the men in the bars, I wrapped the hand-holding teacher with layers of cloth and placed it far away into the edges of my memory. By the time I walked into our house and realised that Mammy had just been paid her salary, those memories were already filed and stored neatly away.

After I had counted Mammy's money, I had to go to this new bar she found for me to buy her rum. Parmanand's was too far away for me to shop there anymore (and so was Grimmond's in the scheme), but luckily there were ordinary, convenience shops here in the town that sell cigarettes – but never loose rum. I still had to go to the rum shops for that. A lot of my school mates lived around here. I would be an outcast in school if I was seen keeping company with rummies, so I had to be very careful. Today I was getting soft drinks as well, because we were having hot curry chicken and rice.

Theresa was posted off to the market to choose a chicken. They keep them all in a pen, so you could do a quick inspection, then pick the one you wanted. After they weigh the bird and you pay for it, you can take it home. When Christopher was younger and he lived at home with us in the house the mechanic bought, he built a hen-coop after learning woodworks at school. Mammy had bought twelve little chicks for him to raise because she said it was cheaper to buy them when they were babies, then bring them up yourself.

My job every morning was to go down stairs and open the padlock on the coop to let the chickens out. This was around the time when I got that hole in my face – which had now turned into a scar I may be stuck with forever. Christopher said that if you let the chicks out early, they'd catch lots of worms and grow up healthy. Later in the morning, he used to come down and feed them with rice and paddy. They ran around in the grass all day long, pooing wherever they wanted. In the evening he went down and locked them up again. When they got bigger and fatter, we caught them, cut their necks, and cooked them.

One day I came down early to unlock the padlock and only noticed that it was already open, when I began to put the key into it. I slowly opened the door of the henhouse with one little finger, but nothing clucked and hopped out. All gone, they were. Even the little skinny one we'd brought back to life when we beat on the empty down-turned basin we'd placed over her.

I didn't mean to step on her, honest. She was just a little, yellow chicken, running to keep up with the others. Christopher had just got his new chicks, and he was showing me how to fling the paddy and rice so it scattered everywhere under the bottom house of solid earth – no grass. I made one little step forward to practise my fling, and when I put my foot down, she was under it. Christopher sent me racing upstairs to bring down this white, enamel basin we used to have. He turned it down over her limp body, and with all his might, began to beat a rhythm on its base. Every so often, he lifted the basin and looked under it, but she didn't stir. He replaced it and pumped the palms of his hands on the bottom, over and over again – heel of hands, fingers, then heel of hands again, followed by a succession of beating fingers. Finally, he lifted it up and she moved. She shook her feathers, uncertainly at first, then she got up and limped away.

"How yuh do that?"

"You like it, no? See wot your uncle can do?"

"How yuh do that?"

"Is the rhythm, mon. You beat them fingers on the drum long enough, and it will wake them up. Did it to a puppy once. Is all in the rhythm, mon."

I ran upstairs and told Christopher about the empty coop. He wasn't pleased at all about being burgled when it was done to *him*. We never raised chickens after that. We'd just buy them from the market. It was hard getting them home because they fought and clucked all the way.

My job was to pluck them after Theresa cut the neck off. Usually, the actual killing was the daddy's job, but since we had no daddy, Theresa had to do it. The hard thing about plucking was you had to plunge your hands into the hot water to pick the feathers off. If you waited until the water went cold, the feathers wouldn't budge.

Later, while we were eating the delicious curry Theresa had made (did I tell you that she was the best cook in the world?), Mammy said she saw Crunchy Neck's daughter, who invited her last-minute like, to their wedding which was next Saturday. Crunchy Neck was one of our neighbours at the last house we were evicted from, and one of the many people I'd go see to ask for food when we ran out. Mammy called her "Crunchy Neck" because she had a very short neck. All her children were "Crunchy Neck's big daughter, Crunchy Neck's second daughter, Crunchy Neck's long hair daughter, and Crunchy Neck's son."

We'd gone to her eldest daughter's wedding when we lived at Fifty-Four. There were buckets and huge basins of food, lots of dancing, and enough red saris to turn the whites of your eyeballs pink. Last time, they made sure to invite the whole family so Mammy had to take us too – they knew how she was. Well, no one on the outside *really* knew how she was, and even if we told them, I was sure they would say we were making it up to get pity or something. All the same, most people knew she didn't like us very much. Maybe it was the way she talked about us.

"Clear the table," Mammy said to me when we were finished. "I doan want Sister Mac to see all this mess when she comes today."

Sister Mac now visited every Thursday afternoon, and my job was to read the Bible passages she picked out because she said her glasses didn't work anymore. I didn't think it was because of the same reason Mammy said she couldn't see with hers – a secret I only recently worked out – but I read for them anyway.

"Revelations, chapter seven," Sister Mac said to me later when she arrived. She always said 'Revelations' and not 'Revelation'. She was in the middle of teaching us about the 144,000 people who were going into heaven. She said most of the Jehovah's Witnesses were going to stay here to inherit the earth because it was less work down here.

"Heaven would be hard work," she said. "We want to inherit this lovely earth. Only 144,000 of us Witnesses are going to heaven, and those people know who they are. They get a vision."

I was intrigued by this. I always thought that going to heaven was a Christian's ultimate purpose in life. Sister Mac also said God will destroy the earth, which made me confused about where the earth-inheriting-people were going to be when everything was burning up.

I began to read. I read about the number of Israelites sealed to go up to heaven and there were 144,000; twelve thousand from each of the twelve tribes. When I got to verse eight in chapter seven, she said triumphantly, "See!"

But she had got me started and I read on silently while they talked. Verse nine said that, as well as this 144,000 people from the tribes of Israel, there were a great multitude, a number which no man could number, of people of all nations, kindred, peoples and languages. I read it again and got the same thing. There were 144,000 of the tribes of *Israel* (not non-Jews like us and Witnesses) *plus* even more than this number of other people there. I just hoped that if I ever taught the Bible to anyone, I would *first* read all the verses. This didn't mean that Sister Mac was bad, though. She walked from house to house every day in the hot sun trying to help people like us, so she had to be a very good lady.

Maureen, our English teacher, was on leave having her baby, but she said we should always read everything before we came to the conclusion. Whenever we have to do a book report, she'd give us a list of books to choose from. Maureen said this is the only way she could get some of us to read anything. This boy in my class didn't read any of the books, but he thought he could cheat, so he read the introduction of George Orwell's Animal Farm and copied it down word for word. Of course, Maureen spotted it right away and he got caught. Since book reports counted a third of our end of term English exams, he failed, so I understood why it paid to be thorough.

"Elizabeth, my tenants moving out at the end of the month," Sister Mac was saying, so I perked up my listening antennas.

"I know you have to move so . . ." but she never finished.

"I'm there the next day," Mammy said.

* * *

THE WEDDING

Usually at Indian weddings all the women sit with the children, leaving the men to sit on their own, but Mrs. Crunchy Neck told all the kids to sit behind the Pandit so we could get a clear view of what was going on. She said since I was the oldest, I should keep an eye on the small ones.

I was glad they'd locked away their dog. He had bitten me twice when we lived nearby, once on the belly and then on the leg. Dogs always bit me, so he wasn't really vicious. Not really.

The Pandit was dressed in a long white dhoti and sat crossed-legged at his important, priestly-marrying-person spot by the fire. The night before, the bride had had her skin dyed with turmeric in order to look fair-skinned on her wedding day. Her hands and feet were beautifully patterned with bridal, henna designs. After the bride - heavy with golden jewellery - had been brought downstairs, the bridegroom made his entrance on a little mule, wearing something like a flower chain, which hung from his hat. He – the mule, not the bridegroom – was dressed in a jewelled sheet, which sparkled and twinkled in the white sunlight.

Hindi songs played on the loudspeaker in the background, and the fire in the centre of the swept, freshly daubed bottom house was lit. We had arrived early, when Mrs. Crunchy Neck's long-haired daughter was still working on the earth under the house. Just like Theresa used to prepare it, she had mixed one-part cow dung to two-parts water. She stirred them together to make a runny paste, and used an old pointer broom – made from coconut trees' leaves – to spread the mixture over the ground. When that was done, she went on her knees and used her hands to smoothen the entire bottom house until it emerged a spotless, light green shade, as smooth as marble, and almost as tough as asphalt. In an hour, the heat of the sparkling sunlight had dried it to a floor you could eat off – not that you would want to. Although, we did already sort of eat cow-dung, since vegetables grew in beds of the stuff.

The ceremony began and the Pandit read and chanted in Hindi. At the end of each sentence he said something that sounded like '*Swaham'*. After this, they threw tiny, ceremonial, plant-like things in the fire the bride and groom sat around.

The Pandit finally made the bride and groom, who had only met each other once before, go round the fire what seemed like a dozen times, after which a sheet was thrown over them so that the groom could put the red sindoor on his new wife's forehead. Roma had told me once that some people steal their first kiss at this time as well.

The bride had to be seen to cry and all that traditional stuff, and then it was time to eat. We were served our food in water lily pads. They grow in the Back Dam trench, so you had to wash them really well, because that was where most people dumped their dead pets.

We had seven-curry, and all of it was delicious. The bride's father got skunk-drunk and vomited over some of the old ladies who were leading the singing. One moment they were belting out Lata Mangeskar and 'Kutchu Gar Bar Hai' and the next, they were wiping slimy, rum-flavoured curry vomit from their long, jewelled hair. They were Naanies and Chachies and Bowgies, so being relatives, they didn't mind much.

CHAPTER 26

THE ESTEEMED COMRADE LEADER

Dear Aunty or Mister,

At the end of the month, we moved in. Yes, it was during my end of term exams and no, Theresa didn't come, because she had a second breakdown. Mammy said it was bad this time, a lot worse than the first time. She had to go into the mental hospital for treatment. Theresa always said she never wanted that to happen because it would mean the end of her life. I cried for her, and for the life she had lost, the life she had not really begun to live.

The house we rented from Sister Mac was right next to the big one she and her husband and grown-up children lived in. She was also raising two grandsons who, every single day, came out to play in the yard between our house and theirs. Ours is a small house with just one bedroom, so Mammy put a bed in the tiny living room for me. The only furniture in the living room – apart from the bed – was a broken-down desk we had once been given by long gone friends, a mirror belonging to those same friends, and one single chair.

The chair was the only survivor out of the set of three my mother had once bought at a second-hand shop. The shiny, metal legs were now rusty and aged, and the only way to make it stay upright was to lean it against the side of the bed. I think if Theresa was here, she would've been able to lie on the floor with arms and legs outstretched and touch the walls of the living room from end to unpainted end.

There was no electricity in the house, and no running water in the kitchen sink – a square, zinc receptacle outside the back window. The window, one of a total of four in the house, opened only if propped up with a piece of wood.

Any water used to wash up the dishes immediately pelted though the wide hole in the bottom of the sink, into the soggy, mud-slime below. When you closed the window at night, the sink remained outside of the house, and the mixture below it made a perfect watering hole for scurrying rats and other small night animals after the dish water had stopped falling.

Most of the rest of our furniture was already broken from all the moving we'd had to do. Mammy put her rocking chair by the only front window we had. This is where the front steps used to be. It had obviously broken off some time back, but had been extracted and taken away, and the front door was then boarded over. The only steps we had to access the house were awfully narrow and looked like they'd been slapped together in one afternoon.

There were no banisters and no back boards behind the stairs themselves. Climbing the rickety structure step by single step was always a balancing act you had to be sure to get right every time. There were no safety nets, and the fall was ten feet below.

Inside the house, there was one other room; a small kitchen with a tiny cupboard-like lean-to with loosely placed zinc sheets for a roof and a concrete floor. This was where we washed ourselves. Like the sink, the hole in the bottom was where the water escaped once you'd poured it over your body.

There was an outdoor latrine which, even though they were out of fashion these days, didn't bother me much. It's not that we enjoyed doing our toilet business outside. We didn't. But Theresa and I preferred being far away from Mammy when we had to do our wee because she kept telling us that doing loud wees meant that we are bad girls with lots of boyfriends.

When we lived at Fifty-four and had a normal indoor toilet, we used to have to hold in our wees if we heard her outside the toilet. That's not an easy thing to do, especially if you really had to go and you'd been holding it in for a long time. But we had learned to do it, even when we were in mid-stream. We felt we had to.

Now, because the 'toilet' is out of her earshot, it was a relief to be able to let go and wee as loudly as I wanted. The stupid thing about this whole matter was that we used to believe her, but then we grew to realise that since neither Theresa nor I had ever had a boyfriend and we still did loud wees, that it was obviously something Mammy had dreamed up so she could have control of our bladders. Of course this didn't stop Mammy from believing it, so we were still at square one.

This place was a lot better than our last one. Sister Mac didn't really want to rent it again because it was run-down and meant to be uninhabitable, but she realised that we were desperate. They had enclosed two thirds of the bottom of their big house, and had rented the front half of that to a butcher, who ran his meat shop out of there every Friday and Saturday. Behind the butcher's shop was a small room, rented by a single nurse with a young baby.

One of Sister Mac's grandsons was my age, and he would sometimes ask me to come out and play with them. He clearly didn't know about us yet.

I walk past him and ignore his questions completely because, not only did I have to stay in, I couldn't even tell him this because I wasn't meant to speak to him.

After a while he looked at me in a sort of amazed-at-the-freak kind of way. I was torn between explaining to him that I wasn't as awful as I seemed, and running past like a fool every time he said hello. I confess I chose the latter because of my crazy compulsion to obey Mammy, my fright of beatings, and my never-ending zeal to please her.

Which is why, every year on her birthday, I make her a special card. I never have enough money so I can't buy her anything. But all year round, I collect anything beautiful that I can find; things like shiny paper, cute buttons, old cards – anything. When I've got everything I want, I design the card, cut out the pieces with old razor blades (we were only recently able to buy scissors), then take the pieces into school and borrow the teacher's glue and sticky tape to paste my creation together.

Mammy's birthday is always in the holidays, just before Connery, her teacher friend, brings her wages. Today as soon as I got up, I gave

Mammy her card I'd made earlier, and told her 'Happy Birthday.' She said the card was nice, but that she could really do with a cigarette after the breakfast she'd just had. I brought out my little match box, filled with pennies I'd picked up around school, and on the street, which had just enough to buy two cigarettes. I went and got them for her as a present. I knew this would make her feel better.

When I came back from the shop, Brother Mac, Sister Mac's husband, was having a heated discussion with himself as usual on his veranda. Sadly, a few years ago he had lost half of one of his legs to diabetics, but because he had children living abroad, he was one of the very few amputees in New Amsterdam fortunate enough to have a false leg. There was just one weird thing about this leg, though.

It was white.

Maybe the people in charge of making limbs thought that only white people could afford them, so they didn't bother making any black ones. He hardly wears it, though. He brings it outside on the veranda with him as if he was going to take a walk, but never does. Or maybe he just liked to give it some fresh air.

Just before Teachers' Training closed for the holidays, we were told that the new Guyana Teachers' Union (G.T.U) hall was going to be finished soon, and who was coming to open it but the Comrade Leader himself. The cool thing was, since I was always at the Teachers' Training, I was personally invited by the lady in charge of the class. Of course all the teachers there, including Mammy, could bring their immediate families.

Before the 'Opening' time gets here Mammy's immediate family will have to include Christopher, because he's moving to New Amsterdam.

Uncle Daniel, the one who became a lawyer, wrote Mammy to say that Christopher had gotten fired after stealing something from the army. He was supposed to be moving back soon. Maybe he would arrive before my birthday, which came almost a month after Mammy's, and bring me something beautiful. I often dream of what it would feel like to wake up one morning on my birthday with presents all around me and be told, "Happy Birthday!"

I know I shouldn't daydream, especially during school in my Maths period, but I can't help it. Our old Maths teacher has gone to work for a bank, and we're stuck with a new one who was just out of school. She is not very good, nor is my

Maths, so I can hardly understand anything. I'll just have to try extra hard in my other subjects to make up for my downward-hill-rolling grades in Maths, because I've now given up trying to struggle with the pack of untamed numbers racing across the blackboard.

Lately, with my birthday around the corner, I've been daydreaming about having a birthday party. I've never had one, you see. Esther said I did when I was a year old, but I can't remember this, even though there is a picture to prove it. Maybe I could have a large group of friends over, and a big, high cake. I only ever have a piece of cake at Christmas time but I don't like it much.

My friends could eat the high cake though, and I could have music and floaty things to celebrate. Maybe I could have a pair of jeans for my present. That would be the best present ever. I promised myself in my daydreams that when I am eighteen, I'll throw a big party just for me. Yes, that is what I will do. I'll have a humungous party, invite all my friends, Theresa and Franc, and I'll buy myself a nice pair of jeans.

"I want to welcome you all back to school," Mr. Nandkishore, our Head Master, said at General Assembly on my first day back. "It's good to see that all of you are wearing the new green uniform. I must say you all look very smart."

At the end of last term, all the form one students – who're now in their second year, along the kids who were newly coming into high school, received free cotton material from the government to make their uniforms. They looked like plastic soldiers in a toy box on account that they all got their uniform material from identical bolts of dyed, green cotton.

Mr. Nandkishore was wrong, though, when he said, "You all." I guess he didn't see a lone, older student standing there with her old blue and white that she'd worn since her first day of secondary school.

This term was a bit different because I didn't usually grow very much. However, I must have sprung up during the holiday like wild grass in the rainy season, because I had to take down the hem of my two skirts. I didn't seem to grow outward at all because the waistband remained the same. I really hadn't realised how tall I had grown until I saw Renee and the other girls who were always much taller than me. When I stood next to them, they now had to look up to me.

We had lots of different kids in our class now, only five of us from our forms one and two were together. Bright girl, Rosie now lived abroad *and so did quite a few kids from our old group. Sita and I were together at last. I know what you are thinking. Yes, I confess, I went and changed my class yet again. I am now in the business stream.*

Later that General Assembly morning, I was sent for, spotted, I suppose, as the lone blue and white on campus. I was sure I was to get lots of talking to about my uniform over the coming weeks – just like the vest thing. I wished myself invisible each day I walked into the school compound, and knew it was bad news every time I was called to the staff room. But I had good news too. Theresa came out of the hospital just in time for The Comrade Leader's visit to New Amsterdam.

Best wishes, xxx

* * *

There was security like hungry packs of stray dogs around town for the High Comrade's visit. When the twelve green Land Rovers came driving slowly up the street, everyone started to move up closer into the road to see which one he was in. I had a look too, but all the men inside all of the Land Rovers were dressed in identical Dashikis, and had moustaches and short black hair.

They looked exactly alike!

Someone behind me said that this was to trick anyone who wanted to shoot The Honourable Comrade Leader, as they wouldn't know which one he was. Me, I wondered if a criminal would really mind if he had to shoot ten men just to make sure he got the one he wanted. Besides, why would anyone want to shoot their leader?

When all of the men alighted from the Land Rovers, one of them walked slightly ahead, with the others following. It was my lucky day, because I got to be the first person outside the circle of identical Comrade Leaders. The real Leader gave a short speech outside the building before he cut the ribbon to the brand new hall. I wasn't listening to anything he was saying, of course. I was just so curious about this man who commanded so much reverence and fear; so much so, it was easy to forget he was a real person.

He was wearing a blue Dashiki. All the men in high positions wore them. I heard they were cool in the hot sun, but smart too.

The most amazing thing about him was the fact that he was moving his hair – I mean just the top of his scalp – as we were singing the National Anthem. In a weird, inhuman sort of way, he was making furrows in his forehead and his whole scalp was going back and forth, back and forth. It was amazing. I'd always thought – after for years digesting these ever-present pictures of him – that he was very tall and walked a bit proud like Mammy, but he wasn't and he didn't. He was simply ordinary looking, which made me wonder why we were all were so scared of him.

He was average height for a man, with an average brown colour. He even bore an average-sized belly like most of the men his age. His build was nothing short of average - everything *just* average, except for his hair which was slightly too black, like Mammy's.

Physically average, but powerful in every other way; so powerful that without saying anything, he had everyone around him walking on the edges of their toes, seemingly afraid to make any mistakes. They were all calling each other 'Comrade' this and 'Comrade' other, and holding themselves tall. It reminded me of Napoleon in George Orwell's Animal Farm, one of my book-report books. But much more than that, it reminded me of the way we were with Mammy.

I looked at the Comrade's shoes, and even they were powerful. The soles and heels were thick and sturdy. Even the front of his shoes looked like they had been re-enforced with the kind of leather I'd never before seen. I looked at my own, which could only be called shoes when viewed from the top. They had lost their meaning, their purpose, their very soles.

I wondered at the man with the charming smile on his face, and made up my mind that all the bad things I'd heard the grown-ups say about him were lies. Surely if his physical nature wasn't the reason I was feeling this awesome force radiating from his body touching mine, it had to be something inside of him. Sure, he made me stand in lines for small portions of rationed food, but like he said on the radio, he was doing it for our benefit, so we could grow into a better nation. A man who could make you *feel* his mind power could do anything!

When we got into the new building, I got an aisle seat. I was glad because this meant I could ogle The Comrade Leader some more. He gave a very long speech about the P.N.C. and things which I blanked out, and then he said he wanted to pick up a collection. He passed a basket around, but he didn't want to hear anyone putting any change into it. He told us to be quiet so he could hear if any 'tinkly' money was falling into it.

No one spoke, no one coughed, and it sounded like we all held our breath. I know, I did. But as the basket went around, he started to sing in a loud, deep, surprisingly melodious voice:

"Bringing in the sheaves
Bringing in the sheaves
We shall come rejoicing
Bringing in the sheaves
Sowing in the morning . . . ."

CHAPTER 27

HOW TO COOK HUMAN FLESH

Christopher *did* move to New Amsterdam. He said he was looking for a job around here.

"Yuh can only stay here for two weeks," Mammy told him. "Yuh know ah doan trust you with all them shenanigans you get up to."

In the bedroom, Theresa, who was now back home, had set up a single fold-out bed next to Mammy's, which meant that there was now only shuffling room between the two beds. Since Christopher had my bed in the living room, I had to sleep with Mammy - again. I slept in one position all night long, with my back turned to her. This was *not* because I didn't want to breathe in her hate-air – well, I didn't want to do that either – but because if I had my hands turned the other way, there was a better chance of me not touching her in my sleep. I was scared of being slapped awake for doing this, so I had to be very careful not to turn in my sleep. It sounds odd, but fear makes you manage impossible-sounding things.

Christopher had suggested we ask Uncle Daniel to buy my school uniform because he had loads of money. So I wrote him a letter yesterday. I also had to tell him the bad news about Mammy being fired from her job. She was told that some teachers were being retrenched, and since she was near retirement age, she was one of them. She wasn't too happy about this at all. I think that this is why she made me stand in the corner waiting for her instructions for longer than usual today, and when Theresa said something like I was getting too big for that now, she answered.

"Doan let that long thing fool you," she spat over her shoulder. "She's still stupid as hell. Look how she's standing there with she long, ugly gaulin neck like she father! She want you to feel sorry for she, but I know better. She's sly and stupid, and a curse to me life!"

I bowed my head, squeezed my eyes shut and waited for it to stop. I was older now, so I knew that if someone could say stuff like that while you're standing right there, what hope did you have when you were not. But Mammy was right. I wanted Theresa to feel sorry for me. I wanted her to feel as sorry for me as I did.

After that, all I could remember was that I was starting to feel very faint. All kinds of dark, bat-like things were crawling around inside my head, gnawing at the space behind my eyes. I didn't know what followed, but the next thing I heard was Theresa saying, "Anne, Anne, get up, get up."

The first thing I did when I came to was to make sure that Mammy was at a safe distance. I didn't want a fat face because it was the day I would find out if I would be made sub-prefect or not. I saw she was busy stirring her pot of boiling 'vegetables' that Theresa had left to come over to help me up – as usual.

"Go and brush your teeth and get ready for school," Mammy said over her shoulder. I got up, took an empty bucket from the bathroom, put on my flip flops that I had mended with new wire only yesterday, and went downstairs to fetch the water for my wash.

When I returned upstairs, I carefully took my slippers off, put them neatly by the side of the door, then carried the full bucket over to the bath cupboard, careful not to get too close to Mammy. It was hard to hide from her in a house where one person had to move to let the other one pass by. This week, there was a choice between salt or the washing-soap bar for brushing my teeth. As usual when money had run out, those were the options. I preferred the washing soap to salt, because even though it had a horrible taste, it made suds - which gave the impression that my teeth were being cleaned. I supposed they were both better than chewing on a stem from a black-sage bush.

I picked up the bar of Zeck's soap and rubbed it on my well-flattened out toothbrush. By the time I'd finished cleaning myself, Theresa was cooking the rice for my packed school lunch on the one-burner kerosene stove. The pot was a large one, almost full to the brim with water. We had to save this thick, porridge-like water after straining it from the rice, so that we could sweeten it and drink it as 'tea'. On its own, it probably wasn't that good, but with a bit of sugar and a touch of hot water, it would go down fine. At least it was something hot and sweet to start the day.

I wrapped myself the best I could with the thin, half-towel I'd had since I was little, and tiptoed to the bedroom, past Mammy by the sink, to get myself ready for school. Walking through the kitchen and the middle space we used as the living room was the only way to get from the little hanging bathroom to the bedroom. I had my skirt around my ankles by the time Mammy shouted out, “Come here!” from the kitchen. I knew she was calling me because she didn’t bother to hang a name onto the end. I yanked up my skirt, stumbling and hopping on one leg several times while I ran to her with it halfway up my legs. I shouldn’t keep her waiting. Theresa had gone outside to the toilet and the rice she’d been cooking earlier was ready to be strained.

We didn’t have a colander, so straining rice was generally a tricky business, especially when you actually wanted to save the strained water. Usually, to catch the boiling liquid, Theresa put a bowl on the kitchen table, positioned the lid of the pot so it didn’t quite close, then tipped the pot over the bowl, keeping the lid down by holding a tea towel taut between the two handles. All the liquid then ran out of the corner of the pot’s half-opened lid and into the waiting bowl.

Mammy however, was going to do it different way. This way involved the same trick with the slightly opened lid and her holding both the handles and the lid with tea towels. The only difference was – I was to hold the bowl under the pot to catch the ‘rice water’.

The scene that played out after this act was one of the most horrible ones in my life yet. It’s the part of the horror movie during which you close your eyes, because it was the part you didn’t want to creep up into your memories later when you were alone.

The scene during which you should close your eyes:

It was a green bowl, not a very big one. It was a lot smaller than the pot, and I wondered if it was big enough to hold all of the thick, boiling liquid. I stood, hands trembling, grabbing on to the sides of the bowl. Mammy tipped the pot over the bowl. The weight of the pot, full of rice and white-hot liquid, shifted the bowl a little, but I steadied it.

I’ve got this, I thought.

A moment later the lid clinked, shifted, then slipped.

A shower of thick, boiling rice water poured down my fingers like white, molten lava off a slowly erupting volcano.

I screamed!

The instinct to let go of the bowl wildly flitted across my mind, but the greater, more ingrained instinct of fear made me hesitate long enough for Mammy to hiss, "Yuh better not let go of that bowl and make this rice water burn my feet, or woman, I will beat yuh life outta yuh."

So, foolishly, I stood there and tried to bite in the panic and screams as the river of the bubbling, gluey substance kept pouring down my hand and the rest of it slipped into the bowl. I watched Mammy move her foot out of the way. I looked up to the galvanised zinc ceiling with its remnants of red paint that had long since flaked off and left, and I yelled inside the pit of my belly. I tried not to feel the lava stick to my hand, and stick and stick.

The imprisoning, all-absorbing pain reached my heart, slowing it down. Maybe it thought I had died.

I went into myself for a few seconds. I had to, in order to escape to sanity – *with* my sanity.

Mammy continued to chew her lip and calmly strained the rice. I ground my teeth and listened to the animal groans coming from inside my throat.

Pour, pour it came, sticking to my fingers and boiling my flesh. I heard it boil, I heard it inside the very back of my ear drums. Then dribble, dribble, came the lava, but she wasn't done.

And it continued to boil my flesh.

But I didn't let go of the green bowl.

It's now safe to look. The scene has passed.

Finally it was over. Theresa came in as I was pouring cold water over my fingers. The pain was indescribable. My right hand was badly burned.

Will I ever be able to do my writing again, all my lovely essays and poems and the secret diary I keep in a Comrade Leader exercise book inside my school bag?

Theresa looked at my fingers and said I probably needed to go to the hospital.

More than twenty years later, I would be thinking that she was right, and that maybe if I had, I wouldn't still be suffering with the pain from the all the damaged nerves. But then I would also think that I was blessed to escape Mammy with nothing but physical resetting. After all, I would think, my body's pain was mine, and didn't hurt my loved ones. What if? What if she had succeeded in dismantling my mind?

In my heart I knew that even though all my other injuries were explained as falling down the stairs, this one couldn't be.

"She will be late for school," Mammy replied. "She should just drink the rice water, have a bowl of rice for breakfast, and go."

After breakfast, I picked up Sita from her house and we walked to school together. But all the way there I couldn't help thinking about my throbbing hands and how ugly they would be when they healed up. I didn't hear Sita shout my name when I walked in front of the car coming out of a side road.

The car stopped, though, the second before it would've hit me. I was spared, but for what other horrors?

Of course, I wanted to think that I didn't walk into the car deliberately, that it happened only because I was so depressed. Sita was talking to another friend we had picked up on the way to school and I drifted into my daydreaming world, except today, my dreams were all about hurt, death and sadness – and burns.

* * *

Uncle Daniel, who didn't go by this name anymore, sent some money to buy my uniform. It was enough for two, but Mammy said she needed some of it. I didn't really mind. I knew how to wear one uniform all week. He wrote me a letter with my name on it. He said he was happy I was doing so well at school and that he would pay my C.X.C fees (this is the most important exam at the end of secondary school) if I just told him when I was ready. I had to read the entire letter to Mammy so she could make sure he wasn't telling me anything bad about her.

Meanwhile, my fingers weren't healing very well. They were still very swollen and some of the soft puffy tissues held water inside them. At least I could still write for a little bit at a time. I was glad I didn't have all those Teacher Training notes anymore. I wouldn't have been able to write so much.

CHAPTER 28

THE BEGGING LETTERS

It had been three weeks since Christopher moved in, a week longer than Mammy said she was going to keep him. Just in time though, he got a job as a fireman and was moving out to live with the nurse girl who lived in Sister Mac's converted bottom-house flat.

"It's only been three weeks," Theresa told him.

"Why yuh think they call me, 'Sugar Daddy?'"

My birthday passed with no cards, no gifts, no party, nothing. Theresa remembered the day though, and kissed me on the cheek when Mammy wasn't looking. At least I wasn't beaten. *That* was something to be thankful for. So I suppose I did get something – peace.

The decision came in, and yes! I am a sub-prefect! I had to wear a green sub-prefect badge under my regular school badge. I was very proud of myself, and now that I wore a green uniform like everyone else, I felt even better.

Last night Mammy made us pack everything of any value to take to Esther's friend's mother for safekeeping. We made two tiring trips on foot, fetching the big glass dishes, the pressure cooker, the record player, all the records, and a few other things.

"Christopher's desperate for money until he's paid," she said. "He's asking me to tek the stuff to the pawn-shop, and ah ain't doing it!"

"Is only Christopher," Theresa said. "He's *all* talk, as you know."

"No, he ain't. He will do them things, I know he will. He told me he will steal them, and tek them to Mr. Davies' pawn shop."

Theresa opened her mouth to speak, but shook her head instead. She had developed a slight tremor in her neck, which she said was because of the tablets she had to take for her nerves.

Me, I couldn't understand why Mammy said no to Christopher, because Mr. Davies had 'held' the record player and the records – even the Elvis and Bob Marley ones – for longer than *we* had.

"Ah sure he will break in and kill me for the stuff," Mammy continued.

"He won't kill you for a few pots and pans. Yuh, imagining stuff."

"Well, ah prefer not to have them. If ah don't have them, he can't tek them," she continued, as if Theresa had said nothing.

"So now *we* have to do without things we need? At least keep the pressure-cooker. It's hard for me to cook peas without it."

"Ah taking everything, and that's final," Mammy answered. A hard-working ball of blit moved quickly between her top and bottom lips. "Ah not having him break in on me and kill me for Esther's things."

Just before we left, Mammy had gone to the toilet. Theresa saw this as her opportunity and went down to Christopher, who was sitting on our stairs playing with his girlfriend's baby. He spent quite a lot of his home-time outside in the yard between the two houses, and often had his meals sitting on our stairs, which was just outside the only door to his dark, damp bottom-house room.

"Yuh know what's happening, don't you?" she asked him.

He did a big, long suck-teeth between his thick lips. "Mammy's mad, Theresa. You and I know that, mon."

"Can you not tell her yuh won't break in and kill her," Theresa pleaded.

"Nah," he smiled, "Let her stew," then laughed with the clicking sound. "Serves she right," he said, bouncing the baby upon his knees and nodding his head at her playfully. "Yes," he continued in a baby-talk kind of voice and the child giggled, "She should stop imagining that everyone wants to kill she."

Theresa began to walk away. She had recently developed a line in the middle of her forehead, which pointed fiercely at Christopher.

"Look!" he said loudly, and she turned back around. "Ah want money, but ah wouldn't get very much by killing her, would I?" Then he laughed again, louder this time. The baby jumped, startled, then she giggled again.

* * *

Dear Aunty or Mister,

Theresa and I were going out this afternoon. We often go on these trips, but I don't like talking about them much because they're way too embarrassing. There is one good thing about these journeys, though. Theresa and I get to spend time together to talk.

Some of the trips require us to walk for an hour sometimes because many of the people we go to live far away. When Theresa isn't here with us and I have to make these trips on my own, I usually go into one of my daydreams to avoid the shame and depression they bring.

To prepare for one of these trips you had to first write a note. As I do all the writing in the house, I write the note as directed by Mammy. It would say, "Dear ----" and then it would go on to ask for items of food or sometimes to borrow money. Mammy never, ever went on these trips. It was always Theresa and me – or just me.

I obviously know the content of the notes, which makes me keep my head slightly bowed when giving them to the people to whom they're sent. The note can be sent to old teacher friends of Mammy's, to Esther's friend's mothers, or old or new neighbours.

Today we were going to an old neighbour, the Persauds, from the scheme where I used to buy ice, and the people who owned the big dogs and the even bigger house. Yesterday we went to that house but were told that they are spending some time at their farm, about four miles away.

Today we're walking that distance with yesterday's note. We weren't looking forward to the end of the journey when the note will be delivered, but we were excited about the long time it would take us to get there and back – time spent away from Mammy.

We have to pace ourselves with whom we ask, as we can't ask the same person all the time. Mammy obviously has a note in her head of likely people to ask, and then goes through it. Don't get me wrong, I always hope for a successful trip, because there is no food or money in the house when these notes are sent out. But I still wish I didn't have to beg for food. Especially since Mammy lost her job and we've been having to do one each week.

Best wishes, xxx

* * *

As we set out on our journey, I noticed Anita coming across the street. She was the cousin of that boy, Steve, who was in my class, who had that terrible toilet accident at school just before he went to live abroad. Anita greeted us, especially Theresa, very warmly and with a huge smile. When she walked away, Theresa said, “You remember her, don’t you?”

I *did* remember her. She used to go to my school, only finished recently, but Theresa didn’t know that.

“Remember when we lived up in the Corentyne? She used to live next door with her parents and brother.”

“Wot? Wot you talking about?”

“I’m surprised you don’t remember. You remember things ‘bout when you were two.”

I did, but for some reason I couldn’t remember Anita from there.

“Remember when we used to go to Joachim’s shop?” Theresa asked me.

“Yes, and he used to make that funny throat sound to scare me. I ‘member I used to peep at him from under the tip of the counter because I couldn’t see over it.”

“See,” Theresa said. “All that you remember. Why not Anita?”

“Dunno. I could only remember that you and me used to go through the hole in the fence and peep at the nursery school children next door. Is that where they lived?”

“Yes,” she answered. “Know how old you were then?”

“No.”

“Two.”

“Really? I remember one time, right, when you were wearing yuh plaid skirt, and your arm got caught in the wire when we were boring back through the fence to come home.”

“Yes, I had to hide me arm all week,” Theresa sighed, “So she wouldn’t see it and beat us for going through the hole in the fence. That was such a long time ago.” She sighed again, as if she was involved in a long, tiring fight and the other person had just won.

Small world, Mammy would’ve said.

“Why doan my father like me?” I asked a bit later, matching my steps with Theresa’s longer ones. Five foot ten inches tall she was, when she was measured for her current National Identification Card earlier this year. That was a whole inch taller than Mammy.

“Ah doan know,” she answered. “But what I *do* know is that yuh father doan take any responsibility for anything about you. He’s blaming Mammy because yuh can't bond with him. Mammy is mad, but that's no excuse for him not to make himself known to you as a dad at all. You know that he's your father, but he never gave you a chance to even like him.

He expects that as soon as he come 'round, once in every ten years for ten minutes, you should run to him with excitement. Remember the last time he visit?"

I nodded.

"You were about seven, right, coz it was the first time we lived at Fifty-four. He come up to you and tried to hold yuh hand, but you fight to get away. He said he felt bad, but you didn't even know who he was before he grabbed yuh hand."

"Yeah, that's right," I agreed. The glasses man with the long, thin limbs and hairy arms had scared me when he yanked me closer to him. I had no idea of what I was meant to do except cower.

"I know Mammy would like him to visit more, coz she would get an extra twenty dollars," Theresa said smiling.

We talked about days gone by when Nizam and Aunty Meena and the girls were still in the country, and how they used to give us Halal meat every time their Muslim holiday came around.

A lot later that day, after a humble but nice meal, Mammy told us the story about her connection to a famous person in England. I didn't know the person she was talking about, but he was an English actor called, Michael Caine.

Mammy said that she once lived very close to the mother of this man's wife, Shakira Baskh. She said that Shakira's mother was a talented seamstress and even made one of her daughter's outfits for the Miss Guyana contest that made her famous. Shakira even went on to secure a very good place in Miss World, the highest that any Guyanese woman has ever had.

Mammy didn't know this, but I'd always wished I could be a model. If it *was* true that I was too tall and thin, and my neck was too long to be beautiful, maybe people wouldn't think I was suitable for cat-walking. I wished I was, though, but I seem not to be able to grow out at all – especially my waist. I now wore my old blue skirt at home after changing out of my green school uniform, and it fit me the same as it did when I started high school – apart from the length, that is. I'd try to grow out a bit, then maybe I could become a model and be as beautiful as Shakira Baksh. Maybe I could even enter a contest when we get away from Mammy.

* * *

It's Saturday, general cleaning day again, which meant that we would be cleaning the house from top to bottom, inside out, turning the beds over, and washing underneath. After all this has been done, it'd be time for Mammy to sprinkle Jays Fluid on the mattresses to stun the bed bugs senseless. Once they were giddy with the smell of the disinfectant, they started crawling out of the hard coconut fibres of the mattress and into the light, paying no attention at all to their hiding places and their safety. It was at this point when Mammy pounced, yanked them out, and squashed them between the nails of her thumbs. The blood they'd drunk from our bodies carelessly spilt on her nails. One down, and she moved on, chewing her bottom lip and looking, searching for the next bug to break the surface, and the killing started all over again.

No one – least of all the bugs – got away from this cleaning method of torture. We had to all stand by to hand her fresh water at the right temperature, hold up any large object she wanted held up, regardless of weight, while she cleaned underneath, and moved things around in spaces so small, even *I* couldn't get through. I got a few slaps, and she dropped a few things on Theresa's hands "to keep her awake."

"That's it!" Theresa said. "I've had enough of all this. This is the last stupid general cleaning day for me!"

"Well, that's sudden," Mammy said, not looking at either of us.

"No, it's *not* sudden," Theresa answered. "It's been coming, always coming. Ah just can't be treated like a child anymore."

"You can't leave here. You got nowhere to go. No one wants a crazy, deaf woman on they hands."

"Ah been asked to do washing for someone and they offered me a place to stay," Theresa said calmly. She was now so used to Mammy calling her 'crazy woman,' that it no longer registered with her like it used to.

"Yuh gon be a servant. Is that all the ambition you got? A servant?"

"I'm a servant *here*."

"How dare you talk to me like that? Go nah! Like I care. I would even pack the bag for yuh."

Desperation caught in my throat, threatening to strangle me to death. With Mammy not working and Theresa not there, I would be in the front line of fire. But I was old enough to know I was being selfish. I bit my tongue so that it wouldn't ask Theresa not to go. I wanted to ask her to stay for my sake, but I didn't. I wasn't foolish enough to think that I was going to stay strong, because my brain had already blown up in a panic, but I couldn't be weak either. I had only to think of that day when Theresa said her life was over, to keep me from capsizing. I didn't want her to be sad anymore.

"Ah won't be far away," Theresa whispered to me later, as she packed. Mammy had by this time forbidden me to speak to her.

"Ah will come back to visit and maybe stay a bit. Once ah got money, she won't say no. But ah had enough, can't take no more."

I knew that was all she could take in her life. We'd both noticed that nowadays, when Mammy made me cry with harsh words or beatings, she always said, "When *you* get yuh breakdown, don't blame me."

With Theresa gone, I suspected I was the next ingredient for Mammy's nervous breakdown pot, the pot she kept stirring, cooking on the heat of violent hatred. Sometimes I could even picture my mind heading down that road, but I will myself to try to steer clear of it before I get to that bend.

It was the bend Mammy had already gone around, so much so, that she had sat down there and licked its armpits. This was made clearer the day she told me that Christopher was no longer welcome in the house because he'd told her a bad thing.

"He's a criminal and a no good," she spat. "If you let him into me house, I will beat the life out of yuh."

That morning while wiping down the wooden steps, something I did early every Saturday morning, I overheard a conversation between Christopher and Theresa, who had stopped by for a visit with her brother. Mammy had already left for the market.

"Ah really doan know how she could do something like that," Christopher was saying, shaking his head from side to side.

"On her own children too," Theresa agreed.

“She’s got so much hatred, mon,” Christopher went on. “People like she shouldn’t have children. She had us to punish us. With her, it’s always want, want, want. And then she comes out with stuff like this when you ain’t looking.”

“Who did she tell?” Theresa asked him.

“One of me work mates’ step-sisters.”

“So she probably didn’t know it would get back to you.”

“Ah doan know, Theresa. You’s me sister, right. You know I wouldn’t do something like that.”

“Wot?” Theresa asked. She had turned away from him to look at me and had missed what Christopher said to her.

“*You* know I wouldn’t do something like that, right?”

“Oh, no, no,” Theresa replied. “You would never.” Her full attention was now back on her brother’s face. “Did she actually say that you interfered with the baby?”

“What he told me was,” Christopher swallowed hard and lowered his voice. Theresa went in closer, her eyes focused on the words that were to form on his lips. “His step-sister said that Mammy said that she didn’t know how Tracy could leave her child with me and go to work when I’m off shift. Said that I could easily interfere with the baby.”

“A baby,” Theresa whispered, “a *baby*?”

“I doan know where she hear these things from. She probably hear ‘bout one of them nasty foreign people who do these things.”

“That’s really evil,” Theresa said. “You mean people really do that?”

“Yeah, yuh see it in those foreign magazines all the time. But Theresa, to think yuh own son can do that, mon? That’s really hurtful to know you mother think you can do that.”

“She only told me her side . . .” Theresa began, but she couldn’t finish because just then, the butcher’s – who rented the front space under sister Mac’s house – young nephew walked up to me at the bottom of the steps. His short, curly hair was, as usual, oiled and neatly parted at the side of his head. The stylish white shirts he wore under his bloody apron and the clean, watermelon smell of his cologne gave the impression that he was rudely and abruptly transported from a catwalk into a butcher shop without his knowledge or consent.

“Mornin’, Anne,” he said.

"Mornin', Gaz."

"You alright?"

"Yeah," I answered, keeping my eyes down, not daring to look up into his face.

"You always workin' so hard."

I didn't know what to say to this, so I just nodded my head.

"You alright?" he said again.

"Yeah."

"Ah so sorry. Now ah got to walk up your nice clean steps. Can I go for the meat?"

"Yeah. Is no problem, Gaz. Honest. Ah could wipe it again."

"Ah will tek me shoes off, right," he said, then bent down, removed his shoes, and balanced his way up the narrow stairs to our kitchen.

Recently, the man who rents the butcher's shop next door, under Sister Mac's house, asked Mammy if he could leave his cuts of beef at our place. He said that in the past, burglars used to break in on Friday nights because they knew he left the large cuts of meat he brings in on Friday afternoons to finish off selling on Saturday. Mammy said he could, that it would be safer at our house.

Little did he know – or maybe he *did* know – that every Friday night after he or his cat-walking nephew had brought the huge pieces of meat and hanged them up from the rafters on our roof, Mammy would get out the knife and carefully slice thin strips of it off. She would then get Theresa to broil the meat in salted water to keep it safe to cook for a couple of days.

Theresa walked over from Christopher's front door to where I still stood at the bottom of the drying steps.

"Ah got a message for Mammy," she said.

"Hi, Theresa," Gaz said to her on his way down. He was carrying the large leg of a slaughtered bull on one of his shoulders and looked like an acrobat on the tightrope of our un-banistered, narrow steps. I tried not to look at the part from where, only last night, Mammy had sliced several thin pieces of fresh, red meat.

"Hi Gaz," Theresa replied. "Back to the grindstone again, ah see."

"Aye, no rest for the wicked," he laughed.

"Ah got a cooking job for Mammy," Theresa told me, after Gaz had disappeared with his meat into the side door of the butcher's shop. "It's with the same lady I work for."

"Is that where you live now?"

"No, I ended up staying with her friend. It's someone who does ironing for her called, Miss Hyacinth."

"So this lady got a washer and ironer, and she wants a cook?"

"Yeah. She's got sick children and stuff."

"Oh."

"Give Mammy that message. Ah doan want to talk to her right now."

CHAPTER 29

MY FIRST THIEVING JOB

Dear Aunty or Mister,

Now that Mammy is working, I sometimes come home to a lovely, breezy, empty house. I'm really happy on the rare occasions this happens, because 'home' to me has always been just an iron enclosure of tension and unhappiness; a place where you keep your head down, stand out of harm's way and listen . . .

And wait with breath drawn, and muscles tense.

I get to take half an hour or so to sit in the rocking chair and look out of the front window. I've been doing very well at school in my new business stream with my friend, Sita. She and I walk home together every day, we still only live a few streets away from each other, so I have to go just five minutes further than she does.

Sita is the youngest of three brothers and one sister. Her sister is engaged to be married to a teacher of the high school she went to, so they'll soon have a wedding to plan. I can't invite Sita to my home, but I stop to pick her up from hers, on my way to school. Her mother has changed her hair from ringlet curls to just a simple ponytail. However, Mammy still refers to her as 'The Curly Hair Girl.'

Well, I was telling you about coming home alone. Apart from on these rare occasions, I usually have to go to Mammy's work place to pick her up after school. The family she works for, the Ferreiras, is Catholic like us. We go to church about twice a year and they – twice a day. The priest was visiting this family's house one day when I got there to begin my wait, and he made Mammy promise him that I was going to start attending Confirmation lessons on Saturday mornings.

"How old is she?" he asked.

"Nearly thirteen, Father," Mammy said in her hoity-toityest voice, raising her head a bit higher, and puffing her chest out that bit further. She now had something the priest wanted. No one could be prouder than her.

"Well, she needs to be coming to church. We have to get her into Confirmation class as soon as possible." He punctuated the last word of his sentence with a deep dip of his head, and a healthy spray of spit from his thin, white lips.

"Oh, yes, Father. I knows that, Father," my grandmother quickly agreed, making sure to use her 'es' at the end of the verb, like she always did when she was talking proper. I didn't think that she noticed his spit, even though I was sure that a bit of it landed on the edge of her sleeve.

When I get to the Ferreira's house to wait for Mammy to finish work, the man of the house usually meets me downstairs, gives me sweets and talks to me as if I was an actual person.

His wife often comes and tells him to shut his trap when she hears his voice, so nowadays he talks quietly, and gets in really close to my face. He never wears anything else but a tee shirt and white underpants, even when he is tinkering about downstairs on his cars.

This is acceptable and normal, though, because it's how most men go about their house and yard. It doesn't bother anyone else. In his chats to me, he mainly inquires about school and stuff, which makes me wonder why such an old man with a head of grey hair and soft, crumply white skin wanted to know about my lessons. But I suppose that he's just lonely, aching to talk to anyone.

His wife is always busy with the two grown-up kids who need special care and attention. Maybe this is what makes her so stressed, and causes her entire body and head to shake so much. Mr. Ferreira seemed to be the only 'normal' person in the family.

Talking about 'family,' Theresa is gone, and Christopher is still living next door, under Sister's Mac's house, in the little room behind the butcher's shop. Every Thursday afternoon after school, Mammy sends me over to his workplace at the fire station to collect two bottles of milk from him.

He and Mammy have worked out a fool-proof plan. A particular farmer grazes his cows on the land next to the fire station, so Christopher was going to sneak over the fence and milk them into two bottles, one for himself, and the other for Mammy. Thursday was the day his boss went elsewhere, so they decided that this would be the perfect day to do the deed without getting caught.

On the countdown to Thursday afternoons, my hands and feet become even more sweaty than usual, and my heart wheezes like an overworked trumpet from the stress of imagining that I'd be caught red-handed.

Christopher waits for me at the fence, bottles hidden inside his firefighter jacket. When I get close enough, he looks around to make sure we're alone, then quickly slips me the bottles and walks off. As I steal away from the compound, each step gets heavier and more laboured. I feel my pulse thump inside my eardrums and I expect to be ordered back and checked at any moment. I look around me with eyes ready to jump out of the cavities in my head.

But I cannot run.

I was warned not to run.

Maybe if I could just race away, I'd feel less tense. But running could be seen as 'suspicious behaviour on Government land.' So I measure my steps and pray with every breath that I dare to take. At last when I make it out of the compound, I allow myself a sigh of relief, having escaped yet again, with the false freedom of a regular thief.

But the tension doesn't go away because I know that next week I come back for more.

It's the same way I feel at nights when I go over to the guard next door to ask for cigarettes. I told you that Mammy sits at the front window in her rocking chair, and looks out onto the Main Road, right? Well, there is this certain night watchman who guards a big hardware shop which is on the other side of our house.

Mammy sits and watches the smoke from his cigarettes rise into the night air. The more she watches the smoke, the sweeter the smell of the tobacco. She says she could smell it calling her, naming her.

He doesn't smoke her Bristol brand, but she says it doesn't matter when you really want one. Then, when she could take it no more, she sends *me out into the dark night so I could crawl over and beg him for one.*

The watchman never says much to me, but sometimes he makes sure our fingers touch when he hands me the cigarettes through the chain-link fence, something that always makes me scrub my hands when I get back home. Every night after the touch, I would slime away, head bowed, feeling cheap and used. A small price to pay – I would think – for the ten minutes of secure peace they would bring Mammy.

And myself – my rotten self.

And I would know in my heart that I've sold myself for one or two cigarettes.

. . . So I would scrub my hands clean.

Best wishes. xxx

* * *

This morning Sita and I were walking to school when we met Jennifer. She was in our class, but was older than Sita, and a lot older than me. She was made to stay back another year for not being able to catch-up with school work, and had a way of rubbing her obvious maturity in our faces.

"My boyfriend, Frankie is this, and Frankie that," was all she talked about.

This morning it was no different. She was telling us about her plans to go to the Mashramani celebrations with him.

"I got a new outfit," she said, patting yet again her straightened then styled hair. None of the other girls in our class had had that done.

"What's it like?" Sita asked.

"Yuh know what?" she asked, as if Sita hadn't spoken. "Frankie kissed me last night."

Sita and I looked at each other and giggled helplessly.

"Look at you two." Jennifer sucked her teeth and knitted her brow. "I doan know why I talk to you. Yuh just two little girls, who know nothing 'bout real life."

"Maybe we're just two *good* little girls who doan get kissed by boys," Sita replied. Laughter erupted in my chest and spilled out of my mouth into warm morning air.

"I'm not walking with you two," Jennifer declared, and started to walk away. "Musketeer," she muttered under her breath as she left.

"You believe that?" I asked.

"No," Sita answered. "Why would her mother let her do stuff like that? She's only fifteen. *My* mother said that girls like that are too wild. That's why they get pregnant before they marry, and sometimes they have kids by different men."

"If I *did* decide to have a family," I told her. "I'd prefer not to have kids than to have them while I was unmarried or with different men."

"Wot you mean, *If* you decide?"

"Ah don't know what ah want to do about marriage and children," I answered. "But I'm sure ah not goin' to have a life with men and children-fathers."

"My mother said that it is easy for girls like *you* to do stuff like that, too," Sita said to me.

"What'd you mean girls like *me?*" I asked. I couldn't settle on which was more painful, Sita saying that without hesitating, or her mother's impression of me.

"You know . . . is like, when you grow up with strict parents or grandparents, suddenly when you get older, and you have all this freedom, right? Well . . . my mammy said that girls like you go wild, coz you don't know what to do with freedom."

So many answers tapped on the window of my mind, dying to be let out into the open, but I swallowed them all down deep into my aching belly. I thought that Sita and I were a team. It never crossed my mind that she was better than me, or that she *thought* so. All this time, how did I never see . . .

I couldn't know it then, but years later I would read my jottings about this incident, and realise this was the point at which I found out that Sita – somehow – was aware of my circumstances of abuse and poverty all along, and used this knowledge and her blessing of a good life, to elevate herself above me. This was the moment our friendship started to become diluted, because I realised that I'd given her my loyalty – all of it, in return for nothing.

* * *

I now went to church every Saturday morning to my Confirmation classes. It was one of the best things I had done in a long time. Instead of staying indoors and sometimes getting beaten or getting my elbows and knees pounded, I'd go out to church and meet new people. Father, known as Father Soley, takes the class. I try to sit as close as possible to him, not because I like the generous fountain of spit that escapes in white sprays when he speaks, but because I long to get a glimpse of his blue eyes, which he only opens while reading to us. When Father Soley looks up to speak, his eyes almost always remain half-shut. And when someone else is reading, he falls asleep.

I suppose he had to concentrate hard so that he could impart all the information we needed to know before we could be confirmed Catholics.

At first I didn't like it that I couldn't answer many of his questions, so I began reading the Bible. I read from the first page in Genesis about the creation of the world, and planned to go all the way to Revelation if I could. I knew I was a bit of a nerd but I supposed that wasn't necessarily a bad thing. I sat by the lamp in the solid darkness of the night and devoured the tiny print, page after page after page.

"One of we relatives went mad reading the Bible," Mammy informed me several times. "He thought he was Jesus and tried to get them neighbours to worship he."

I remained silent, but stopped reading to show that I was listening. I wasn't expected to have an answer for this, but I was meant to stop what I was doing when she was talking.

"Don't *you* bother going mad thinking you're Jesus, shouting out, 'I'm Jesus! I'm Jesus!"

Still, I didn't have an answer. There was nothing I could say.

I had gotten to the New Testament. The Old was very good, but I didn't like the Chronicles – the books about the kings and stuff.

I really didn't want to know about them, so I skipped some bits when they became too boring.

On my journey through the book, I marvelled at the parts where the Old Testament prophets talked about Jesus. Even though I knew a bit about Jesus, I'd never realised that they talked about him in the Old Testament as well.

So excited I was about Jesus' story that when I discovered his brothers, I smuggled the Bible to Father Soley and pointed it out.

"Look, Father!" I prodded the thin pages of the old family Bible we'd had sitting on a ledge in the bedroom for years. "I found Jesus' brothers!"

"Don't you worry your head about that too much, Anne." His eyes were half shut, his head nodding, as words and spit spluttered out of his mouth. "Holy Mary was a virgin all her life. She didn't have any more children. Jesus was all she had."

"But Father, it says in the Bible . . ."

"No, Anne," he said, pointing at the book in my hands. "Why aren't you reading your catechism notes? That wasn't on your list of things to learn and read."

"But, Father," I prodded weakly at the Bible.

"You won't get the information you need to be confirmed if you don't read the things you were given," Father Soley patiently explained to me through a series of nods, while he played with the contents of one of his overfilled pockets. Change, maybe keys, jingled and echoed in the grand hall, watched by stone statues of the saints to whom we prayed.

"Don't worry about that, Anne. Just read your Catechism book."

Father Soley looked tired. I shouldn't have bothered him so. It was not the first time I had come to him with one of my discoveries, all of them found, not in the Catechism notes I should've been learning, but in the Bible I shouldn't have been.

I thought I would've pleased Father by learning from the Bible, but if the Catechism notes are more important . . . but hold on – I could read both! I'd been reading both anyway. Of course, I have to know answers about the sacraments and stuff, things I wouldn't know if I just read the Bible, so maybe Father is right. But so was I, I thought.

I was only thirteen and didn't know enough to know what I should or shouldn't do. Father did. I just wanted to pass my Catechism class and be confirmed, because you can't be a nun if you're not. I can still be a teacher because lots of nuns are teachers. When my uncle Christopher went to primary school, all his teachers were nuns. They were bad nuns, though. They used to punish the children by locking them up in dark toilets until they ate their own poos. They weren't allowed out until they either tasted it or got whipped – an easy choice really.

I think that if Mammy was a nun, she would've been given special prizes of excellence, as she would know just how to measure out punishment. She could've been like the head of the Department of Witchery and Evil Punishments, or the coordinator of the Poo Eatery and Make Them Vomit scheme.

Maybe I was punished for not doing the Catechism thing right, because bad things seemed to happen whenever I was there. One Saturday morning a boy came to my house. It happened this way – as he told me later:

Davindranauth was one of the best Spanish students in the whole of the third forms. Since there was only one Spanish teacher in the school, only two of the four third forms were offered Spanish, mine and Davindranauth's class. It happened that Dave, as we called him, was ill and out of school for two weeks. When he returned to school that Friday, he asked our Spanish teacher if he could get hold of the notes for all the classes he'd missed.

"I don't have the notes," Sir had told him. "I have the lessons that I teach, but in that format, they'll be no good to you."

"What will I do?" Dave had asked him in desperation.

He said that Sir gave it some thought and said to him, "Tell you what, find someone who knows where Anne from Business Class lives." I was absent that afternoon. "I'm sure she'll have all the notes."

Apparently someone *did* know, and that someone gave Dave my address. On Saturday morning while I was at Confirmation class, he came to my house hoping he could borrow my book and copy the notes over the weekend. Theresa was there that weekend so she told me what happened next.

Dave came to the door and was accosted by Mammy.

"Good afternoon, Aunty," he said. "Can I see Anne, please?"

"No," she said in her anger-rocious voice. "She not here."

She said this loud enough for Theresa to hear, even though she had her back turned to her. When I came home, Mammy took the hammer because she couldn't find her wood. 'Somebody' had taken it again.

She beat me with the wooden part of it, on my knees and elbows, and even on my now badly scarred and ugly hand. She didn't scour all over my body like she used to. I suppose it wasn't easy to do so to someone who was now almost as tall as she was. When the hammer met my bones, I heard them groan. And as I cried my stupid, stupid, silent cry, sharp, loud pain shot through my arms and legs.

I could never describe the pain I felt, not the physical pain, of course – because even though that was unbearable, the emotional pain of my early teens was much, much worse. I didn't understand why, but I felt as ashamed as if she had just made me take my clothes off again.

The deepest, most awful pain of all was the fact that when she said, "Put out yuh hands!"

I did.

And when my knees collapsed from the blows and she said, "Yuh better stand up, woman!"

I did.

Again.

Dave got his notes, but ironically, the Spanish teacher left three weeks later, so we couldn't do that subject anymore.

Another bad thing – for me that is – that happened while I was at Confirmation class, was someone asking for me; not just anyone. It was Gaz, the butcher's nephew.

On Saturday while I was at class, Theresa brought home two bags of shopping she had bought for us with the money she had earned that week. On her way up the stairs, Gaz approached her. "Hi, Theresa. Got a load of shopping there. Need help with yuh bags?"

She said she had bent over to hand him one of the bags so he could take it upstairs for her.

"Where's Anne today?"

She said she hadn't heard him, so she'd asked him, "Wot you say?"

“Where’s Anne today? Didn’t see her this morning.”

By then he was halfway up the stairs, and Mammy, standing at the open stable door, heard his question.

She couldn’t contain her boiling rage to wait for me to return, so she sent Theresa to drag me home.

I was at the front of the church by the altar with the other children in my class. Someone saw Theresa and nudged me. I looked back to where she was coming up the left corner aisle. The pain on her face was so transparent I knew something bad had happened. When she told me, I felt defeated and angry - angry at Gaz for having asked for me, especially since we’d never had but passing conversations about slabs of dead meat.

I walked home with Theresa to receive my punishment for this dreadful, adulterous crime that I had committed.

CHAPTER 30

A RACE TO THE BREAD LINE

As usual, every day after school when we had money, I'd go to Harvey's bakery shop to buy bread. You could no longer get wheat flour from the shops, but somehow the bakeries managed to get hold of this illegal white stuff in bulk. This meant that anyone who wanted any bread had to make a daily trip to line up in front of the shop in the hot sun for just one loaf – no more than that was allowed. Sometimes it would take me hours to get my bread, and at other times, just twenty minutes.

Today there was a huge queue. I tucked myself in a place in the line around the back of the shop where it had curved around like a colourful anaconda. About half an hour later, someone came up, whispered something to someone else, and a rumour started to spread. A few people in front of me carried on a quiet conversation.

"Guess wot I hear, mon."

"Aye?"

"The bread almost finished in there. They only got a few more loaves left."

"Yuh joking, right. Where you hear that?"

"Naw, I ain't. That man just come up and said so."

"Ow, mon, that's not good. We been waiting here in the hot sun for hours."

"He also said that Somal's bakery round the corner selling bread today."

"Really? He don't usually sell bread on a weekday."

"But he selling bread today, mon. And the line ain't even as long as this one."

"Should we go up there and see?"

"And lose we place in this line?"

"Well, if we won't get any bread here anyway, we ain't got nottin' to lose."

"Makes sense."

"You goin'?"

"I think I might go."

"I goin', only if *you* goin'."

"Should we pass the word around, or go quietly?"

"I say, go quietly, Comrade."

I don't know which part of 'go quietly' the crowd missed, but the word had obviously passed around in several little groups all along the line because in a beat there was a crowd of us tearing down the road towards the other baker shop. I was slow – I told you – and wearing broken, wired-up flip flops didn't exactly help my speed, so I was towards the back of the crowd with the old people. Just as I was getting into the street towards Somal's bakery shop, I saw the fast crowd mowing down the asphalt, back towards me.

"Is a trick! Is a trick!" they were shouting.

I and the old folk turned around with them and raced back to Harvey's bakery, puffing and panting and sweating like leeches on a spit. Back there, I managed to slip under, wriggle, then slide into a place in the line amid all the shoving and pushing. I was now all the way at the end of the street, twice as far as where I was before I left. Apparently, someone had spread the false rumour just so they could get a place in the front of the line. Everyone was naturally upset and I think this was the reason for what happened next.

I know you'll appreciate why I didn't leave my place in the line to see what was happening. I can't tell you much, except to say that it involved two wigs and as many bras. There was an enormous fight going on at the front of the line. Lots of people were angry at what had happened to them and didn't mind letting their, erm, hair down. Lots of black women wear wigs, not because they didn't have any hair – they had lots – but because it was the easiest thing to do if you were having a bad hair day when you got up in the morning. Mammy had one but hardly ever wore it. Sister Mac had lots of them, and *she* never wore anything else.

When the discarded bras eventually pitched my way, I was surprised that they actually came in those sizes. I didn't wear them yet, but Mammy's and Theresa's were small, so I thought they all looked like that.

The bread lasted one day but the memory of that line will last for a very long time. Though, it did hit a spot straight away, because that night Mammy told us a story about herself.

That night Theresa came by to make dinner for us, and Mammy told us about when she had her first of two nervous breakdowns. She said Daniel had come to the end of secondary school and was getting ready to do his G.C.Es.

"He was studying at the table by lamp light," she told us, settling into her rolled up wad soaked with mentholated spirit. She unfolded it, then re-positioned it so that she could sniff a fresh bit of the aged piece of cloth, and inhaled deeply. Doesn't it burn her nostrils, I wondered again. When she asks me to soak her piece of sniffing wad with the spirits, the smell that forces its way up my nostrils, even from a distance, is almost unbearable.

"I was in another room," she told us between sniffs and blits. "And I doan know what come over me. I just picked up a knife and I knew then and there that I was going to kill him."

"Did he see you?" Theresa asked.

"Well, I got up close, like. But before ah could get to the table he was sitting at, he looked up and saw me. Dunno how, but he's a lucky boy. By the time ah could push the knife into him, he jumped up and backed away. Ah had him in a corner of the kitchen with nowhere to go, but he turned round, quick as a flash, jumped through the window, and was off."

"Did he fall down hard?" Theresa asked. "How high was the window?"

"You probably can't remember that house, but it was one of them flat one-story estate houses," she answered with a flip of her slack wrist. "You could stand outside and look into the window. Yuh know, he didn't come back that night," she continued with that looking-inward sort of stare she had. She took another long, deep breath on the mentholated and licked her lips.

Later, when Theresa and I were washing the dishes in the kitchen, I mouthed to her, "I didn't realise that nervous breakdowns made people want to stab their children."

"Nervous breakdowns don't make you do that," Theresa whispered. "It's your heart that does."

Maybe she was right. I just hope that Mammy didn't have a breakdown one night when I was sleeping in my bed, because I knew that I wouldn't have the guts to get to a window. Even if I did, what if she forbade me to jump? What then?

* * *

Sister Mac invited us to their Passover celebration at the Kingdom Hall, with strict instructions not to take any of the Passover bread.

"No one is worthy to eat it," she said.

"Wot yuh pass it around for then?" Mammy asked her.

"Well, it's like this," Sister Mac explained patiently. "It's just to represent the Passover. That's *why* it's called the Pass*over*."

"Oh, I see," Mammy said.

I wracked my brain trying to remember what the Passover in the Bible was all about. I thought it had something to do with putting blood on a porch or something, but I'd taken in too much of the Bible all at once. Maybe that was why I was confused. Maybe Mammy was right about that relative going mad because they were reading the Bible.

"None of us is worthy to eat the Passover bread, Elizabeth," Sister Mac was saying. "I ain't. You ain't. And, I tell yuh, even the preacher at our Kingdom Hall ain't."

"I see, sister," Mammy repeated.

"Only two men! Only two men in this entire country can tek bread from the Passover feast. They're from the Georgetown meetings, and they were given visions about their acceptance into heaven. Yes. *Visions*."

I knew this one about taking the bread. I'd read this only recently. A person was meant to examine his own heart as he took the bread, never looking at other people to try and determine if they were worthy or not. I wondered what would happen if I reached out and took the bread at the feast. But I wasn't brave enough to do so.

After all, if you were told *not* to do something by your host, it was bad manners to do it. I knew this because Theresa borrowed a book about etiquette and lent it to me.

There was no problem about what my outfit for the feast would be, because I only had one – the pink cat suit. It was a bit short for me, though, and it had been getting a bit tight recently, especially around the hips.

* * *

Dear Aunty or Mister,

It's the last week of the school term. I was a successful sub-prefect, so I will be made a proper prefect when I return to school to start my fourth year. I thought my grades were really going to suffer from having a bad Maths score so I tried extra hard this term. Good news! My teachers thought I did so well, that I was given a Certificate of Excellent Academic Achievement. These are really scarce commodities, like wheat flour, cooking oil and toothpaste, so you know that they don't come easily.

I was awfully pleased and very proud of myself. I showed Mammy the certificate but she didn't really say anything. I know I'm always going on and on about school and exams, but please understand that I have to keep these assets very close to my heart since they are the only things that make me feel valuable and important. If I didn't have them, I'd be a nobody, just a lost, little no-good, cigarette-grabbing thief.

Things are going well with my Confirmation classes. Father Soley said that he liked my reading so much, (I've stopped asking him Bible stuff. Don't want to be like the cat) that he wanted me to read his Homily scripture reading once a month on Sunday mornings during Mass. I know I should be excited and honoured about doing this reading, but I'm not. It's not the reading that's the problem – he said that I was one of the best in the class. It's just that I'm embarrassed to leave my seat in the middle of Mass and walk up to the altar in front of the entire congregation in my tight, pink cat-suit.

You see, nowadays, we have to go to church more often, now that I am to be confirmed. It's not about wearing the same thing all the time. It's about wearing the same tight thing – for which I'm too tall – all the time; especially since it rides up into places where people behind me can clearly see. I'm supposed to be getting a white dress for my Confirmation ceremony (I wrote Esther a letter and Mammy said to tell her to bring one.) I hope it's a big one so it tents me over and lasts a long time.

You know what are really cool? Jeans.

Lots of girls don't wear them to Mass, but I won't mind at all. Jeans are super. Maybe Esther will bring a pair for me when she comes. Theresa said that I should ask her to bring them when I write the letter, then when Mammy asks me to read it back to her, I should skip that bit. I am too cowardly, though.

I wouldn't know where to fit in my little message between Mammy's dictations and her watching me write what she says. If I take a long time to write something, she usually asks why. After every few sentences, she asks me to read it back to her to see if I've put everything she said in it. Esther is hers, you see, not mine. I'm not allowed to tell her anything that came only from me. At the end of the letter, I have to read it all again. I think this is so that she can make sure I haven't written anything of my own in it. Do you think I should ask for jeans?

Tomorrow is meant to be our end of term class party, so last week we were all asked to bring a gift to exchange with a classmate. Mammy said she didn't have any money, but of course, I couldn't tell the teacher that. Everyone else was bringing something, so I felt I had to, too.

I got an old hair bubble that Franc used to wear. It was made from clear plastic, and had a glittery surface. The elastic had long since unravelled in places, and years of wearing had erased most of the original shine. I took a page out of my exercise book, drew patterns on it with my red and black Bic pens, then coloured them in. The pens would have to do, you see, I hadn't had markers for years.

After careful colouring and wrapping, I tore an old piece of scotch tape off one of my Comrade Leader exercise books, and wrapped my present the best I could. When Mammy wasn't looking, I quickly made some paste from a bit of flour and water, and sealed up the rest of it. It was a tiny package, but I was once told that good things, great things, often came in small packages. This of course, turned out to be a big, fat, doody lie!

This morning when I got to school, I was called into the Lab by the teacher who was planning the party. He told me that he was going through the presents, deciding who was going to exchange what with whom, and came across my oddly shaped one.

"I opened it," he said.

I swallowed the blob of bile that had suddenly climbed to the roof of my mouth.

"I was surprised at what you'd brought," he continued. "I'm putting it mildly, Lyken, when I say that you hadn't tried your best."

I had, I really had, but kept this inside my heart. He must not know, because he will not understand.

"You can see how any normal person would come to that conclusion, couldn't you?" he asked.

I could.

I nodded, and felt my senses drowning in utter embarrassment at being caught.

"It's now too late to get anything for the party tomorrow," he said, running a finger over the present that I'd brought. Somehow this movement made me sink even further.

"I'll have to work something out," he said at last. "Go back to your classroom now."

Best wishes, xxx

* * *

It was Saturday again, time for cat-walking Gaz to collect his joint of beef, time for Mammy to go to the market, and for me to go to confirmation classes. I wasn't made to collect any milk last Thursday because Christopher was caught stealing for the second time and finally lost his job. The farmer complained. I'm sure the 'little red girl' was mentioned in the firing meeting, but no one called her – the little thief – for questioning.

I was sorry that he'd lost his job, but happy I no longer had to steal the milk. Or maybe I *wasn't* sorry about his job. I was getting ready to go out to my class, the place in which I was most happy, the place where I could breathe with abandon and sing as though my joy would burst my heart. I'd even made some friends, a beautiful girl called Althea, and another younger girl called Aaran.

I didn't think Aaran and I could become great friends because we were from such different backgrounds. Her uncle, Merrick, was one of the major Altar Boys – one of the ones who sat close to Father to wake him up when he dozed off – and her entire family was extremely active in the church. Little did I know, that in the future, Aaran and I would become inseparable and remain best friends for many years, and that her young uncle, Merrick, would become my first silly crush when I decided that I didn't need to be a nun to worship God.

Mammy had returned from the market, and I was just about to leave for class. I put my hand on the closed bottom section of the stable door, getting ready to open the bolt. A strong, warm burst of air brushed across my face. I had to get past the butcher shop without Gaz seeing me, so I always had to plan my escape carefully. I could only leave when customers were milling around and he was slicing beef.

"Anne," a small voice said from behind the door. She wasn't tall enough yet for her head to reach over the top of it. I had been so intent on stealing out, that I hadn't noticed her standing there.

"Franc!" I screamed, startled, but it took a second to occur to me, what her presence meant. Of course! Esther was here again!

We brought in bags and bags of stuff from the hired car, piling them on beds and on the table top as we were so short of floor space. Mammy, too, was happy to see Esther and Franc.

"Oh, yuh both so fat and nice," she said, admiring the weight they had both put on since the last time we saw them.

"Yeah, thank you," Esther replied.

In a carnival of activities, everything was well again. Cartons of Bristols made welcome guest appearances out of bags, Shop Lady was paid, my nice, unbitten nails were admired, milk – not stolen – was brought into our diet again, cod liver oil was proudly restored to the kitchen ledge, with a few bottles stacked away of course. Before the week had finished, Esther had – whatever the opposite of 'exiled' was – Theresa, batteries were put into the record player, Jim Reeves was singing again and all was indeed well.

I shouldn't forget that the celebrity that was Colgate was re-introduced, too. It was the start of the August holidays, so we feasted on several Indian movies. Amrish Puri was the preferred Baddie these days. Rishi and Shashi Kapoor, a bit older now, weren't as popular, but somehow Amitha Baachan was still getting most of the lead roles.

Amid the blur of movies, food, Colgate, and things going well, I even slipped out of Mammy's radar and got myself taken to Georgetown for one night. When Esther said she had to go to the city to take something for a relative of her friend who lived in French Guyane, I didn't have the audacity to even *think* that it would involve me. Surely, stuff that involved fancy things like travelling *couldn't* involve me.

When I overhead her telling Mammy that she was going to take me, I just knew I hadn't heard her right. Me? On a trip to the capital city?

No way!

Then she said it again – to me this time.

A strange – and when I say strange, I mean strange as in *freaked out* – feeling mauled my mind. I was sure it was something like panic, except it didn't feel scary. It was a sort of feeling that made me want to scream and stamp my feet at the same time, a feeling which left my breath caught in my throat, and my eyes wide and peeling. I couldn't remember ever experiencing that feeling before.

It was going to be my very first visit Georgetown. I'd always heard of the 'Capital City' and the 'The Garden City' on the radio, and I never knew I would one day go to it. It was supposed to be an enchanted place, far away, where Eddy Grant once made his music, and where the Queen of England and her husband visited.

In Georgetown, we didn't visit anywhere else except Esther's friend's house, and travelled back home the next morning, but this was still the best experience of my life. On the way there we went past the Saint George's Cathedral, the tallest one-story wooden building in the whole world. I sometimes saw pictures of it in the papers and it was unbelievable to look at it with my own two eyes from the window of the mini-bus. The whole experience made me feel free, like the wind was blowing in my hair (it was actually, I had the bus window open). I was liberated! My arms were open wide! I was the luckiest girl in the world! I couldn't believe it was possible to feel so good – and free.

This trip reminded me of when I went to Suriname. It was just before I started primary school. I couldn't remember why, but Esther took me with her for a couple of weeks, maybe close to a month. I stayed with the Palentacks, the people who owned the bar where Esther worked. There, I was the little girl I wanted to be. I played with their children in the yard, shouted and laughed and did everything they did. But then it was time to go back to where 'home' was supposed to be.

". . . I say a little prayer . . ."

Dionne Warwick was singing on the radio while Esther told us all that she had met someone very nice.

"He's named Fred, and he's a good man," she said.

"So, you goin' back to see he?" Mammy asked her.

"Nah, he doesn't want me to go back to French Guyane. He said ah should stay here, and that he'll come here to meet me."

"Oh, ah so excited," Mammy said. "Things now working out for me."

I thought it was Esther that things were working out for, but I kept my mouth shut.

"He left the same time I did," Esther continued. "He's gone back home to Germany and will tell me when he's comin' here."

"Then I could tell him ah liked the watch he sent for me," I chimed in. "It's the best watch I ever had."

"It's the *only* watch you ever had, Anne," Esther said smiling.

"It's the *best*, only watch I ever had," I repeated.

Esther had also brought me two new outfits, a white dress for my Confirmation, and a really freaky one that looked like you should wear it to do something opposite to confirmation –whatever *that* is. I hoped that I never had to wear it. Why couldn't I get just a normal pair of jeans!

This strange outfit consisted of three parts, a short, strappy top that ended just under my rib cage, pants – yes pants (or maybe they were hot pants; they looked like pants to me) – and a sarong thing that didn't wrap. It was a small piece of material that covered around the back, but was opened at the front with a button at the waist band. This was so you could show off the 'pants' whenever you took a step.

Why can't I just have a normal pair of jeans? I shouted inside my head when I saw it. I knew I was just an awful and ungrateful teenager who dreamed for things, and when she got them, wasn't thankful in the least. I was tired of worrying about my Silver Fox shoes, or my tight, pink cat-suit which rides up into places, or this brand new, indecent outfit which I will be forced to wear, but which will cover a grand total of less than half my body. Help!

CHAPTER 31

THE RAPE CASE

"In the summertime . . ."

I liked this Mungo Jerry song. It played quite frequently on the radio and made me and my friends wonder about what it felt like to live in a country which enjoyed different seasons. Maybe people who lived in those climates dreamt about ours as well.

'In The Summertime,' was just halfway through when the world suddenly collapsed into total silence. You could always tell when there was a blackout in the daytime because everything, everything suddenly became . . . silent.

Still.

Motors, fridges and engines all stopped working all at the same time. Of course, there was no guessing when it happened at intervals every evening because the night suddenly became black. Then seconds later, universal, dejected Comrade-Leader-hating moans penetrated the air – not that night-time blackouts affected us any.

We'd used our trusted kerosene lamp ever since the day we got kicked into Edwards' broken down house a few streets away from here. Daytime power-cuts were a different story, however, because it meant we didn't get any ice. Even the shops didn't get away scot-free either, because even before they could get their fridges cold enough to cool the drinks, there would be yet another blackout.

The power-cuts were a sore point when going to the cinema too, as you lived in hope there wouldn't be a blackout while you were watching your film. There was always a fifty-fifty chance – or make that a sixty-forty chance in favour – of going home disappointed without actually seeing the movie. Sometimes, depending on how much of the film you'd already watched before the power-cut, the cinema people would give you a part of your money back.

On the other hand, if you'd seen more than half the movie, you could forget it! No amount of screaming or whining would get you anything short of banned by the cinema owners. Then where would you go? There was only one other cinema in town, and that one showed different kinds of films. If you had relatives in Georgetown who had television sets, I suppose you could go to them a year later, after the film had been released in Guyana, to watch it on a pirate TV station.

Last time when we went to the cinema to see 'Pyar,' all was well and spirits were high. There had been a four-hour long blackout all morning, so we expected to be able to watch the entire film without trouble.

We shuffled into our places in the middle section of the cinema house, with the other middle section people. Then we stood at attention when the National Anthem played before the start of the trailers – a law all cinema owners had to abide by if they wanted to stay open – before relaxing into our chewing-gum-covered seats to enjoy the show.

The man in front of me had fired up his cigarette as soon as the anthem had finished, but so did Esther, so it would've been stupid for me to complain that his smoke was blocking my view of the screen.

About twenty minutes into the film, once everyone had their feet safely tucked up onto the back of the seat in front of them, all suddenly went black. Groans crept up from every corner of the solidly dark room. People started to shuffle around to open the wooden windows lining the sides of the building. A second later, there was a muffled announcement over a loudspeaker.

"Attention!"

Everyone went quiet except for a few suck-teething patrons from the pit section of the cinema.

"Attention, everyone! Please stay in your seats. The electricity is going to come back on in fifteen minutes."

By the heavy swearing in the building, it was clear to me that no one liked the sound of that. I heard people getting up from their seats and feeling around for the latches on the window. A few seconds later, bright, burning sunlight flooded into the hall, in pockets of white light.

Fifteen minutes passed, then another.

"Is half an hour, mon," someone shouted. "Ah want me money back!" Before he could be joined by the rest of the patrons, something flickered on the screen and the movie coughed to life.

"Rewind it a bit, no," someone shouted, but the man on the loudspeaker paid him no attention. The windows were quickly closed, everyone settled in, quieted down, and got into the movie again.

Another fifteen minutes after that, just as the rats were feeling safe enough to start peeping out of their hiding places, the screen disappeared, burying us all in a pit of complete darkness. Quiet. Nothing. Then people started to scream, shout, and stomp their heels in frustration as usual. This time, there was no loudspeaker. The noise in the building built up from the groaning of angry customers to the desperate shouting of people trapped in the solid blackness of the cinema.

Someone opened a window again and flooded the hall with cruel daylight. Ten minutes later the lights came on. "Light, yeah!" the crowd screamed and cheered.

The windows were quickly slammed.

CHEER!

Then the lights went off again.

CHEER!

The end part of the National Anthem played on the loud speaker.

BOO!

The film started to play – not from where it stopped.

CHEER!

But only for about fifteen minutes.

We went home that day like many other days, without seeing the middle, let alone the end of the movie. Christopher had said once that sometimes when the people at the G.E.C – the electricity board – turn the various switches off, they do the wrong ones by accident. He said that when they realise their mistake, they're made to come back and do it right. Maybe that day, the boss at the G.E.C. was showing some trainees how to turn the switches off and had a particularly dull one who couldn't quite get it.

"Now let's try again, okay," he must have said. "Yuh got to flick it up to turn it off, and down to turn it on. Now *you* try."

Trainee looks baffled, scratches his head and makes his move.

"No, yuh eediot. Me said up for off, and down for . . . wait," Boss says. It's his turn to take off his boss-man helmet and scratch his important-looking head. But he continues, "Wait, it's up for . . . hhmmmm . . . what did ah tell you first? Ah little bit forgetful, mon."

"Ah hear that the cinemas are supposed to be bringing in their own generators soon," someone said when the crowd finally realised that the cinema boss had locked up his ticket office and had already left with all their money.

"Comrade, this is what we get for nationalising everything," someone else said after he had kicked at one of the benches we sat on, which were solidly bolted down on the floor of the cinema house.

* * *

I will be back at school tomorrow, my first day in form four. I looked forward to it. In fact, I always looked forward to going back to school, as school was my sanctuary, my special place where I was liked and wanted, and where I was treated as a person with an actual mind.

Esther had gone back to French Guyane. I didn't know why. She didn't tell me. I was still waiting for the arrival of Fred, the man who gave me my first watch, but that never happened, and no one told me why. Today, I was papering all my books with old newspaper, and writing my name on the front covers in fancy, chunky letters. We always got lots of free, new exercise books from school at the end of every term. The old picture of the Comrade was still firmly placed on the front of every one of them.

There was a knock on the door. I put the book I was papering down on my bed and got up to see who it was. It was a man, an old-ish man, whom I'd never seen before.

"Is Martha here?" he asked. I wondered if Mammy had gotten herself a man. She was forever talking about the things she was going to be able to do when she got herself one of those.

"Yuh in your fifties," Theresa tells her. "Ain't that time to forget about getting a man?"

"Wot's wrong with you, yuh fool? I is still young and attractive enough for men to want me. I had priests running after me to get with them."

This man looked about her age, so maybe he wasn't her man after all.

"Ah doan want no old man to dribble on me," she'd said too many times. "Ah too good for that."

"Martha here?" he asked again, pulling me out of my daydreaming. His accent sounded different to mine. It was a nice twang, in good English. I turned to go get Mammy but by then she was almost at the door. I bumped into her and felt that familiar repulsion as her cold flesh touched mine. She looked at the man oddly.

"It's me," he says, "Your brother, Emmanuel."

I knew who 'Emmanuel' was, though I'd never seen him. He was Mammy's youngest brother who went to England to study to become an architect, and had once told her that he never wanted to see her again. He sounded a bit like an English man I once knew, who lived in the scheme. I used to see him every day on my way to school. It was good manners for children to say 'Good morning' to adults they crossed in the street. Every time I greeted him, he always smiled widely and said, "Good morning, m' dear."

He was the only person in my whole life who had ever called me, *dear*. Uncle Emmanuel wasn't dressed like him, though. English people wore knee-length khaki shorts, black socks and brown sandals. Or maybe Uncle Emmanuel decided to change his dress when he came back.

It turned out he had been back for over a year and was living in Georgetown with an English pension.

"So who are these children?" he asked.

"Esther's two girls," Mammy replied.

"You don't look like your mother when she was your age at all," he said to me.

"She's everything of the father," Mammy replied. "Same long, stupid neck, and lanky body."

"I think *you* look a bit like your mother when she was little," he turned to Franc, "Except for the complexion, of course."

He somehow managed to frown at Mammy and smile at us at the same time.

“This is me youngest girl, Theresa,” Mammy introduced Theresa to him and they shook hands. He had something important to talk to Mammy about, so the two of us kids had to go and sit on the steps outside.

“He been here all this time and never contacted me,” Mammy said to us after he’d left. “Only come to see me coz he want me help now.”

“What he want?” Theresa asked.

No one was paying any attention to me or Franc, so we sat down on the bed next to Mammy smoking in her rocking chair and listened:

“He say that he in trouble,” Mammy told Theresa after a long drag on her Bristol. “He said that he had Melly living with him for a while, but he didn’t like she behaviour…”

“Melly,” Theresa said in shock, “Our Melly? We thought she was dead.”

“Yes,” Mammy said impatiently, blowing the grey smoke from her lungs out and through the open, wooden front window. “She was living on the street, and he tek her to come and live with him and his wife and daughter. He say she’s obsessed wid rape and always accuse lots of different people.”

“Melly,” Theresa said, as if still in a dream, wiping the sweat from the back of her neck.

“Anyway, he asked her to move out, and now, she accused him of raping she,” Mammy continued, blit working hard from her bottom to top lip.

“But he is she uncle,” Theresa said.

“He didn’t do it, though. So now he want me to go to Georgetown to the court case to give evidence for he.”

“But what about Melly?” Theresa asked, “Suppose he did it?”

“He didn’t. Melly is a crazy woman!”

“But how you getting to Georgetown?” Theresa asked.

“Emmanuel gon pay my passage, and I gon stay at his house.”

The minute Mammy left for Georgetown, I asked Theresa to tell me about my aunt Melly. She was one of Mammy’s middle daughters, born just a year before Lorna, who died of a belly ache when she was nearly twelve years old. Theresa said every time

Mammy beat Melly, she would run away and stay out for days. She said one time when Aunt Melly was about twelve, after a particularly bad beating, she had left swearing to never return. *But where does a frightened twelve year-old girl go, if not home?*

When they found her a few days later, she was hidden away in a recluse's house, a man who everyone thought had done something really bad to her. But no one could get Melly to say *what.*

"Melly left home a few years after that," Theresa told me.

"Wot? So young?"

"Yeah. But she did come back for yuh christening. That was the last time we saw her."

"So she knows who I am?"

"Sure. It was she who brought yuh christening outfit."

"Does she look like you?"

"Nah. Not really."

"Who then?"

"Who she look like? Hmmm, let me see," Theresa pondered.

"Like Esther?"

"A bit. But Esther's mostly smiling. When Melly was home she used to be sad all the time."

"Well, she'll be sadder now, won't she?"

"Yes," Theresa answered, scratching her scalp through her thick, wool-like hair. "Yes. She will be sadder now. It's not right for Mammy to testify against her own daughter, even though Uncle Emmanuel gave her so much money, especially since she hadn't seen her for so long."

"Will she tell us what happened at the court?" I asked.

But Theresa had turned her back to see about Franc and didn't hear my question.

CHAPTER 32

LITTLE GIRLS *DO* CRY

After the August holidays, when I went back to school, I noticed a new, but slightly familiar face in our class. When Mr. Paltoo, who was now our form master as well as P.E. teacher, introduced her as Bibi, it suddenly occurred to me that I knew who she was. She used to be a student at Overwinning Primary, and was in one class above mine, the class Marleen and Marla were in before they stayed back for that extra year.

She was the girl with the long hair down to her bum, except now it was shoulder length. No wonder she looked so different. Bibi had gone on to the school she'd got the points for, which incidentally, was the school the twins eventually went to. She had written her Secondary School leaving exams (C.X.C) but was not completely satisfied with her grades, so her parents had her transferred to B.H.S, where she could be offered a good chance to do better. We became friends instantly, since I was the only one in the school who vaguely knew her. I introduced her to Sita. After that, Sita and Bibi and I would walk home together. After Sita and I got home, Bibi would flag down one of those Morris Oxfords to take her the rest of her way home.

As usual on Monday mornings, we had to present ourselves at the General Assembly. And considering it was the first assembly of school in a new term, the occasion would be much grander than usual. Mr Nandkishore makes a big announcement of the names of last years' leavers, who did extremely well at their C.X.C final exams. We usually listened for names of the people we knew, and found in the past that lot of them were prefects. Bibi and I were excitedly catching up on the latest news she brought about Marleen and Marla, and we got carried away in the moment. By the time we got into our spanking new auditorium, everyone was already singing the National Anthem,

". . . Of Rivers and Plains
Made rich by the sunshine

And lush by the rain . . ."

We found a place in the standing crowd, giggling as we tried to make ourselves as small as possible.

". . . Your children salute you
Dear land of the free.
Green land of Guyana
To you will we give
Our homage our service, each day that we live
God guard you great mother
And make us to be more worthy our heritage
Dear land of the free."

The singing stopped and the mumbling died down. We, the older students, standing at the back of the auditorium, made use of the fresh air flowing through the hall's opened doors. Mr. Nandkishore welcomed us all, especially the tiny first formers, who stood in the neat rows up front, wearing different shades of green. We at the back were less impressed by the formality. We had long since acquired a bored impression of everything.

A couple of the new students – children fresh out of primary school – saw me this morning after I collected my sparkling, extra-special, red, prefect badge. They were giggling with each other, probably saying something rude by the look of it. They nearly walked into me, and when they saw what they probably thought of as a towering prefect, they stopped giggling and stepped out of the way so fast, it made me laugh. I couldn't believe a badge could make people act in such strange ways. It made me wonder if the badge represented me, or who they thought I was. Whatever it was, that was cool. I'd remember to look sternly at them the next time I spot them around on campus.

I thought I could have some fun wearing this badge for the next couple of years.

Mr. Nandkishore began his annual, lofty speech. He insisted that naming the students who excelled last year was not a waste of time because. "Other students can be encouraged to try harder by the example of excellent performances of the top students." He usually starts with the names of students with high passes in four subjects – out of a possible total of six – and then move upwards.

Considering that we were told that a measly grade three – the lowest passing grade – is no lower than sixty-five points out of a hundred, I suppose those students did deserve to get to bore us with their good news.

"You've got a problem," Mr. Nandkishore would say every year. "You've got a problem if you don't strive for the best grades, because there is only one University in this entire country. They have a right to be extremely picky with grades. They only take students with good passes in five subjects and up."

"We did well again, as expected," Mr. Nandkishore said, addressing the hall. "Well above the other schools!"

Then he puffed out his chest and read out the names of the esteemed students. Those with high grades in five or six subjects got an enormous cheer from the teachers and students, almost raising the roof of the new auditorium. There were seven of them this year.

* * *

"But if he wants to kiss you, would you say yes?" Sita asked me on our way home from school. The three of us ambled home in heat so intense, it seemed to bounce off the asphalt and radiate off our skin. Bibi and Sita both had parasols, as Indian girls were supposed to protect their whiteness at all cost.

"No, I won't," I giggled, almost looking over the top of her head. At some time in the past year, she had stopped growing, but I had carried on . . . and on . . .

Sita enjoyed saying that Ravi liked me. He and Tony were friends and Sita had a crush on Tony, the hairiest boy in year four. He shoots her a smile every chance he gets.

"He's nice," I answered. "But I don't think I want a boyfriend. I hope he likes me though."

"Wot? You don't like him, but you want *him* to like you?"

"Well, it's nice to feel that people like you, ain't it?"

"S'pose so."

"He *must* like you, Anne," Bibi said, her honey-coloured eyes looking up to me with something that reminded me of Theresa. "Look at you. You're pretty, and you got the best hour-glass shape I ever, *ever* seen. *Everyone* would like you."

"Really?" I asked, pretending to look around. I briefly thought about what Mammy had said about the way I looked, but let it dart from my mind as fast as it had come. Were Mammy and Bibi looking at the same thing? How could two people look at the same thing and have such opposite opinions of it.

"I know that Tony really likes me," Sita continued.

These days I had my wanting-to-be-a-nun days interspersed with wishing-for-a-family ones and I couldn't help being totally confused. I couldn't tell Sita this, though. She would laugh at me because even though they were Catholics, her mother's Indian, and marriage was very important in their culture. It was a system where you never had to worry about finding someone to marry because you were assured that your parents or brothers would find someone for you.

"Maybe you could have a double wedding," Bibi said, and we all giggled. Then she turned to me and took a double take.

"The sun's reflecting off that scar on your nose," she said, pointing at my face. "I 'member you used to come to classes with a big bandage on your face in primary school. Everyone thought you'd lost an eye."

"Yeah," I mumbled under my breath and tried to smile.

"Did you scratch it on the stairs when you fell down?" Sita asked.

"Did you fall down?" Bibi asked.

"Yeah, she told us she fell down the stairs," Sita answered.

"I did," I lied. "There was a nail or something. It happened very fast."

"Did you scream?" Bibi asked, pushing her short fringe behind her ears, a habit I remembered from primary school.

"Yes," I said, knowing this would be the normal thing to do.

We soon started giggling about the boys again. I got to my own house soon after Sita got home, and said goodbye to Bibi.

"You must eat lots of downs," she said to me, pointing to the large fruit tree that stood in our front yard.

"Yes, lots," I lied again, knowing it was the normal answer that would be expected from me. She wouldn't think that I'd be locked in as soon as I entered the house and not even expected to sample the spongy, yellow fruit that grew right outside our wooden front window.

"We cookin' on Sister Mac's fireside this afternoon," Mammy said to me when I was barely up the stairs. She was in the kitchen, looking over at Christopher's flat out of the open door.

My heart fell. The smoke would be enough to make my chest wheeze for days, but Mammy also insisted on me bringing up the hot pots all the way from Sister Mac's old fireside on the far side of her bottom house. She always said that allergies were only a way for pretentious and sly people to get out of hard work. When she was a teacher, she used to rage at 'fat bum' teacher for saying she was allergic to dust.

"She pretends to sneeze only coz she never wants to sweep up the floor after them kids," she used to say.

I usually had to go downstairs to the fireside to get various pots and cooked dishes to bring upstairs. In itself, there was nothing bad about this, but in Mammy's world, you weren't allowed to hold hot, aluminium-handle pots with a cloth. She said everyone should be able to hold them like she did. Sadly, if you lived with Mammy, you *had* to live in her world.

Bringing a hot, aluminium-handled pot all the way from the fireside from the far side of Sister Mac's bottom house, through the yard between the two houses, and up our stairs, is not something that even fright could make it possible for me do.

A little rest I thought, when I could stand the pain no longer. *I'll just take a little rest.*

But she was watching me from the open stable door.

When I picked up the pot again, I glanced guiltily upwards, and saw her eyes. They were hotter than the handle of the pot I'd just taken from the open fireside. Her red anger glowed even brighter than the old pieces of wood I'd found and burned in order to cook that pot of rice. I dropped the pot down into the wet sink when I came into the kitchen, and she closed in.

Yesterday I was confronted like this for something totally different. Franc liked to open the curtains and look out at the boys playing in the yard, but she knew enough to realise that Mammy couldn't catch her doing this. When she heard Mammy coming, she'd drop the curtain and disappear under the bed – whose one side and head are against right-angle walls – where Mammy couldn't get to her. Mammy tried to get her out the first few times by blindly swiping the coconut pointer broom under the bed. The more she swiped, the angrier she got, but Franc had found a good spot.

In the end, she quenched her rage and frustration by beating me instead. By now, Mammy realised it was a waste of her time to even try to get Franc. She'd just beat me – the coward she had groomed all her life – to save time. Yesterday was one such day.

"Why don't *you* see she doing it to make she stop?" she shouted at me when she closed in. This way she could pretend to beat me for *not* doing something I should do. Otherwise it would seem as if she was breaking me for nothing at all.

As Mammy came closer to me for today's hot pot confrontation, Sister Mac walked up the steps, in clear view from the open top-half of the wooden stable door. But I'd made Mammy too angry to stop, and as Sister Mac got to the top of the stairs Mammy folded her fist and punched me in the face. This was the most natural way to beat someone who had grown to almost your own height.

"Oh, doan hit her!" Sister Mac cried, but she didn't look surprised.

"Is wot she like!" Mammy shouted, "People feeling sorry for she!"

And as she said the word 'she' she cuffed me again. This time her fist hit me on the side of my jaw. I had just turned to look at Sister Mac so that I could tell her with my eyes it was not a good idea to say anything else – not if she didn't want to make it worse.

Instead, I stood there with tears running down my cheeks, too humiliated in my own teenage way to stay, but too scared to move away. Sister Mac had come to ask us not to put so much wood into the fireside because the flames were getting too high.

* * *

Dear Aunty or Mister,

Tonight's story was about what happened to Aunt Melly at the court hearing in Georgetown.

Mammy had stayed at Uncle Emmanuel's grand house, near the centre of the Garden City. She had a posh dinner and was taken care of by her sister-in-law, whom she had just met for the very first time. However, it was enough time for her to decide that the lady had cheated on her brother, because their daughter looked nothing like her father.

Apparently, Aunty Melly had stayed with Uncle Emmanuel and his family for a long time before she was asked to leave. In court, Uncle Emmanuel's defence lawyer wanted to know if Aunty Melly was "delusional and inclined to lie and make up fantastic things," all of which Mammy confirmed.

A nun who was found innocent of a rape charge a few years earlier was also brought to the stand. She was accused of rape by Aunty Melly after she had her stay at her home for a couple of years.

"Emmanuel won the case, no problem," she beamed.

"You shouldn't ha' done it, though," Theresa said. "Let them win their own case without you. Melly is your daughter."

"It serves her right!" Mammy replied. "She abused me outside the court yard. She said I not her mother and she never want to see me again."

"She felt sad," Theresa persisted. "She hadn't seen yuh for a long time, and the first time she does, yuh swear that she's a liar."

Mammy said she didn't care but I am sure I noticed something in her face, something that looked like regret.

"Stop pulling me curtain," Mammy shouted at Franc, who was busy looking outside to where the house next door was flooded with light, quite unlike our dark one. Franc dropped the curtain bent over, pulled her pants down and showed Mammy her bottom. Then she waited for Mammy to get up to chase her.

Mammy had been trying to break Franc into her mould ever since she came back from French Guyane, but I think she's realised that a couple of years away from her can break that evil and horribly cruel spell. I think she got this sudden sucker punch in the belly of her pride the day she pushed Franc down the steps.

Already, it was a hazard climbing the narrow stairs to our door. Add the fact that there were no banisters or safety boards behind the steps themselves, and you've got yourself an accident stacked on the shelf, and ready to be shipped away. If you went up or down the stairs, especially when it rained, or just after I'd brought up the day's water, you would know what I was talking about.

One afternoon just after Esther had left, we were coming back home from the cinema. Theresa went up first, because she was holding the key, which was tied to an old, sticky rubber band. Franc was standing with her, Mammy was behind Franc, and I was bringing up the rear.

Mammy always said not to stand next to each other on the stairs because they were so narrow. Franc never bothered, so I think Mammy had been waiting to teach her a lesson. If you know Mammy, you would know this was the kind of thing she did. Theresa couldn't get the key into the old, rusty padlock on the door because it refuses to bother opening sometimes. All the faffing about got on Mammy's nerves, so she reached up and yanked the key away from Theresa. As she did this she swept Franc aside and said, "Move outta me way, you!"

As there were no banisters on the stairs, Franc went flying through the air and landed in the dirt - about nine feet below - with a loud thud. One minute this little infant was standing on the stairs waiting to get into her home, and the next minute, like a doll, she was lying flat on her back on the dusty ground below.

I ran down to get her but she had already begun to scream. Mammy? She didn't even look back. How could a human be so cruel to a four year old.

When we got into the house, Mammy shouted at Franc to stop screaming. Remember I told you about Franc's screams when she was a baby? Well, now they were even louder and more deafening. Franc stood by the door and screamed and screamed, then retched and screamed again. Mammy held her little body in one hand and beat her all over with the next, but Franc kept on screaming – kept on fighting her cause the only way she knew how.

Every time Mammy let go of her, she went to the door and screamed. Mammy locked the door and beat her again, and when Theresa pulled Mammy off her, Franc went to the front window and screamed, all the time showing her anger by stamping her feet and generally making lots of noise.

I think that Mammy was secretly panicking, because Franc was turning purple and holding her body so rigid that she shook violently. Finally, Mammy backed down, saying that the neighbours were going to call the police, but Franc kept on screaming for over an hour. If this sounds impossible, it's because you haven't yet met Franc.

After that night, Franc screamed at the slightest provocation by Mammy – even a cross look would set her right off. Mammy had found her match. When it came to fight partners, Franc was the bigger, more powerful one.

Checkmate!

CHAPTER 33

AN ENCOUNTER OF THE MAD KIND

Dear Aunty or Mister,

The mere fact that Mammy has asked me to do the general cleaning this month, shows how busy working she really is. I was shocked because I know how much she enjoys having this kind of control over things. I was surprised at how easy it was to do, though - cleaning one room at a time.

First I swept and dusted everything, then I washed every surface, cleaning all the stuff on the ledges and walls. Lastly, I scraped the greenheart wood floor until it was spotless. Whilst it was drying, I started on the next room. I then went back after a while to replace everything. By the time Mammy had come home, I was scraping the last few stairs outside.

This term has really gone by quickly. It's almost the end of my fourth year of high school, which means I have to do my big exams next year. The imminent end of every term signals a very unpleasant ritual in our house - castor oil drinking! You see, even though we go to church more now than we used to, we don't go every week, so Mammy plans a church-free Sunday in favour of a castor oil one.

At dawn the household is awaken, while the blue-sakies are barely stirring in the large downs tree in the front yard. We are then required to fast until the middle of the morning.

At about 10 a.m. Mammy pleasures herself in whisking up a horrible mix of stinky drink. I don't recommend it myself, but if you'd like to make it for some perverted appetite you've been nursing, here is what you do. Mix half a glass of castor oil with a fresh raw egg – though I don't suppose that a bad egg would taste any worse. Get a fork, and whisk in a few tablespoons of cassareep. This is a black substance made from cassava, which looks a bit like molasses, but half as thick.

Now chug it down – slowly, mind.

There was one glass for each of us. We're told to drink it up in one gulp, then to rub some on our navels. We then have to wait until we have a bowel movement before we eat anything. This is so gross that I feel like I am going to be sick as I write this.

The castor oil has a vile smell, and floats on top of the raw egg. The black cassareep makes a terrible background for this hellish, evil mixture. As you drink, you can actually feel the lumps and slime going down your throat like blobs of stale, overnight snot.

It feels exactly like on those occasions where you find a glob of phlegm in your mouth. You look wildly around, but important people are watching and there's nowhere to spit. You steel yourself and your oesophagus, you squeeze your eyes shut, and then . . . you swallow it. Yeah, phlegm ain't cool.

But it gets worse. Now imagine that your phlegm was someone else's. Then imagine that that someone had put in a glass, mixed it with a raw egg and two tablespoons of soy sauce, and made you drink it. But they're not finished, imagine that after you'd drained the glass, you had to rub the left-overs on your belly button.

Why?

Then imagine the smell.

My throat was never good at swallowing blob-food like mashed 'anything.' Even porridge used to send me retching all over the place when I was a baby. Esther said that I was sick or got the hiccups at the slightest thing. I still do.

I remember one time last year, one of Esther's friends, Bibi, came to visit us from Georgetown. While she was here, I had the hiccups which lasted the entire day. After drinking dozens of glasses of water and trying every other hiccup remedy I knew, I went to sleep, defeated. When I got up the next morning, they were still there.

Bibi offered to try and cure them. She said her father was a Muslim priest and that he used to cure hiccups all the time. She got a glass full of water, then she said a Muslim prayer in Arabic and blew on the water a few times. "Drink all the water," she told me. I did, and when I was finished, so were the hiccups. Impressive stuff, whichever way you look at it.

This term I passed my confirmation classes, too. I had one more important question to ask Father before the ceremony. There was just this tiny thing, but it kept nibbling, like four-eyed fish at my mind, so I couldn't resist the question.

Remember that part in the Bible where it tells us not to worship idols? Well, I had a feeling that I was doing it, because I and the other people in the congregation, kissed the statue of Mary and bowed down in front of the other statues of Joseph, Jesus and St. Christopher at the back of the church.

"Am I worshipping idols, Father?" I asked, "Coz I don't wanna worship idols."

"Oh, of course not, Anne," he answered, eyes half-closed. "The Bible isn't talking about the statues we have here," he spread his arms, taking in the multitude of statues we sprayed with holy water and bowed down to during the stations of the cross. "By 'idols' the Bible means that some people have statues in their hearts, like money and material things, which they've set up in place of God. These are the things we should not worship."

Later on, I went to confess about a lie I'd told. I knew that Father Soley was asleep on his side of the curtain in the confessional, because he had been sitting in there for more than five minutes at this point. He woke up in time to give me a penance of a few 'Hail Marys' and a couple of 'Glory Be.' As I got up from my knees and walked away to do my penance, I hoped that someday when I got older, I would understand the idol worship thing.

Best wishes xxx

* * *

"Trouble!" I shouted to Sita and Bibi when I spotted her coming from a distance. Some of the less violent mental patients from the asylum nearby were allowed passes to walk around town. A lot of them hopscotched aimlessly around, just walking their invisible dog, or sightseeing. Others took a more exciting approach by scampering about naked, by crazily shouting (well I couldn't expect them to *sanely* shout) at us, or by pelting us with dry grass, sticks, and occasionally – stones.

Mad Mary was different. She had been known to run after students, to try and pull their uniforms off, or just to beat them across the head. Just last week she grabbed Renee's bag from her shoulder and ran off with it.

Mad Mary wore her bright red wig today. She had quite a few of them. There was a very believable rumour around that she had been a successful actress in Georgetown. We thought that would explain why she had so many dress-up clothes and stylish handbags.

She carried a bag that matched her wig. In true Mad Mary fashion, she was swinging it out, as far as her arm could stretch out from her body. Princess Elizabeth Road was the one we took to school. It was such a narrow road that even when you walked on the right hand side, you were in danger of being hit by traffic coming towards you on the left. Nevertheless, we took our chances and crossed over the road to avoid an encounter with our town's embodiment of an urban myth.

When Mad Mary was about ten feet away, she took care to look left, right, and left again then walk carefully across the road – which was more than we did. She projected a mad, frothy smile at us from the dark, roomy hole of her famous – or maybe infamous – toothless mouth. Her lips, and the not-so-close vicinity of the area. were covered in bright red lipstick. Mad Mary's shadowy legend said that doctors had to extract her teeth because she kept trying to eat their hands when they attempted to treat her. Since both Frank and his mother, who worked at the mental hospital were now living abroad, there was no way of finding out if this was true.

Mad Mary came towards us, wriggling her hips like a dance scene born out of an Indian movie. We tried to go back across the street, but at eight o'clock in the morning, there was no chance of that happening any time soon. She continued walking towards us with that face of mischief, and we knew that something scary and oddly funny was about to happen.

We edged into the grassy bank and into the dry gutter but it was no use. Mad Mary yanked her wig off and took a swing at us with it. It didn't connect and somehow we all managed to scramble by, screaming our heads off. She obviously became frustrated that we'd escaped, but didn't seem to be in a running mood, so like a toddler she stamped her foot and spat at us, and caught me on the bum. We ran away laughing and screaming, "Mad spit! Mad spit! Get it off! Get it off!"

When we had gone a safe distance, Bibi and I scrambled up some dry grass together, and with shaking hands we rubbed the mad spit off my bottom. There was nothing like an encounter with one of the mental patients just before the first period.

We had barely got into the hard court on the way to our form room when Ravi from our class came running up with some news. A sub-prefect from one of the third forms had died.

"How?" Bibi asked for all three of us.

"Sardines," he said.

"Sardines?" I asked puzzled. Esther had brought a few tins of sardines for us when she used to go to Suriname. They looked harmless to me.

"They opened a few tins a couple of days before, but they had too much, so they kept the rest to eat another day," Ravi told us.

"But . . ." began Bibi.

"What happened was that they left them in the tins," Ravi continued. "You not supposed to leave opened sardines in the tins overnight.".

"I didn't know that," I said.

"Me neither," Sita joined in. "Whenever we have sardines we always have them all, but we have a big family."

"Wow!" Bibi said in amazement. "They all died?"

"Only the two children. The parents had given them more of the sardines. I guess they thought they were doing a good thing."

"How you know all this?" I asked Ravi.

"I live up their road. My mam was at their house and at the hospital all weekend. Is really sad."

We all thought so too. Even though she wasn't our friend, we all knew her.

I was still thinking about the sardines when I got to my Confirmation ceremony rehearsals. While I was there, I felt so overcome with thanks that God had brought me through everything, and still kept me sane enough to like who I was. As we were all kissing the feet of the statue of the Holy Mary, I made a vow to her that I would be just like her. I would serve always and be good. I would always be close to her in prayer and the rosary. I didn't expect to cry but I did a bit. Only Aaran saw, so I told her what I'd done.

She must have told the others because Andrew and Peter and a couple of the other boys came up to me and asked if it was true that I wanted to be a nun. I said I wasn't really sure, but they insisted that I shouldn't. Maybe they were right. I later said a prayer to God because I didn't know what to do.

My Dear God,

I know you will lead me in the right way. I am doing this now because it's all I know how to do. I think this is all wrong, but just in case it is right, I am going to do it for You. Please help me to know, Lord. I am going to say my rosary every day and keep close to the Holy Mary. I love you Lord, please make my life easier to live. Amen.

CHAPTER 34

A VERY WEIRD FAMILY INDEED

Because I had to go to Mammy's work place to wait for her to finish work, I spent a lot of time with the Ferreira family. If I had my way, I'd rather have hung around in the street than being there, because it had become very stressful and even scary at times. The son thundered through the house mumbling under his breath. When he passed next to me, the weight and speed of his body's air pressure alone sent me scurrying to a corner of the kitchen.

"Don't get near him, and move out of his way when you see him," his mother told me the very first day I went there. "He can get violent and may hit you."

"Dem family cursed, ah tell yuh," was Mammy's diagnosis of the situation. "The son's a mad elephant, and the daughter's got a sewage-baked mouth on her."

I hated admitting it to myself, but she was right.

"All day long, ah got to mek several flasks-full of tea," Mammy continued. "A red one for the daughter and blue one for the son, but Mrs. Ferreira can't let them know that every time I mek a new batch, she comes around and secretly grinds up six different tablets into them. She say that they won't take the medicine otherwise."

Jo Jo, the daughter, was an angel to look at and even knew all the Latin prayers and songs we sang at church. She loved wearing white and spent hours in her bedroom continuously brushing her straight, blonde hair. Her steps were careful and slow – calculated. 'Busy' was not a friend she played with. Her eyes were two still, grey marbles buried deep below baby-soft brows. Even her speech was gentle and soft at all times, *except* for when she was at home. There she spat torrents of curses at all the furniture, the floor, her mother, Mammy, the food, and everything else, even the ice in the fridge. She had a good supply of swear words. Maybe she knew some in Latin as well, because she never ran out of stock.

One day, while I waited for Mammy, Jo Jo came into the kitchen for a drink of her tea. While she carefully and posh-tastically poured the tea into the lid of her flask, her mouth, as a separate entity, muttered curses under her breath. The moment she took one sip of the tea, Jo Jo and her mouth suddenly re-united into one body and threw the flask at her mother who was standing at the sink. She then used eight words to shout, "This tea tastes like poo!"

She swanned gently off in what looked like the bridesmaid's dress she was fond of wearing. She didn't change half as often as her brother, though. He had to change his clothes every time he made a round of the house: living room, dining room, through his bedroom door, come back out, knock-knock on it, go into bedroom, go into rest of bedrooms, come into kitchen, knock-knock on dresser, go into bathroom and kitchen, come back out, pull up trousers, go and change, then start all over again.

This was his day. It was sad to watch, but too enthralling not to.

Last Friday, I got the shock of my life. Seema from our class, who lives a few doors from the Ferreiras, had seen me going into their yard.

"Saw you going to that house where that mad, old man lives," she told me excitedly.

"He's only is his twenties," I said.

"Not the son, stupid," she said. "Why do you think I go to Daddy's shop every afternoon after school?"

"I thought you went to help," I replied.

"I go coz Mr. Ferreira shows himself to any young girl who goes past on her own. He stays under his house all day long pretending to tinker with his cars. As soon as he sees a girl – any little girl – he pulls his underwear down and shows his . . . you know. He never does that to you?"

"No," I answered slowly, realisation dawning on me. No wonder his wife kept such a close eye on him when I was there. No wonder she always came downstairs and didn't go back up until I was safely upstairs, where she could watch, not me, but *him*. She was protecting *me*. So *she* was the normal one!

My mind began to drop little pieces of puzzles into places I never knew they could fit, but Seema wasn't finished.

"One day when I was about ten, I was walking past and he called me up to the gate for a sweet – that's how he gets you close." Seema's breathing increased in speed to match mine. "So I went up to the gate to get the sweet, coz he was our neighbour, right?"

"Yeah, yeah, of course," I answered.

"But when I got up close, he dropped the sweet and yanked down his underwear."

"His underwear?" I took a deep intake of breath through my open mouth.

"Yes! You know those white, Y-front things he wears?"

"So he pulled his underwear down in front of you?"

"Yes!"

"And you saw his . . .?"

"Yes!"

"I don't believe it! Well, I believe *you*, but what did you do?"

"I screamed and ran back home to tell my mother, but he was calling me back for the sweet. Imagine the audacity! He was bribing me with a sweety."

"Or paying you for services rendered," I laughed. We both laughed, but we didn't think it was funny; not funny in the least, especially since my little sister went to his house too. How could his wife allow that?

I can't go there now without first steeling myself; always hoping against hope that he wouldn't be there, but he always was. I snatch the sweets as quickly as I could, and run upstairs to relative safety where son was on the loose and daughter was swearing, but most of all, where Mammy was waiting to take control. After all, wasn't that the reason I came here in the first place? I had walked home on my own since I was five, so it wasn't for my companionship, *certainly* not for my safety. Theresa had stopped working for them a long time ago. She said she wanted to move on. Only after telling her Seema's information did she say she left because of Mr. Ferreira, and that yes, the information was true and Mammy knew it to be so. It was the street young girls avoided because of the 'wicked old pervert.'

* * *

Dear Aunty or Mister,

As tomorrow is a religious holiday, we're allowed to play Phagwa in school. It's no longer just a Hindu holiday, because everyone gets involved on account that it's so much fun. Some kids bring little buckets to school, and the Hindu kids bring the powder to make up the rich, colourful liquid Paghwa is played with. They mix the different colours with water and splash it on everyone else.

Because of all the soaking and splashing, we're only allowed to play in the afternoon after the Paghwa concert we have every year. Most people just play with water, as this gives you all the fun without the commitment of the colour stuff. I don't mind getting wet, because I dry off in the sun while I walk home from school. Talcum powder isn't that bad either, as not only does it make you smell nice when you're covered in the stuff, it's also easier to clean than the real, brightly coloured powders.

At our annual concert, many girls model beautiful saris and sing Hindu songs. Traditional plays about Prahalad and the origin of the holiday are put on, interspersed with sensational Indian dances, which girls learn by copying from the Indian movies they watch.

Paghwa is always the best celebration in the school year because it's so colourful and spectacular, but mostly because everyone can get involved. There was just one thing marring the celebrations for me this year. For the past week, Mammy has been nagging me to borrow twenty dollars from Bibi to help pay the rent.

She knows where her family lives, and concluded from the size of their house that they had a lot of money to spare. I've been putting it off, but Mammy suspects this, so she is building up to a burst of anger which is promising to erupt at any moment. Last night before I went to the watchman next door for a cigarette, she warned that I'd better ask Bibi today. Now I'm left wondering how to ask my young friend to borrow money for my family.

I finally did it on the way home, just the way I was told to. I lied to Bibi, telling her that I needed some money for medicine. She said it was alright, that she had some savings at home and would give the money to me when we saw each other again after the holiday. Of course, I was relieved that it was so simple, but I felt that bad way you feel when you lie to a friend. She didn't even ask for details, and this just made me feel worse.

The day we went back to school after Phagwa was a strange and scary one for me and a certain other prefect called Simone. There was something massive going on at our school with a form three girl – who was probably just about my age or so – and a pregnant belly. Apparently no other school girl had ever been pregnant before, which made it all the more important for us to chirp about it.

We wanted to see her to find out what her belly looked like. It's not that we had never seen a pregnant belly before. Oh no, we had seen lots and lots. It's just that we'd never had to chance to see it on a girl in school uniform.

Our form four was in one of the buildings on the opposite side of the compound from the form threes, so we had to have an excuse to go around there. We had the perfect one.

We all took turns going to her class to buy Lawas because, as it happened, a girl in her year did a bit of business just before the lessons started and at break times.

It was Simone's and my turn to go this morning. Simone had enough money to get one Lawa for each of us. As with every new thing, Lawas were all the craze for our entire school. We'd had rice every day for all our lives, but we'd never had them as roasted rice balls, cooked with sugar and a touch of food colouring to give them fun, psychedelic colours.

We were twitching with excitement when we left the pregnant girl's class after we'd done our business. She was standing at the time and we could actually see the shape of her round belly. Not all of our classmates had been this lucky. Mr. Shivnankumar, our new Sri Lankan Maths teacher, was already there when we got back to class, so we took our seats quickly, forgetting that I still had both lawas.

Mr. Shivnankumar was taking our register today because our Form Mistress was out. As he slowly went through the names, pronouncing each syllable with a grind in his 'arrs' and a 'vee' in his 'double yous', Simone called out to me, "Anne, you still got my Lawa!"

"Vwot?" asked Mr. Shivnankumar, looking up from the register suddenly, his eyes like a jaguar's, ready to pounce on its prey.

"Anne's got me Lawa, Sir," Simone repeated more loudly and clearly. You had to talk slowly and a bit loud for Mr. Shivnankumar, you see, because he was a foreigner who had just arrived into the country, and it's hard for foreigners to understand our accent.

"You arr a velly rrude little girl," Mr. Shivnankumar told her.

"No Sir," Simone said, "That's not rude at all. Anne's got me Lawa, I'm just asking for it back." The whole class laughed.

"Both of you!" he shouted, standing up and extending a very stiff arm in the direction of the school office. "Go to the Head Masterrr nowv."

When you got 'sent up' to the headmaster, it was time to start rubbing your hands together if you were a girl, and if you were a boy, well, a good bit of stuffing in your trousers might come in handy. We were both puzzled. We didn't feel that we had done anything wrong, well, apart from ogling the pregnant girl, but he didn't see that.

We wasted a lot of time on the hard court debating whether we should wait there until the end of the period, then pretend we'd forgotten, or do what we were told. As Mr. Nandkishore's office was overlooking the hard court, we decided that a couple of prefects hanging around when no other students were there would certainly draw attention to ourselves and get us into even more trouble.

"Come in," Mr. Nandkishore said firmly when we finally built up the courage to timidly knock on his office door.

He looked up from his papers with his lips pursed, but when he saw Simone and me, he relaxed into a smile.

"Hi, Lyken and Jackson. What can I do for you today, girls?" He stood up and smoothed his blue Dashiki over his slightly rounded belly. It was the same colour as the one The Comrade Leader was wearing the day I got to stand so close to him.

"We got sent up, Sir," we both mumbled.

"You two? Why?"

We told him what had happened but he seemed to be more interested in what Simone said to me in class than what Mr. Shivnankumar had said to us.

"How did you say, 'Lawa?'" Mr. Nandkishore asked again.

"La–wa," Simone pronounced it again.

"Right," Mr. Nandkishore said, clearing his throat. "As you two girls have never got sent up to my office before, I'll give you a chance to prove yourselves. Go and call Mr. Shivnankumar, Lyken, and I may be able to fix this thing."

When I got back with Mr. Shivnankumar, Mr. Nandkishore called him out into the staff room, leaving us in his office, maybe to have us at hand if he decided to cane us after all. Through the half-open door, we saw Mr. Nandkishore say something to Mr. Shivnankumar, at which point the Maths teacher scratched the back of his head and looked to the floor.

They talked for a bit longer, both men shifting from leg to leg and rubbing the backs of their heads. Mr. Shivnankumar even covered his mouth like a girl in shock at one point. Mr. Nandkishore then came back into his office and told us to go back to our class.

Because of something he said to them after we had left, our classmates in the meantime had worked out that Mr. Shivnankumar thought Simone and I were shouting about our lovers.

The 'lover' incident seemed to be a theme for the day because later in the day, the girl who sat in front of me, Mandy, noticed that I had a heart-shaped scar on my forehead. I didn't believe her because I had never seen it. Seema, who sat next to her, looked at my face and confirmed that it was there, right in the centre of my forehead, "As if it was taking your stare away from that other nasty scar on the side of your nose."

When I got home that afternoon, I searched the mirror to see if they were telling the truth, and no, they weren't. The heart was *almost* in the centre, but not quite. I couldn't remember getting a scar there, but Mandy had said that an angel must have come in the night and stamped that heart on my forehead. I want to think so too, especially when I think of that short, bald man who, all those years ago, took his belt off to save me. It made me feel all warm inside.

CHAPTER 35

MASHRAMANI

Christopher left right after Mashramani this year to go to Suriname to find his fortune. He said he was sure there was so much there he could do. He said he was going to get out of this country, that he was tired of all this rationing and shortages of food. He said he couldn't see how much longer people were willing to put up with the food lines and the blackouts and stuff. Theresa asked him if his leaving had anything to do with the fact that his nurse girlfriend had broken up with him. He said he was the 'Sugar Daddy' and that nothing like that affected him.

We all went out to see the Mashramani parade. We stood on the side of the street with the thousands of other people, gawking at the huge floats and the colourful, massive crowd of revellers dressed in all sorts of costumes under the sun. Some of the costumes towered into the clear sky and looked mighty heavy. It was a wonder the people under them could even bear the weight. To be honest, some of them *did* look like they were struggling under the huge burden in the heat of the sun. But as usual, the party had to go on.

The Mighty Sparrow's Soca music was blaring on the loudspeakers. This feverish tempo created a sense of electricity – conducted through the hot and humid heat hovering over the procession. There was a certain joy-itch in your bones that infected you as soon as you stepped out into the street. Theresa had to lift Franc up unto her shoulders so she could see what was going on behind the masses of people who coloured the side of the street.

The crystal steel pan beat was ear-shattering and almost vibrated into the clear, blue sky. The day was burning hot and we could see tall, colourful floats for miles. *The Mighty Sparrow's* song was the one about the intruder at The Palace in London. Everyone in the parade was swinging their bodies to the overpowering Soca fever, which burned in your flesh and put you in a trance-like state of bliss as soon as you heard the steel pans in the distance.

The first float was a huge butterfly made of sparkling, glittering rivers of colours, calmly flowing in the breeze as it was pulled along the fiery hot asphalt of the Main Road. This float was displayed by Bermine, now called Guymine after its nationalisation.

The Bermine floats were always a source of awe and excitement, as theirs were often made by overseas-based Guyanese designers. Behind the butterfly danced hundreds of Bermine workers, all dressed in equally vivid little streams of flourescent shades. It was perfect! Franc was screaming and pointing at this float, twisting her little body from side to side as the itch hit her, the itch I was never allowed to scratch.

We learned in Primary school that 'Mashramani' was an Amerindian word for celebration or freedom - or something like that.

Before we left the house, Mammy said she could remember when, "These big celebrations used to be on our Independence Day, just like all them other countries' big Independence celebrations. Nowadays, there's nothing happening on we Independence Day coz The Comrade changed all 'o dat. Why the whole country gat to celebrate his birthday like this, I doan know."

". . .Phillip my dear . . ."

The 'Mighty Sparrow' continued to tell us about the man trying on the royal costumes.

The sugar workers' float came next as another waterfall of dashing, angry colours. This was a red tractor, dressed up to look like a boat. This 'boat' pulled a trailer packed with people depicting the many working place scenes of the sugar industry. There was the cutting of the cane, the transport and shipment, storing and grinding, then finally, the conversion into sugar. Again, hundreds of sugar workers pranced – some of them already drunk, maybe to depict the scene of when sugar is converted into rum – to the constant spiritual beat of the steel pans.

There were dozens more, but by the time we had settled into the parade, Mammy said she was tired so we had to drag ourselves home with her.

It would be the last time I would hear his voice for more than a decade when Christopher shouted over all the noise and bustle to say that he was going to stay and walk on to The President's Park, where all the floats were headed for the judging and prize awards. When he came home that night, I had already gone to bed, and when he packed his stuff, I was at school. I wouldn't see him again for thirteen years after he'd left prison and after my whole existence had been ripped apart, turned inside out and stitched back together again. But of course at fourteen, this was the other part of my story that I couldn't know about yet.

We trudged on home, and when Franc realised what was happening, she screamed to rival the steel pans.

" . . . A man in de bedroom . . ."

We reluctantly stumbled home.

I listened to this song about the monarch on the blaring loudspeaker, and thougunht that if 'God Saved the Queen,' whatever it was that He saved her from, He would save me too. After all, I was named after her daughter.

When we walked into the yard, Brother Mac, sister Mac's husband, was sitting on his veranda having a very amicable conversation with his false leg. By the time we got upstairs and opened the door, he'd gotten up, chucked his white leg under his black arm and walked inside with his cane. As the years had moved on, I'd grown up enough to realise that this man was just as normal as anyone else, he just liked to have a good conversation sometimes. There was nothing in anything else that he did or said to indicate otherwise.

And I should know stuff like that, since I was now in the middle of my last year of high school, getting ready to go on study leave soon.

My uncle Winston paid my exam fees, I'd been registered, and had gone through the revisions. Now it was all up to me. Everyone in the exam classes seemed perpetually sad, or maybe scared, I couldn't be sure. My English teacher had great faith in me to make her proud, so I hoped I would. Maths was compulsory in the exams, so I *had* to do it even though I knew I probably wouldn't do so well at it. I wasn't a great problem solver.

This Maths weakness meant I had to make extra efforts in the other subjects. We were given our exam time-tables and stuff yesterday – another thing to dump more fuel on the nervous pyre.

Sister Mac invited us to yet another Passover thingy at the Kingdom Hall tonight. Mammy had taken out the outfit that I was too embarrassed to wear from her drawer under her bed – the one with the skirt that opens out and the awful matching hot pants get-up. I wished I was allowed to sew up the entire thing. Theresa showed me how to sew so if she was busy, I could do my mending for myself. She had a very clever way of sewing that looked like you did it with a sewing machine. I was learning to do this too, which was probably a good thing on account that Mammy couldn't sew, unless inch-long stitches on the outside of the garment counted as sewing. Sometimes I did her stuff as well, but I couldn't sew on days when my hands got beaten because I couldn't bend my fingers properly then.

I wasn't looking forward to going. Maybe I'll get poisoned or fall downstairs and break my neck before this evening.

Maybe.

Talking about being poisoned, something very funny happened earlier. Theresa was spending a few days with us, so when she got paid yesterday afternoon, she secretly gave me one dollar to get a treat for myself. She said I should get something nice when I went to the shop to get the rum for Mammy.

Money = curried chicken + rum. (And you thought I was bad at Maths).

A lady had a little stand outside the optician's shop. She sold tamarind sours, plantain chips and black pudding. As I went past, the black pudding and the tamarind sour looked especially nice from the distance. My mouth sprouted water just thinking of them together on a nice piece of grease-proof paper.

The shop I was sent to was quite near our house so I had to be quick. On the way back, rum in hand, I went to this lady and spent my dollar on a small cut of black pudding – not forgetting, a touch of tamarind sour on the very top. Since I was in such a hurry, all I had time to do was to gobble it up quickly and make sure it was all gone before I got home. Mammy couldn't know I had the money, you see. It wasn't until the black pudding had gone down that I realised there was something putridly wrong with it.

When I got home, as I was taking my slippers off at the door as usual, Mammy told me to get out of her house and wash my slippers downstairs.

"You stepped on dog dung!" she shouted, taking the rum from my hands. "How come you can't smell that horrible smell?"

I went down and washed my slippers, but I knew that the smelly culprit was a long way from my feet.

After a while I came back up and kept my mouth tightly closed. I figured that if I could manage to keep it shut until we had the lovely curried chicken, the hot spicy curry sauce would cover up the bad 'dog dung' smell coming from within my now contaminated mouth and stomach. As soon as I entered the house again, Mammy sent me straight back out.

"Ah can still smell that dung! Wot them people give them dogs to eat these days, eh? Wash yuh feet this time!" she said, getting ready to tuck into her curry as she poured her rum out into a small glass.

"Day O!"

Harry Bellafonte sang on the radio as I walked downstairs for the second time. If *only* I could get my toothbrush! Theresa came down to tell me that my food was getting cold and I mouthed to her that I had eaten rotten black pudding. She came in to smell my breath but as I opened my mouth, she reeled back violently. This made us both burst out in silent laughter. We had to rest our hands on our knees to stop ourselves from falling down with the storm of laughter that was trying to loudly spill out from between our lips. When she had managed to swallow most of the giggles, Theresa said she was coming back, and ran upstairs. Seconds later, she came back with a bar of Zex washing soap and some toothpaste hidden in the palm of her hand.

"What's the soap for?" I asked.

"Ah had to tell Mammy I was bringing the soap for you to wash your feet with," she answered.

At last I was able to go up and eat my nice curry. My mouth was watering despite the taste of Colgate on my tongue. Mammy gave us all a sip of her rum. It burned my tongue a bit but it wasn't too bad.

Everyone finished eating before I did, and as I sat finishing my dinner, listening to Tom Jones on the radio, I was thinking that maybe we would get a story tonight, after all.

"Anne!" Mammy shouted so loudly that her voice broke in the middle of my name. I knew I was in trouble even before I saw her face. I left my food and leapt up in a panic.

"What's this?" she shouted, holding up a piece of hair.

Oh no! It was the hair I cut off!

Earlier that week I had cut off a bit of my hair. I had never had it cut before and I just wanted to see what it was like. Mammy always did spot checks on the few cherishables I had in the old cloth pocket which was tacked onto the living room wall. However, since she had done one just recently, I didn't think she would find the hair. I was just waiting for a chance to throw it out.

What is she going to do to me?

She came at me and grabbed my ponytail in her fingers. My head dived down with the force, and my hand instinctively went to my head. She pulled me into the kitchen, working her fingers tightly into the length of my hair, hanging on with strength I never imagined a person her age could have. She pulled me bent double to the stove (where the rest of the chicken was being broiled so it could be safely kept until the end of the week) and shouted, "Yuh want me to burn you with dis, you sly devil?"

She was spitting with rage and all the time my stupid brain was shouting, "*It's my hair! It's my hair!*" But my cowardly mouth couldn't get it out. I kept very still, biting in the pain, because I didn't want to knock the pot over by accident. She dragged me away from the cooking pot over to the sink. She obviously didn't really want to burn me. Again.

She snatched the wood that was holding open the sink window, and when I felt it make contact with the side of my thigh, I was relieved that it was the pain of a tormentor I knew rather than the contents of the pot – a tormentor I once met but wanted to forget.

Since the bloody incident with my nose, she hardly hits me in the head, but today she didn't care. When she was finished, I saw her looking at the side of her wrist. In her utter rage, she had hit herself as well. As I stood there, curry abandoned, re-combing the hair I had just recently done before she pulled it apart, I cried to myself in the mirror wishing to die. I didn't know if I really wanted to, but wishing to took some of my overpowering sadness away. I couldn't explain why.

As I walked into the Kingdom Hall that night with my aching spirit and body, I tried to hold the two bits of my 'skirt' together so that my legs didn't show. I looked at all the people in the hall, all smiling and happy, shaking hands and hugging, and knew I would do almost anything to have their life.

CHAPTER 36

LEAVING MAMMY

When Mammy used to work and I was on study leave, I would sit by the front window in the rocking chair and study all day long in preparation for my exams. Now that they were over, I had nothing to do but wait for my results. Mammy lost her job last month. She wasn't very happy with that. I was going back to school next term for a year whether or not I did well in my exams. I was called to the Headmaster's office recently to discuss my future because of the unique situation of my age. I was always younger than my classmates because of the skipping class thing. Now I had gone through to the end of secondary school, had done the leaving exams, and was only fifteen. Mr. Nandkishore was concerned about this.

"I'm sure you'll get good grades, Anne," he said to me. "But you won't get a job and certainly won't be accepted into University at this age. I am concerned about what you *can* do at fifteen."

I knew I wouldn't be allowed into University even if I was the right age. We had no money.

"Come back next year, Anne," Mr. Nandkishore had said. "No matter what your grades are, you can repeat the last year. We'll be glad to have you." So I was going to do just that.

Meanwhile, I was to go on one of those note-taking journeys today. This time the recipient was going to be one of Mammy's old teacher friends. This one had two daughters who were slightly younger than me. I was aware they knew *exactly* why I came, so I never liked going there. Sometimes on note days, I'd go past their house to see if they were playing in the yard. If they were, I'd go home and say their mother wasn't there. They looked at me in a funny way, and sometimes I knew their mother told them to say she wasn't home when they spotted me coming.

Although, if I remembered correctly, she was the person who once gave us more than we'd ever got from a single begging. She had loaded my plastic bag with a whole eggplant when before I'd only ever gotten half of the vegetable. On that same occasion, she'd given me a pint of rice and more than a drop of cooking oil in the bottle I'd taken to her house. The rice had weevils and white worms in it. The weevils were bigger than usual, but I suppose big weevils aren't much different from the smaller ones we were used to in the rice we bought – or even the flour we used to have when I was little.

Back then we used to sift the weevils and white worms out of the flour and dump them in the bin. This lady had even thrown in half of an onion at the last minute. Many people didn't bother giving us nice things like onions. A bit of rice, a handful of peas and a couple of pinches of salt was the best we could hope for.

I was washing my face to cool down before I went out into the heat of the afternoon, when Mammy shouted, "Who's at the door?" I'd heard it too. Someone was frantically opening the bolt of the bottom door.

"It's me," Esther said walking into the house. "Help me bring in the bags."

* * *

Dear Aunty or Mister,

It's four days later and Esther seems to be in a bad mood, she has been this way ever since she arrived. She's just announced that we're moving out. Theresa knows someone down by B.H.S way, whose house we can stay at until we find a place. It was as if Esther had come ready to make this move. When was all this planned? Was Esther waiting until I finished high school? Until she turned forty? Did something bad happen?

I had always imagined that if this day ever came, that Mammy would beat us all out of the house, and we'd be screaming, running up the road, and crazily yanking our hair out. However, while helping Theresa and Esther, who from tomorrow will be 'Mum', to pack up our things in the boxes we got from the hardware store next door, I was crying. I wasn't sad because we're moving, oh no!

You know how much I've been aching to go. I'm sad because lots of bad things were said, things I don't want to tell you because they drain so much of my life out of my body. I can barely finish this letter now because I'm so weak. All this stuff has made me very tired, and extremely sad.

You know how much I have wished for a normal life and stuff. I don't want to be rich and I certainly don't want to be important. I just want to be like you, you know, just normal, and have people who want me. People who know that I am alive and care that my heart is beating inside me and that my spirit can get really low. You know what I mean, Aunty or Mister?

All I ask is to be like you. My life has always been refereed by Mammy. She's always standing there with her whistle poised, ready to bring attention to each tiny fault I make while struggling to play her weird, mad game. It was a game for which she wrote new rules, even before the latest ones had a chance to dry on the paper.

My life has been just a dot to dot picture spelling sadness. Each day, each dot got me closer to the completion of the essence of what sadness is.

And fright. Yes, fright ruled me more than everything else. My life is spent in a straight jacket of tension, waiting for the next sudden outburst of anger.

And murderous beatings.

But my sadness hasn't been alone, because a lot of sadness can bring a lot of hope and I've got bags and bags of both. My life has been overrun by desperation and this low feeling that abandons you in a slimy dungeon that is way beyond worthlessness. But I know that if I can manage to crawl out of this sac and leave it behind, together with its bitter and poisonous amniotic fluid, I could one day help people like me who are also overpowered with agony and shame.

My short life of fifteen years has brought me so much desperation and fright. I can't shake off the fright of her. Sometimes when my flesh is being torn apart, I think there can't be anything more painful in this world. But then the beating stops and I realise that I was wrong.

I know you must know about this, too, because there is pain in everyone's life. What I want to say is that when your mind hurts and your shame is so great you can't carry it anymore and you have to hang your head, you realise how fleeting physical pain is, even though it hurts so bad while it is happening.

You know, sometimes you feel like you could just put your heavy head down and go to sleep and never wake up again, leaving all the stuff that squeeze the life blood out of your heart, all the tears out of your eyes, and everything that was ever pleasant and good out of your mind.

This is how I've been feeling all my life. I feel like all my energy for living comes from my fear of Mammy. I feel like this fear is a propeller on the back of a boat called Anne. There are no paddles or anything, just this sharp terror that moves the boat forward each day. And just when all the bad things are about to cover me like a very thick blanket of fog, and cut me off from all distant glimpses of twinkling light, I somehow get more hope.

It's then that I realise that God has given everyone people like Theresa to lift us up and carry us. This makes me realise that I don't really need that stinking propeller, just hands like hers to keep holding onto.

And then I start to see that if God sent her, He must have known I would need her, and if He knew I needed her, He must know other things about me too. This is what keeps me going, and this is why I have hope. I'll go now, but I promise I will be back to write about my new life so I can tell you what happened to me and all my hope. Please hope with me that I don't lose mine as I go off to sample what life is like when it's not lived in fear.

God bless you.

Best wishes until we speak again.

xxx.

EPILOGUE

Dear reader,

All of the events that I've recorded in this book have happened to me in real life, each and every one of them and more. I have changed most of the names of the people in this memoir (but not my late aunt Theresa's – yes, she died young) because I did not wish to cause them any embarrassment. Apart from these names, nothing else has been changed, although a few of the events may not have appeared chronologically.

I have recorded these episodes of my life to show that regardless of your past, with God's help and a few good people, you are potentially able to rise above it and can consciously decide not to allow it to affect who you are at present.

It's an agonizing affair, but I believe that if people who've been abused in their childhood allow their entire lives to be ruined by it, they have, in effect, surrendered their right of self to their abuser. Abusers are aware of the devastating powers of their actions, so if the victim continues to live his/her life in the shadow of that abuse even after it has ceased, he/she is enabling the abuser to succeed in destroying their life, thus achieving their goal.

I wrote this book in the progressive developmental language of a growing child to provide an opportunity for the reader to visualise the intimate thoughts of an imprisoned child of that age. This, I hope, would offer a tool which could help to identify a child who is being abused.

This approach also enabled me to show how abused children can grow to believe the lies they're told, and actually sympathise with their abusers in some respects. You would've also noticed how easy it is for children to believe the ignorance with which some adults saturate their thoughts and lives.

In addition, I wanted to express my experiences in the way I saw them as a child because I was not willing to add my adult opinions to this story. Firstly, because it allowed the person I am now to take a step back and write the story objectively. Also, it meant that I did not have to painstakingly analyse a lot of the behaviours and beliefs demonstrated in Sunday's Child, patterns which, although I could not understand them then, are clear to me now because of my training, Child Psychology qualifications, and work experiences. For legal purposes, I want to mention also that some of my then juvenile political assessments of the government were not necessarily factual. They are merely what I *believed* to be the truth, based mainly on the opinions of the adults I overheard, and also on the effects their policies had on my young life.

I know how formidable a task it is to muster the strength to change the direction in which your early nurturing points you, but if you know any child who is going through a difficult life, tell them about my story, and tell them to believe and pray, and then try with all their might to be the best they can be for themselves and their future children. And if they can't do it for that reason, do it just to lay bare the depravity of their abuser, and to show him or her by shining brightly, that they've lost their sadistic, evil hold.

What better way to avenge yourself than to laugh in your abuser's face by living an exemplary life? What better way is there to expose their cowardice of taking advantage of a weaker person than to exhibit bravery in your life? Overcome your abuser, because your suffering doesn't hurt them. It's your happiness that does. xxx

From present Day Anne.

P.S. Look out for, 'Fair Of Face' (the follow-up to Sunday's Child) coming soon.

THE END

The first edition of this book was published by U.S publishers, from whom I requested my publishing rights be returned to me.
Steve, thank you for telling me I *could* write this book. Tim, thanks for doing the cover picture.
Find my other books at my author pages on Amazon.

Printed in Great Britain
by Amazon.co.uk, Ltd.,
Marston Gate.